LOUISIANA

A notable collector of art related to Louisiana history, Leonard V. Huber is the author of many books on the state, including *New Orleans: A Pictorial History*. He has received great acclaim for his leadership in preserving Louisiana's historical heritage, including an honorary degree from his Alma Mater, Tulane University.

A Pictorial History

Louisiana

LEONARD V. HUBER

CHARLES SCRIBNER'S SONS

New York

Louisiana *A Pictorial History*

Editor *Norman Kotker*

Editorial Assistant *Alice Trapasso*

Designer *Ronald Farber*

Title Page: Nottaway, a fifty room plantation house near
White Castle in Iberville Parish, was built for a rich
sugar planter in 1857.

Printed in the United States of America
Library of Congress Catalog Card Number 74-14011
ISBN 0-684-14008-X

In memory of

René J. LeGardeur, Jr.

scholar, mentor, friend

Contents

Foreword

Louisiana has had a long, varied and colorful history since it was first visited by Hernando de Soto in 1542. Its French founders, beginning with René-Robert Cavelier de la Salle in 1682, left an indelible imprint upon the land which they first settled and governed for somewhat less than a century. When Spain established her sovereignty in 1769 over the land that she had accepted by treaty from France in 1762, she was unable to change the basic French character of her new colony. For years after its cession to the United States in 1803, Louisiana remained bilingual, officially and practically, with laws, legal documents and newspapers being published in both French and English. The strong French influence in her architecture, cuisine, festivals and customs is still apparent in this state, an influence that helps to make Louisiana unique among the states of the American Union.

Much has been written about Louisiana, from the journals of its early explorers to the latest novels. Histories have been published; LePage du Pratz in 1758, Martin, Gayarré and Fortier in the nineteenth century and many more in the twentieth. Books have been written about its architecture, its politics, its religion, its folklore and its legends. Many of these have been illustrated, some with crude early woodcuts and engravings, some with portraits, paintings and accurate sketches and drawings and in this century with magnificent photographs as well. Never before, however, has a truly pictorial history of this remarkable state of Louisiana been produced.

Leonard Huber's extensive collection of illustrative material has already been drawn upon and given to the public in his recently published *New Orleans: A Pictorial History* in which the history and lore of his native city were pre-

sented. More than a thousand illustrations with accompanying text traced the story of the Crescent City from its founding to the present day in a handsome volume that has been called his "magnum opus." Tireless in his efforts to see the history of his city and state presented factually and authentically, he has continued his research and the collecting of illustrative material in libraries, archives and private collections both in this country and abroad to complete his ambitious project by producing a sort of sequel to his New Orleans volume. His own collection has, of course, supplied the basic material for this monumental pictorial history of Louisiana.

His introductory historical sketch is remarkably concise, interesting and entertaining, well calculated to prepare his reader for the vast amount of information on all aspects of Louisiana's history and development—its cities and its people, its problems and its progress.

Leonard Huber, successful businessman and widely known Louisiana historian, has made the study of his state's fascinating history and culture his life's avid avocation. His pictorial collection embraces almost every facet of New Orleans and Louisiana life and history and his numerous published writings have covered many aspects which range from a postal history which appeared in 1949 to works on its cemeteries, its great river, its historic buildings and its carnival. Some of these works have been in collaboration with others; in most cases, he has been the driving force behind the project. Besides all these time-consuming works, he has found time to devote much of his energy to civic and cultural affairs, to historic preservation and museum activities. Louisiana is fortunate to have such a knowledgeable and dedicated biographer.

SAMUEL WILSON, JR., F.A.I.A.

Acknowledgments

Most historians of the past have written their books and then gathered pictures to illustrate them. In *Louisiana: A Pictorial History* I did the reverse; gathered pictures of events, customs, people—the whole gamut of life in this state as seen by contemporary artists and photographers and then strove in the text to provide an authoritative narrative to make the illustrations meaningful.

As a long-time collector of all sorts of illustrations pertaining to the region, I quickly found that there were many areas in which I needed help and I soon enlisted aid not only of my friends but of libraries and museums both here and abroad, of Chambers of Commerce, universities and commercial organizations. I wish to express my debt of gratitude—first and foremost, to the late René J. LeGardeur, Jr., researcher, rhetorician, expert in Louisiana history, whose editing and friendly criticism were invaluable. His death in 1973 removed a bright star from the firmament of Louisiana historians. I owe a debt to Mrs. Connie G. Griffith, former Head of Manuscripts and Special Collections at the Howard-Tilton Memorial Library of Tulane University and to her staff for unfailing aid in research. Collin B. Hamer, Jr., Head of the Louisiana Department of the New Orleans Public Library, was most helpful in the search for pictures in his well-organized department. To Manuel DeLerno, a photographer-historian who provided photographs from his own collection, and skillfully made prints from century-old negatives I owe much, as I do to Raymond Cresson and his staff—Beverly Cook, Raul Acuna, Ludger Landry and Leo Scheuermann. Guy F. Bernard, an expert amateur photographer and authority on Louisiana iron work and cemetery architecture helped greatly with the loan of pictures. Anita and Henry Pitot on their annual trips to Europe found important illustrations in France for this book. To them many thanks. The Comte Le Moyne de Martigny of Paris, a descendant of the Le Moyne family, gave permission to publish photographs of the paintings of Bienville, Iberville and de Serigny in his collection. The photograph of de Chateaugay's portrait was kindly sent from the Museum of the City of Mobile by its director, Caldwell Delaney. I am also indebted to Lloyd Poissonot and Ted O'Neil of the Louisiana Wildlife and Fisheries Department for their aid.

David M. Kleck's talent and skill are evident in the several beautiful photographs which he so kindly loaned. Albert L. Lieutaud, antiquarian, generously gave advice and furnished source material. For his permission to use on-the-spot pictures of Acadian life in the twenties and thirties, I am thankful to Dr. Lauren C. Post who was born in southwest Louisiana and who tirelessly recorded the life and customs of his Acadian neighbors. Boyd Cruise, Director of The Historic New Orleans Collection, assisted greatly in the selection and photographing of some of the treasures of that collection which appear in this book. Mrs. Austin Fontenot sent pictures, some never before published, of her home town, Opelousas. Alexandria scenes and data were generously furnished by Mrs. Charles Lafayette Brown and Mrs. Robert H. Bolton. H. Parrott Bacot, curator of the Anglo-American Art Museum at Louisiana State University, helped greatly with photographs of the Rural Life Museum on the campus of that institution and in searching out rare photographs in the library of the University.

For their invaluable help in furnishing pictures of Louisiana celebrations and places many thanks are due to Bob LeBlanc, Gus Cranow and Mrs. Joyce Yel Del LeBlanc of the Louisiana Tourist Development Commission.

The following museums, universities and libraries were generous in their help: Louisiana State Museum, New Orleans; Louisiana Historical Society; The Henry Francis du Pont Winterthur Museum, Winterthur, Delaware; The Historic New Orleans Collection; New Orleans Public Library; Emile Kuntz Collection; The Museum of the City of Mobile; The Newberry Library, Chicago; Confederate Memorial Museum, New Orleans; The Library of Congress, Washington, D.C.; the United States Navy; The National Archives, Washington, D.C.; The National Gallery of Art, Washington, D.C.; Bibliothèque Nationale, Paris; Musée d'Histoire Naturelle, Le Havre, France; Archives Nationales, Outremer, Paris; Musée Condé, Chantilly, France; Museo Nacional de Historia, Mexico City; Wallace Collection, London; The Dwight D. Eisenhower Library; Louisiana State Exhibit Museum, Shreveport; The Vieux Carré Survey, New Orleans; New Orleans Museum of Art; Orleans Parish Notarial Archives; Louisiana State University, Baton Rouge; Louisiana State University, New Orleans; University of Southwestern Louisiana, Lafayette; Southeastern Louisiana University, Hammond; Northwestern State University, Natchitoches; McNeese State University, Lake Charles; Centenary College of Louisiana, Shreveport; Dillard University, New Orleans; Tulane University, New Orleans; Nicholls State University, Thibodaux; Louisiana Tech University, Ruston.

I am grateful also to these commissions, chambers of commerce, and trade associations: Southern Forest Products Association; Louisiana Department of Agriculture, Commerce and Industry; Louisiana Tourist Development Commission; United States Department of Commerce, Bureau of the Census; Louisiana Superdome Commission; Department of the Army, New Orleans Corps of Engineers; Department of the Navy, Washington, D.C.; Louisiana Department of Wildlife and Fisheries; Louisiana Department of Agriculture; Board of Commissioners of the Port of New Orleans; Louisiana State University Press; Shreveport-Bossier Convention and Tourist Bureau; Baton Rouge Chamber of Commerce; Monroe Chamber of Commerce; Greater Lake Charles Chamber of Commerce; Jennings Association of Commerce; Greater Lafayette Chamber of Commerce; Alexandria-Pineville Chamber of Commerce; Natchitoches Chamber of Commerce; Chamber of Commerce of the Greater New Orleans Area; Freeport Sulphur Company; Kerr-McGee Corporation; Shell Oil Company; Kaiser Aluminum and Chemical Company; Southern Pacific Lines; The Boeing Company; Cadillac Motor Car Division, General Motors Corporation; The Times-Picayune Publishing Corporation; Louisiana Landmarks Society, New Orleans Chapter; Ursuline Convent; Albert L. Voss Collection; New Orleans Public Service, Inc.; Southeastern Bell Telephone Company; Crown Publishers, Inc., New York; The Keyes Foundation.

Henry W. Krotzer, Jr., made sketches of the first colonial buildings in Louisiana from plans in the National Archives in Paris. To him I am also greatly indebted. Others who contributed their picture information or skill are Capt. Fred Way, Jr., Miss Esther Cooley, the late Edward D. Rapier, Henri A. Gandolfo, George P. Mead, Mrs. Ben C. Toledano, Hugh Smith, Dr. and Mrs. Robert C. Judice, Dr. Ambrose H. Storck, Dr. Jessie Poesch, Professor Robert W. Neuman, Dr. Jack D. L. Holmes, Dr. Mark McKiernan, Mr. and Mrs. Robert S. Eddy III, Mrs. Louis Früchter, Sidney L. Villeré, Walter C. Flower III, Dr. T. Harry Williams and Alfred A. Knopf, Inc., the late Dewey A. Somdal, Professor Joe G. Taylor, Professor Philip D. Uzee, René R. Nicaud, Dr. Joy Jackson, Dr. R. S. Savoy, Richard Remy Dixon, Mr. and Mrs. Beauregard L. Bassich, Joseph Merrick Jones, Major Henry M. Morris, Donald F. Schultz, Mrs. Ferdinand H. Latrobe, Mrs. John Dart, Jr., Charles L. Dufour, Mr. and Mrs. Samuel Wilson, Jr., Thomas A. Greene, Miss Margaret Ruckert, Miss Mary A. Waits, Mrs. Bernadette H. Hellmers, G. William Nott, Arthur L. P. Scully, Jr., Angelo J. Mariano, Ray Samuel, Earl Cancienne, Comtesse Paul de Leusse, Robert Polack, the late Hugh M. Wilkinson, Mrs. Albert F. W. Habeeb, Mlle. M. H. Menier, Dan S. Leyrer, Gerald E. Arnold, Stuart Lynn, Carroll Fuller, Charles L. Franck, Monsignor Henry C. Bezou, Edwin Gebhart, Dr. Sherwood Gagliano, Maurice Ries, Herbert E. Long, and Bernardo Parlange, Mexican Consul General at New Orleans. My thanks also go to Goodloe Stuck and Thomas F. Ruffin of

Shreveport who loaned photographs and sent detailed information on the Shreveport region. To Norman Kotker, Alice Trapasso, and Ronald Farber, I am greatly indebted for their scholarly work in the editing and design of this book. Last but not least I am thankful to my wife, Audrey Wells Huber, for the patience and understanding she exhibited while I put this book together.

L.V.H.

Louisiana—1850

An 1850 map shows Louisiana's division into parishes and marks the canals, roads, and steamboat routes crossing the state. At upper right is an inset map of New Orleans.

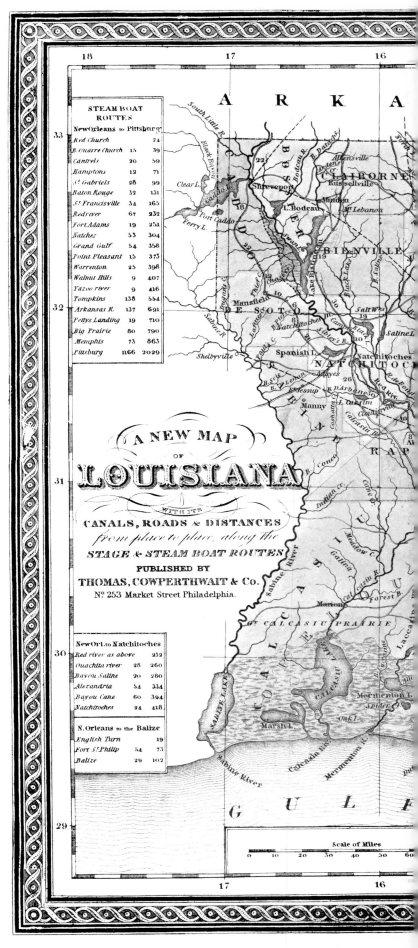

A NEW MAP OF LOUISIANA WITH ITS CANALS, ROADS & DISTANCES from place to place, along the STAGE & STEAM BOAT ROUTES PUBLISHED BY THOMAS, COWPERTHWAIT & Co. No 253 Market Street Philadelphia.

STEAM BOAT ROUTES

NewOrleans to Pittsburg

Red Church		24
B. Ouarre Church	15	39
Cantrels	20	59
Hamptons	12	71
S! Gabriels	28	99
Baton Rouge	32	131
S! Francisville	34	165
Redriver	67	232
Fort Adams	19	251
Natchez	53	304
Grand Gulf	54	358
Point Pleasant	15	373
Warrenton	25	398
Walnut Hills	9	407
Yazoo river	9	416
Tompkins	138	554
Arkansas R.	137	691
Pettys Landing	19	710
Big Prairie	80	790
Memphis	73	863
Pittsburg	1166	2029

NewOrl. to Natchitoches

Red river as above		232
Ouachita river	28	260
Bayou Saline	20	280
Alexandria	54	334
Bayou Cane	60	394
Natchitoches	24	418

N. Orleans to the Balize

English Turn		19
Fort S! Philip	54	73
Balize	29	102

Scale of Miles
0 10 20 30 40 50 60

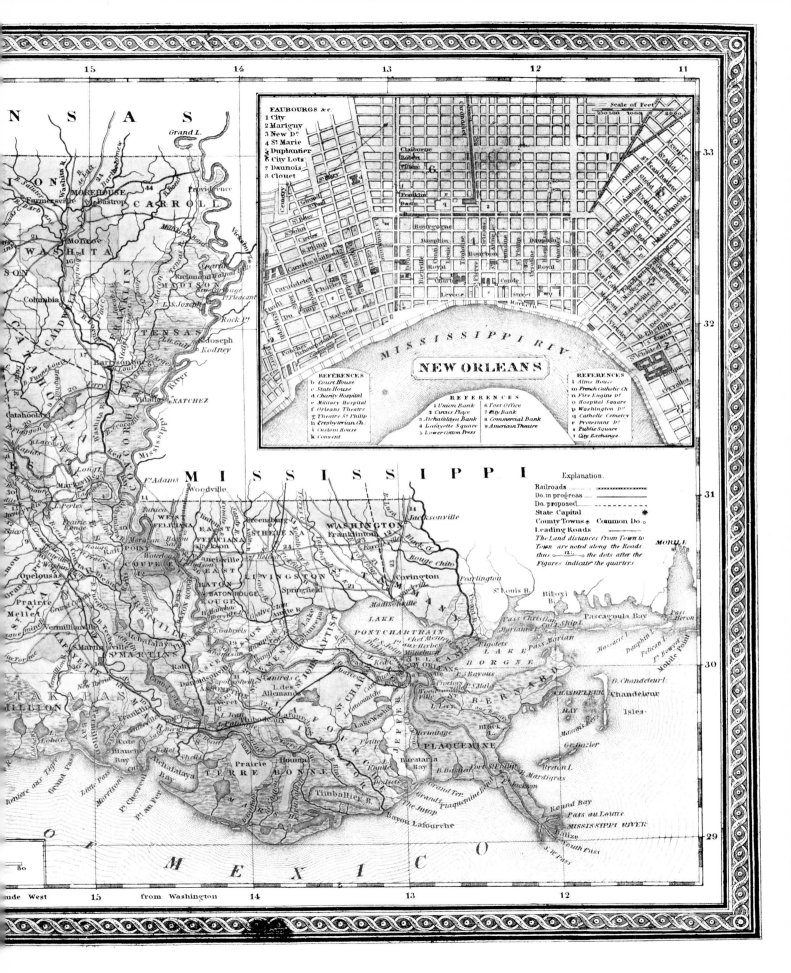

LOUISIANA

Introduction

The word "Louisiane" fell for the first time on human ears on April 9, 1682, at the mouth of the River Colbert—which was later to be called the Mississippi. It was uttered as the name of the new land by René-Robert Cavelier, sieur de La Salle, after he had planted a wooden cross and addressed his followers, taking possession in the name of his king of a territory so vast that not even a hundred and twenty years later did men realize its full extent. La Salle's successor, Iberville, coming to the Gulf Coast in 1699, founded French settlements in what are now the states of Mississippi and Alabama. It was not until 1714 that the first permanent post within the boundaries of the present state of Louisiana was established at Natchitoches.

In 1803 the immense Louisiana Territory, for more than a century a pawn of French and Spanish rulers, was acquired by the United States through purchase. The next year it was carved up by Congress into two units: the vast District of Louisiana and the Territory of Orleans; this latter portion, below the thirty-third parallel, eventually became the state of Louisiana. This book endeavors to trace in pictures Louisiana's colorful and dramatic story from its discovery to the present day.

Louisiana is a state of contrasts. Generally the northern part is hilly and the southern part flat. Some of its cities are unlike each other: Monroe in the north and Lafayette in the south have distinctive characteristics and New Orleans, with its French-Spanish background, has a flavor quite different from the state's second largest city, Shreveport, which is said to resemble Dallas. New Orleans was a great melting pot. Its original white Creole families were augmented by the coming of settlers of Anglo-Saxon blood and by the infusion of Irish, German and Italian immigrants. Negroes of all shades were part of the local scene from earliest times. Westward from New Orleans live the descendants of the Acadians; farther west are the great-grandchildren of German and Scandinavian farmers who migrated to Louisiana in the 1880's from the Midwest. North of New Orleans in two of the most beautiful parishes, East and West Feliciana, are descendants of English colonists who came there from the seaboard states. The north, central and northwest are largely peopled by the offspring of immigrants from Mississippi, Alabama, and the Carolinas who "went west" in search of new lands. South of New Orleans are the descendants of the Islenos, whose forbears came from the Canary Islands in Spanish times.

The state has had a history of epic proportions. In the nearly two and three-quarter centuries since its founding by the French, Louisiana has been the pawn of kings and speculators; it witnessed the first revolt against a European power in North America, was transferred from king to king and then sold to the United States, saw the coming of the steamboat, the development of the plantation system, and the almost magical growth of its principal port, New Orleans. During the Civil War it suffered the fall of its principal city, the ruin of its shipping business, and the paralyzing of its plantations. The blight of occupation and reconstruction left scars which took years to heal; then came the slow and painful struggle back to normality. Meanwhile, Louisianans have endured semi-tropical heat and mosquitoes and struggled with epidemics of cholera and yellow fever and with floods, fire, and hurricanes.

Hernando De Soto, with his expedition of gold-seeking soldiers, had probably been the first white man to set foot on the soil of the future state of Louisiana. After three futile years spent fighting Indians in Florida, Alabama, Georgia, Mississippi, and Arkansas, De Soto died on the banks of the great river that he had discovered a year earlier. The place was opposite present-day Natchez; the date May 21, 1542. Incredibly, one hundred and thirty-two years passed before other white men (Jolliet and Marquette) rediscovered the Mississippi as they traveled down from Canada to the mouth of the Arkansas River, and it was not until 1682 that La Salle, also starting from Canada, traced the course of the Mississippi to its mouth and took possession of the vast Mississippi Valley for France, and named it in honor of his king, Louis XIV.

To forestall English hopes for expansion and to find "a port where the French might establish themselves and harass the Spaniards in those regions whence they derive their wealth," La Salle proposed to undertake a new expedition to found and fortify a settlement on the Mississippi about 200 miles from its mouth. Setting out in 1684, he sailed too far westward, however, landing at Matagorda Bay, Texas, in the belief that it was a western mouth of the Mississippi. La Salle abandoned the search for the river and set out on foot for the Illinois country; but just a few weeks after he had begun his journey he was treacherously assassinated by some of his own men.

After the disastrous La Salle expedition the French lost interest in Louisiana, but the publication of Father Louis Hennepin's flamboyant *Nouvelle Découverte* (1697), and warnings that the English were pushing into the Mississippi Valley, caused a reawakening of interest in the territory at the court of Louis XIV. Previous voyages had been largely exploratory; now the court determined to establish a permanent outpost of France in the New World to guard against further expansion by the English and Spanish.

The king's minister of marine, comte de Pontchartrain, chose Pierre Le Moyne, sieur d'Iberville, as the leader of a new attempt to find the mouth of the Mississippi and to establish a colony near it. Iberville was a Canadian, a man eminently fitted for the task, a brilliant soldier-sailor who had worsted the English in sea and land battles in Canada.

The expedition, consisting of two men-of-war and two coastal vessels, sailed from Brest on October 24, 1698. Arriving at Mobile Bay in February, 1699, Iberville learned from the Indians that the great river was a short distance to the west. He anchored his fleet off Ship Island and with a party in small boats set out for the mouth of the Mississippi, which they entered on March 3, 1699. On the next day, Shrove Tuesday, or "Mardi Gras," they started upstream and made camp for the night at the first great bend in the river, "on a point on the right of the river which we have named Mardi Gras point"—the first place-name on the mainland of Louisiana. Two days later, after battling high winds and the strong current, the explorers passed a site located on a beautiful curve of the river; this place, an Indian guide told the Frenchmen, was a portage between the river and the lake, which flowed into the gulf where their ships were anchored. Young Bienville, Iberville's brother, surely must have been impressed with the site, for two decades later Bienville was to found New Orleans there.

Iberville, however, was still not sure he was on the Mississippi because he could not locate a fork in the river which he had been told existed. He pushed farther upstream. He and his men were received warmly at the Indian village of the Bayagoulas and Mougoulachas, about 30 miles south of the present-day city of Baton Rouge. Iberville was surprised to see the chief of the Mougoulachas wearing a blue serge coat and a red cravat, which unmistakably were of Canadian style. The coat had been given to the chief by Henri de Tonty in 1686, thirteen years earlier, when Tonty had paddled down the Mississippi, searching in vain for his friend La Salle.

When Iberville reached the vicinity of the mouth of the Red River an Indian told him that Tonty had left a letter with the chief of the Bayagoulas; the chief was to give it to any man who came upriver from the sea. So Iberville started his return journey. He decided that the river did not fork. He divided his party into two groups. His group returned to their ships by way of lakes Maurepas and Pontchartrain; his brother, Bienville, continued downriver with another party and retrieved Tonty's letter, obtaining it in exchange for a hatchet. Tonty's letter was addressed to "M. de La Salle, governor general of Louisiana." One can imagine the great satisfaction Iberville derived from reading it.

From the village of the Quinipissas
20 April 1685 (1686)

Sir,

The post on which you had affixed the arms of the king, I found to have been overturned by the driftwood [washed up] by the tides and I had another one planted farther northward about seven leagues from the sea. I left a letter in a tree next to it in a hole in the back, with a sign above it.

The Quinipissas having danced the calumet for me, I left this letter with them to assure you of my humble respects, and to inform you that . . . I descended [the river] . . . I close by telling you that it is with great disappointment to me that we are leaving this place with the misfortune of not having found you, after two canoes skirted the coast thirty leagues toward Mexico, and twenty-five toward the Florida cape . . .

Iberville now had the confirmation he needed. The river was indeed La Salle's Mississippi!

As supplies were dwindling Iberville chose a site on the Bay of Biloxi and constructed a fort which he called Maurepas, at the present site of Ocean Springs, Mississippi. The fort was garrisoned with 76 men under the command of Sauvolle, with Iberville's 19-year-old brother Bienville as second in command; and on May 3, 1699, Iberville sailed for France to report on his mission.

When Iberville returned to Biloxi on January 8, 1700, he learned that the English had appeared on the Mississippi. The previous September Bienville had come upon the British ship *Carolina Galley* anchored in the river, awaiting favorable winds to proceed farther upstream. Young Bienville ordered the English captain William Bond to retire immediately, with the warning that there was a large French force stationed upstream. This was a ruse, but it was successful; the Englishman pulled up anchor and sailed downstream. The bend in the river where this incident occurred has since been known as English Turn, or *Détour à l'Anglais*.

Iberville constructed a little wooden fort on the river which he named Fort Mississippi, near present-day Phoenix. Bienville was placed in command with a force of 15 men and an armament of four cannon. This fort, shown on some maps as Fort de La Boulaye, was the first establishment built by the French within the limits of the present state of Louisiana.

Iberville made a third voyage to the colony in late 1701. At this time he ordered that an establishment be laid out on Mobile Bay and that a fortified town be built on a bluff on the Mobile River, and that Fort Maurepas be abandoned. The new Fort Louis de la Louisiane was completed before Iberville left for France. Bienville was put in charge, and Fort Louis became the capital of the Louisiana Territory. It was not to remain so; the French, for various reasons, moved their capital down the river to the edge of Mobile Bay in 1711, then back in 1720 to a new site near old Fort Maurepas on Biloxi Bay, and finally to New Orleans in 1722.

The French colonists in the first two decades of the eighteenth century were hard put to survive. Many times there was a scarcity of food; there was sickness and often death; there was the indolence of *voyageurs* from the upper valley and the *coureurs de bois;* there were inefficiency in management, quarrels among leaders; there was boredom. And there was a scarcity of women until 1703 when a group of marriageable girls was sent to the colony.

Nevertheless, some progress was made in exploring and in treating with the Indians. Attempts were made to colonize the province. The French court had visions of large revenues in gold, silver, and pearls; but disillusionment soon set in. When the colony's maintenance proved to be a constant drain on the royal treasury, the king in 1712 farmed out the exclusive trading rights to his counselor, Antoine Crozat, the secretary of the royal treasury and a man of immense fortune. The 15-year contract called for importing more colonists and slaves from Africa. Crozat intended to make the venture successful through mining and trading with Mexico.

During this period another French explorer, Louis Juchereau de Saint Denis, traveled extensively in western Louisiana and in Mexico. It was he who in 1714 established Fort Saint Jean-Baptiste (now Natchitoches) to protect French territory in the Red River country.

Crozat sent over a new governor to succeed Bienville. He was Antoine de La Mothe Cadillac, a pompous Gascon who failed, in the four years that he governed the colony, to find gold or silver mines and to effect any considerable increase in colonization. Cadillac was recalled, and Jean Michiele, sieur de Lépinay, was sent to replace him; he lasted just six months. When he was recalled Crozat petitioned the ministry of marine to take back Louisiana; his unfortunate venture had cost him more than two million livres.

Just when Crozat was abandoning his concession a new figure appeared on the scene: John Law, the Scottish financial wizard who had gained enormous influence in France and proposed a grandiose financial scheme to pull the bankrupt country out of debt. As part of the scheme, Law founded an organization called the Company of the West, which received a 25-year charter granting a complete monopoly on trade in Louisiana. The company was capitalized at 100 million livres; Law's extravagant publicity lured thousands of investors who wanted a share of the quick wealth that the gold and silver mines in Louisiana were expected to provide. Philippe d'Orléans, the regent of France, enthusiastic over Law's enterprises, made Law's private bank into a state institution, and France became a partner in Law's financial organization.

The charter of the company provided that 6,000 white settlers and 3,000 slaves should be brought to Louisiana within ten years. In 1718, 300 concessionaries with land grants arrived on American shores, but by the next year Law and his associates began to realize that volunteer immigration would not succeed and that the company (now renamed the Company of the Indies) would have to resort to forced immigration. For about six months ne'er-do-wells, prostitutes, convicts, and smugglers were transported to Louisiana until the regent put a stop to it. Then, in order to improve the quality of immigration, Law's agents visited Germany and distributed glowing pamphlets about life in Louisiana. As a result, hundreds of hard-working German peasants who were promised land, tools, seeds, and livestock to begin farming left their homeland and set sail for Louisiana. Law, now comptroller-general of France, sent the greater part of more than 2,000 Germans who survived the arduous and dangerous sea voyage to land upriver in the present-day state of Arkansas.

One of the first of Law's plans was to establish a city on the banks of the Mississippi "thirty leagues up the river, a town that should be named New Orleans, which one could reach by the river or by Lake Pontchartrain." Accordingly, in the spring of 1718, Bienville came to the Mississippi River, and with a force of 40 men—30 of them former convicts—started the work of clearing the land and laying out the new city. Leaving Major Jacques Paillou de Barbezan in charge, Bienville returned to Mobile, but very little work was done during the next three years until the engineer Adrien de Pauger arrived in 1721 to lay out the streets. Pauger had been sent by his chief, Leblond de La Tour, who had made a good plan of the future city. Pauger cleared a considerable area of land and built a large warehouse for the king's supplies —food, trade goods, and, in all probability, weapons too.

Meanwhile in France John Law's house of cards, which had grown higher and shakier by the day, finally tumbled. On May 21, 1720, an edict reducing the value of the company's bank notes by one-half caused a run on his bank and brought utter ruin to bank and speculators alike. "The Mississippi Bubble" had burst; Law had to flee for his life, and France was again bankrupt.

Law's Germans in Arkansas, now abandoned without even having harvested their crops, descended the Mississippi to New Orleans and demanded to be repatriated. Bienville's handling of this disenchanted group, and perhaps also the fear of another horrible sea voyage back to Europe, convinced them to settle on the west bank of the Mississippi, about 25 miles above New Orleans. Establishing themselves in two villages, they soon had small farms under cultivation. This and the founding of New Orleans was the beginning of a stable Louisiana— something that had taken the French almost a quarter of a century to accomplish. But by 1721 New Orleans had a population of 470, and there were about 1,200 more Louisianans scattered up and down the river near the town.

In 1722 a hurricane struck Louisiana, and two-thirds of the buildings in New Orleans were destroyed. Despite the catastrophe, that same year the capital of Louisiana was moved from Biloxi to New Orleans. The next year saw the construction of the first levee to keep the rampaging Mississippi from flooding the town, and a year later Pauger could report to Paris that "at present everyone works, vying with one another. Workshops and buildings are seen to rise everywhere so that New Orleans is growing before one's eyes and there is no longer any doubt that it is going to become a great city." Pauger was never to see the completion of his work; he died two years later and was buried under the church of St. Louis, which he had designed.

The year of Pauger's report saw the introduction to Louisiana of the Code Noir, or Black Code, a very important piece of legislation which had been drawn up in France. Designed to regulate the conduct of slaves, it laid down laws to protect them from injustice and cruelty. The Code's 54 articles dealt with working conditions, holidays, and marriages, ensured that adequate subsistence and housing be provided for slaves, and fixed penalties for runaways.

These early years were marked by continual quarrels among the leaders of the colony. Bienville, who had been a peacemaker with the nearby Indians, seemed to have a marked capacity for making enemies among his superiors and subordinates alike. Criticisms of his conduct reached Paris; an official investigation was made, and the "father of Louisiana" and founder of New Orleans was recalled from his post in 1725.

Etienne de Périer, a lieutenant in the king's navy, was sent to succeed Bienville. Périer inherited a colony racked with dissension, and with quarrels between Capuchins and Jesuits over religious jurisdiction. Two events lifted the spirits of the colonists, however: the arrival of six Ursuline nuns in 1727 to found a school for girls and tend the hospital, and shortly thereafter the entry of a cargo of marriageable girls who were placed in the nuns' care. In 1729 an Indian massacre of 250 colonists at Fort Rosalie, the present-day Natchez, threw the capital into a panic, and Périer ordered the construction of a rampart and a moat and issued arms to citizens. The defeat of the Natchez tribe next year under French leadership ended the threat of invasion.

In 1731 the Company of the Indies, profitless and beset by a multitude of problems, petitioned

Louis XV to take back the colony; once more Louisiana became a charge of the monarch. Périer was recalled and in 1732, Bienville, then in his fifty-second year, was summoned out of retirement by the king to become for the first time officially governor of Louisiana. After an absence of eight years Bienville returned to New Orleans in 1733. He found the colony short of provisions, merchandise, and money, and the Capuchins and Jesuits still feuding. The population had decreased, and the attitude of the Indians toward the French had sharply deteriorated.

The last ten years of Bienville's tenure in Louisiana saw improvements in his relations with his associates and the colonists, but the governor was continually vexed with Indian problems, particularly with the troublesome Chickasaws. In 1743 Bienville reluctantly asked to be relieved. He retired to Paris, where he lived for another 24 years.

The new governor of Louisiana was Pierre de Rigaud, marquis de Vaudreuil. Vaudreuil, a 45-year-old Canadian, and his 60-year-old wife immediately captivated the Louisianans with their good taste, elegant manners, and elaborate entertainments. The governor was named "The Grand Marquis," and the ten years that he governed Louisiana (1743–53) was a period of concord and prosperity. Peace with the Indians was restored, contending religious orders stopped their quarrels, and there was even some growth in the colony. This period was marked by the establishment of a social elite. Among the wealthy in New Orleans and in the plantations nearby there were balls, soirées, banquets, and entertainments on a scale not seen before. Economic life flourished too. Experiments had been made with sugar-cane planting as early as 1742, but in 1751, during Vaudreuil's governorship, the Jesuits undertook planting on a more ambitious scale. Though their efforts were not a conspicuous success, their venture marked the modest beginning of the great sugar industry which was to become a major source of prosperity for Louisiana in later years.

In 1753 Vaudreuil was appointed governor of Canada and left New Orleans. His successor was Louis Billouart de Kerlérec, a distinguished naval officer who had in his 25-year career already seen service in Louisiana. Kerlérec soon found himself frustrated by a shortage of goods to trade with the Indians and by the incompetence of the French troops under his command (which was a particularly worrisome problem since the Seven Years' War had broken out), and he was fearful of an attack by sea from the English.

Unfortunately for the governor, a conniving *commissaire-ordonnateur,* Vincent-Pierre-Gaspard de Rochemore, was sent to Louisiana to report on the progress of the colony. Rochemore became Kerlérec's bitter enemy and sent back reports to Paris charging Kerlérec with wastefulness and extravagance. At the same time he himself, with power almost equal to that of Kerlérec's, permitted favored merchants and officials in certain circles to accumulate fortunes through speculation and through sharp and sometimes illegal trading. This laissez-faire policy in the colony sowed seeds of rebellion which were to bear fruit in the next decade. Eventually, Rochemore was removed and another intendant, Nicolas-Denis Foucault, succeeded him. But Foucault was as great a troublemaker as his predecessor, and his charges of malfeasance against Kerlérec resulted in the governor's recall and imprisonment in the Bastille.

At the conclusion of the Seven Years' War France had lost Canada and all of Louisiana east of the Mississippi except the "island" of New Orleans. The duc de Choiseul, Louis XV's foreign minister, was determined to rid France of Louisiana too, a colony that had caused nothing but trouble since it was founded. Choiseul urged the king to make a gift of Louisiana to his Spanish cousin, Charles III. Louis agreed, and Charles, seeing the gift as a useful buffer against English expansion toward Mexico, consented too. Louisiana was ceded to Spain by a secret treaty of November 3, 1762. Eighty years had passed since La Salle had come down the Mississippi and claimed for France the land drained by the great river.

The Bourbon cousins kept the treaty of cession secret for a year and a half; nearly two years were to pass before the Spanish government finally made efforts to take possession of Louisiana. In October, 1764, Jean-Jacques-Blaise Dabbadie, who had succeeded Kerlérec in 1763, announced to the stunned Louisianans that they were to pass under the rule of Spain. Shocked and disappointed, leaders in New Or-

leans and delegates from the surrounding countryside held a mass meeting which resulted in the sending of a wealthy citizen, Jean Milhet, to Paris to petition the king not to relinquish Louisiana. Milhet received no encouragement at the French court and was not even able to reach the king to present his petition. Hope vanished when word reached New Orleans that Charles III had taken over in earnest by naming a governor of Louisiana, Antonio de Ulloa, a captain in the Spanish navy. Ulloa, a savant of great repute, disembarked in New Orleans on March 5, 1766, with an entourage of three civil officers and only 90 Spanish troops. The Spaniards had held the mistaken idea that the French troops in Louisiana would join their forces; but they had not reckoned on the temper of the colonists. Because of the meager forces the new governor had brought with him and because of the absence of any apparent effort on his part to assume command (in fact, he held himself aloof from public view and delegated his authority to the French commandant), some of the colonists began to imagine that the transfer was not intended to be a permanent one and that the colony would soon again come under French rule. Among these were merchants and planters apprehensive that the application of restrictive Spanish commercial regulations would deprive them of the easy profits they had enjoyed in recent years as a result of the permissiveness and connivance of the French intendants. Some of the more rebellious leaders decided to take matters into their own hands and formed a conspiracy to expel Ulloa. The French commandant, Charles-Philippe Aubry, did everything in his power to restrain the plotters; but on October 28, 1768, a number of excited New Orleanians, with the help of some Acadian colonists from the outlying parishes, "took" the city. Aubry managed to save Ulloa and his family by helping them escape on a Spanish frigate which was providentially anchored before the city. There was much excitement and loud talk, but fortunately no bloodshed.

The Spanish, so slow in taking over Louisiana, were quick to react to Ulloa's expulsion. To avenge Ulloa, Charles III sent one of his favorite generals, Count Alexander O'Reilly, an Irishman in the service of Spain, with 2,600 troops and 50 cannon. O'Reilly arrived on August 18, 1769, his troops deploying from 24 vessels. With church bells ringing, cannon booming, and flags flying, they marched to the Place d'Armes, where Aubry handed over the keys to the city in an impressive ceremony. The flag of France was lowered and that of Spain raised.

Although O'Reilly had had reports of the conspiracy, he made an independent investigation, and acting on instructions of the king, tried the 12 ringleaders including one who had already been killed while resisting capture. Six were sentenced to death and six to imprisonment. After the sentences were carried out, O'Reilly wisely granted amnesty or pardon to all the others who had signed the petition to expel Ulloa. The short-lived "freedom" that the Louisianans had enjoyed thus came to an end. The first revolution on the North American continent by European settlers against a European power had ended in failure.

O'Reilly abolished the superior council of the French and substituted a group called the Illustrious Cabildo. The Cabildo, similar to that in other provincial colonial Spanish towns, was partly a legislative and partly an administrative council. The main laws came directly from Spain, or from the captain-general in Havana, or from the governor himself; there was no real legislative body.

O'Reilly ordered a census taken, which demonstrated that there were 3,187 persons in New Orleans. The results showed:

Free persons, including 31 blacks
and 69 of mixed blood   1,902
Slaves   1,225
Domesticated Indians   60

There were 468 houses in the city, and while no census was taken of the inhabitants in the various parishes, or counties, that then comprised Louisiana, the historian François-Xavier Martin later estimated that at that time there were about 9,500 inhabitants in the area of the present state, excluding New Orleans.

O'Reilly did little to disturb the lives and customs of the Creoles, who continued to retain their characteristic French speech and ways. The population quickly became reconciled to Spanish rule. Luis de Unzaga, who had come to Louisiana with O'Reilly, was proclaimed governor by him at the first meeting of the Cabildo on December 1, 1769, but O'Reilly continued to

exercise his influence until he sailed for Spain on October 29, 1770.

Unzaga, a man of considerable ability, soon realized that a strict interpretation of Spanish commercial laws would strangle Louisiana. He therefore winked at the contraband trade, largely British in origin, which had supplied many of the necessities of the colony. He showed marked sympathy for the French language and the customs of the Creoles as well as for the French Capuchin monks; when the French Capuchins' spiritual leadership was challenged by the leader of the Spanish branch of the order, the governor took the part of the French. In other ways he helped reconcile the essentially French community to the rule of Spain.

In 1777 Unzaga was succeeded by Bernardo de Gálvez, a dashing young soldier then only twenty-nine years old. Gálvez further relaxed trade restrictions and permitted American agents to establish bases in New Orleans, through which they provided the rebel Atlantic colonies with supplies and munitions in their struggle with Great Britain. Although Gálvez was helping the Americans, his prime purpose was to hurt the English, in order to recover possessions that Spain had lost to Britain in the Seven Years' War.

In 1779, during the American Revolution, Spain was an ally of France, and found itself at war with England. Gálvez led successful expeditions against British-held Manchac, Baton Rouge, Natchez, Mobile, and Pensacola. By May, 1781, both East and West Florida were added to Spanish Louisiana, and for the first time in its history the area now comprising the state came under one flag. The northern boundary of West Florida, set at thirty-one degrees by the Treaty of Paris in 1783, ultimately became the northern border of the portion of Louisiana lying east of the Mississippi.

In 1785 when Gálvez was named viceroy of Mexico, Esteban Miró became governor. An affable, goodhearted, and honorable man, Miró married into a prominent Creole family, and under his administration the Creole population became fully reconciled to Spanish rule. It was in Miró's administration that the great fire of March 21, 1788, laid waste to the greater part of the city of New Orleans. Eight-hundred and fifty-six buildings were destroyed, and the population, then about 5,000, suffered from a scarcity of provisions which taxed the resources of the governor to supply.

Another noteworthy event which occurred in Miró's time was the movement of more than 1,600 Acadians from France to Louisiana. These exiles had languished in France and had for years led a hand-to-mouth existence, neglected by the king from whom they had expected help. In 1784 a former resident of Louisiana, Peyroux de La Coudrenière, then living in Nantes, France, induced the king of Spain to transport these unhappy people to Louisiana. In 1785 they came, 400 families in seven ships, one of the largest transatlantic movements of colonists in the history of America up until then. The Spanish authorities assisted them with land, seeds, tools, and farm animals, and soon they were among the most prosperous and sturdiest of colonists. This wave of Acadians settled along the Mississippi, in the Attakapas, at Donaldsonville, Opelousas, and along Bayou Lafourche. Many of them intermarried with Germans, the older Creoles, and the Anglo-Americans, and it is estimated that there are today about half a million Louisianans who have "Cajun" blood in their veins.

Baron Francisco Luis Héctor de Carondelet, a Belgian in the service of Spain, succeeded Miró, taking office on January 1, 1792. Carondelet was an energetic and determined man who effected many improvements in Louisiana. Under him the city of New Orleans had its first newspaper (published in French), the *Moniteur de la Louisiane,* of which he was the real editor; its first street lights—80 oil lamps suspended on chains across street corners; its first theatre which was opened in October, 1792, by the brothers Henry; and its first night watchmen and police commissaries. Carondelet erected two forts, St. Charles and Bourgogne, at the city's outskirts, since he was fearful of attacks by the British or by the Americans from upriver. He ordered the digging of a canal (known in later years as the Carondelet Canal) from the headwaters of Bayou St. John to the center of the city. This ditch was made to relieve New Orleans streets of flood water from the rains; it was eventually widened and deepened to become a waterway used by vessels from the Gulf Coast and towns across Lake Pontchartrain.

Carondelet, the Louisiana Spaniards, and most of the Creoles were monarchists, and they were fearful of the results of the revolution that erupted in France in 1789 and the slave rebellion that broke out in Saint-Domingue. War broke out between France and Spain in 1793, and the governor was concerned with the possibility of invasion by the French and Americans and uneasy about plots from within, particularly after the close of the war in 1795, when French vessels once more came to Louisiana bringing some of the more vocal troublemakers. These people were eventually sent away to Havana.

During the years 1793–94 Louisiana was struck by three hurricanes, and on December 8, 1794, a second disastrous fire destroyed practically all the remaining French colonial buildings in New Orleans; some 200 houses were consumed by the fire, which had been started by some boys in the yard of a building on Royal Street.

In Carondelet's time Louisiana was separated by the pope from the bishopric of Havana and a new see established at New Orleans, with Louis Peñalver y Cárdenas as its first bishop. The church of St. Louis became a cathedral. Also notable in Carondelet's administration was the planting by Jean-Etienne Boré of the first commercially successful crop of sugar cane. Boré's venture firmly established the sugar industry in Louisiana.

A most important political event also occurred during Carondelet's governorship. Louisiana had come to depend more and more for the bulk of its commerce upon trade with settlers in the Ohio valley; yet the flatboatmen bringing products of field and forest to New Orleans were sometimes denied passage through Spanish territory. Seizure and confiscation of cargoes irritated the Tennesseans and Kentuckians particularly, and they proposed taking New Orleans by force or seceding from the Union and joining Spain. But eventually a treaty was signed between Spain and the United States which, among other things, granted Americans the use of the port of New Orleans as a "place of deposit." This allowed the Americans the privilege of exporting their merchandise or produce without paying duty. Subsequently, the treaty of 1797 was not formally renewed, but the Americans, with the tacit consent of the Spanish government, continued to use the port until October 16, 1802. At that time, the intendant, Juan Ventura Morales, suddenly revoked the privilege and closed the port. This precipitated a crisis, since it severely curtailed American trade down the Mississippi. The United States began to look for ways to get control of the mouth of the Mississippi.

Carondelet, who had gone on to assume the presidency of the Royal Audience of Quito in 1797, was succeeded by Brigadier General Manuel Luis Gayoso de Lemos, the former governor of the Natchez district. Gayoso was an affable and kindly man whose short tenure in office was unfortunately hampered by frequent disputes with the intendant Morales, a troublemaker. Gayoso died of a fever suddenly on July 18, 1799, at the age of forty-eight. He is the only colonial governor, French or Spanish, to be buried in Louisiana, his remains being entombed in the Saint Louis Cathedral in New Orleans.

The last Spanish governor, General Juan Manuel de Salcedo, arrived in 1801. Salcedo was well advanced in years and, as an observer noted, "somewhat infirm in mind as well as in body." His term came to an end when Louisiana was transferred to France on November 30, 1803, following thirty-four years of Spanish rule. The transfer took place on the insistence of Napoleon Bonaparte. He wanted a colonial empire in America, and bullied Spain, which was under his thumb, to hand over Louisiana.

After its bloody beginning, Spanish rule had been quite satisfactory to the Creoles. At least one historian called it a wise government, and without a doubt the Spanish governors before Salcedo were exceptionally able men. The population of New Orleans and that of the territory quadrupled, and the commerce of the port of New Orleans saw substantial growth. But one fact stands out: the Louisianans resisted all efforts to transform them into Spaniards. They remained French to the end of the regime.

Surrendering to the continual demands by Napoleon Bonaparte, then First Consul, Spain retroceded the "Colony or Province of Louisiana" to France by the Treaty of San Ildefonso in 1800. When President Jefferson learned the news he requested Robert R. Livingston, United States minister in Paris, to try to find out what France intended to do. The President wrote: "There is on the globe one single spot, the possessor of which is our natural and habitual enemy—it is New Orleans through which the produce of three-eighths of our territory must pass to market." His fears were well justified, for Napoleon was preparing to transport an army to occupy Louisiana. He sent Pierre-Clement de Laussat as colonial prefect to New Orleans to prepare for the arrival of the French troops under General Claude Victor, but yellow fever, the slave uprisings in Saint-Domingue, and a winter of great cold delayed Napoleon's scheme and forced him to alter his plans. Yielding to the persistent efforts of Livingston and James Monroe, Napoleon, fearful that he could not hold Louisiana against the British with whom France was soon to be at war, offered the Americans not only New Orleans, which they had been authorized to buy, but the whole territory of Louisiana. After considerable haggling a price of 60 million francs ($15,000,000) was agreed upon, and on May 2, 1803, the Louisiana Purchase was consummated.

Laussat had been welcomed with mixed emotions by the Louisianans. Some of the Creoles, unreconciled to the French Revolution, considered him a dangerous revolutionary, and a number of the Ursuline nuns became so frightened at the prospect of an anti-Catholic government that they left for Havana. Word reached New Orleans in August, 1803, some four months after the prefect's arrival, that Napoleon had disposed of Louisiana, and Laussat's dream of colonial splendor vanished. Chagrined, he was only able to consummate the transfer of Louisiana from Spain to France and its almost immediate cession to the United States. The transfer from Spain to France took place on November 30 at the Cabildo in New Orleans, the headquarters of the Illustrious Cabildo, the city's governing council, and on December 20, 1803, a similar ceremony took place in which the unhappy Laussat signed the *procès verbal* with the American commissioners William C. C. Claiborne and General James Wilkinson. The French flag was lowered and the American flag raised, and the vast Louisiana Territory became part of the United States.

At the time of the purchase, it has been estimated, barely 50,000 persons made their home in the immense territory called Louisiana. New Orleans had about 8,000 inhabitants, half of whom were black. Aside from New Orleans and settlements at Baton Rouge, St. Martinville, Opelousas, Vermilionville (Lafayette), Ouachita Post (Monroe), New Iberia, Alexandria, Natchitoches, and a few isolated trading posts, the area of the present state of Louisiana was mostly undeveloped. The population was centered along the waterways—the Mississippi and Red rivers and the southern bayous. What the region lacked in numbers, it made up in the diversity of its inhabitants. Along bayous Lafourche, Teche, and Vermilion, and in certain stretches on the Mississippi above New Orleans, lived the Acadians. Also on the Mississippi above New Orleans were descendants of the Germans who had been brought over by John Law's Company of the West. Below New Orleans at Bayou Terre-aux-Boeufs and along Bayou Teche were the Isleños, come during Gálvez's administration from the Canary Islands. In West Florida and on the east bank of the Mississippi north of New Orleans were Anglo-American settlers who had migrated to the region between 1763 and 1779, when it belonged to Great Britain. Situated on generous grants of land along the Mississippi in the northern part of the present state were French royalists who had fled France after the Revolution. However, the vast area to the northwest had been penetrated only by trappers and hunters.

Louisianans, particularly New Orleanians, were not completely happy with the transfer of the colony to the United States. They had been fairly content under Spanish rule, and American customs—particularly the use of English as the official language—were not well received. The first American governor was William C. C. Claiborne; he could not speak French and surrounded himself with Anglo-American officials. At first he was unpopular with the inhabitants. The natives looked askance on immigrants who might come from the United States; their acquaintance with the tough and rowdy flatboatmen who came downriver to New Orleans had not left a pleasant impression.

In 1804 Congress divided up the Louisiana Purchase: the immense area lying north of the thirty-third parallel became the District of Louisiana, and the southern portion was called the Territory of Orleans. When the purchase treaty had been signed its description was vague: "the colony or province of Louisiana, with the same extent it now has in the hands of Spain, and that it had when France possessed it; and such as it should be after the treaties subsequently entered into between Spain and other states." This brought immediate difficulties. Spain claimed West Florida as well as the Sabine River area almost as far as Natchitoches, and both Spain and the United States sought to strengthen their claims to the disputed western strip by military occupation. Fortunately, war was averted when Spanish and American commanders agreed to evacuate the contested area and shift the controversy to their respective governments.

The crisis was hardly over when Louisianans were thrown into a near panic by wild rumors that a filibustering expedition under Aaron Burr was headed downriver for New Orleans. It was reported that Burr with a formidable force intended to separate either Mexico from Spain or the Louisiana Territory from the United States, using New Orleans as a base. Under the supervision of General James Wilkinson, an erstwhile friend and confidant of Burr, who had exposed Burr's plans, New Orleans was fortified. Burr, with less than 80 men under his command, succeeded in getting his flotilla of flatboats as far as Bayou Pierre near Natchez. There he was arrested and his band dispersed. Concern over a possible insurrection soon faded.

Many American settlers had arrived in West Florida before the Louisiana Purchase, and the more restless among them had tried, unsuccessfully, to seize the section from Spain in 1805. In 1810 a full-blown revolt took place, and the West Floridans marched on Baton Rouge, which was still under Spanish control, seized the fort, and killed its commander. On September 26, 1810, these revolutionaries declared West Florida a republic, set up a constitution, and applied for admission to the United States. President Madison ordered Governor Claiborne to move with troops into the area. Claiborne took possession despite some opposition and annexed the region to the Territory of Orleans, thus forcibly settling the dispute with Spain over the eastern boundary. The parishes in this part of Louisiana east of the Mississippi are known to this day as the Florida parishes.

According to the census of 1810, the territory of Orleans had a population of 76,556. Much of the population growth came from immigrants arriving from the United States or the West Indies. In 1809 alone 9,000 West Indian refugees came to New Orleans. The population was well over the 60,000 required for admission to the Union. Agitation for admission crystallized on January 11, 1811 with the proposal by congressional delegate Julien Poydras for the admission of the territory as a state. There was prolonged congressional debate and the bill came under violent attack by the New England Federalists who thought of Louisianans as an alien race; but Congress finally authorized the Territory of Orleans to organize itself as a state. Forty-five delegates representing 19 parishes met in convention in New Orleans and drew up a constitution modeled after that of Kentucky. On April 30, 1812, Louisiana became the eighteenth state in the Union. The eastern boundary was Pearl River; in 1819, when Spain finally relinquished its claims to the territory east of the Sabine River, the Sabine became Louisiana's western boundary.

Claiborne, who had been appointed and reappointed territorial goveror six times by presidents Jefferson and Madison, was elected the first governor of the newly constituted state of Louisiana by the legislature. Claiborne was chosen over General Jacques Villeré, a distinguished Creole of an old Louisiana family. This was a surprising victory for one who had been unpopular with the Louisianans on his arrival just nine years earlier.

In the same year that Louisiana became a state, the United States declared war on Great Britain. This war, which went on for nearly a year and a half without any decisive military action, suddenly came alive when the British were able to turn their mighty war machine toward the United States after defeating Napoleon in April, 1814. Admiral Alexander Cochrane led an expeditionary force to raid Washington; he burned the White House and attacked Fort McHenry at Baltimore. Sailing for Jamaica he was joined by a fleet transporting English troops under the command of General John Keene, and the armada, consisting of 50 ships carrying 1,000 guns, headed for the Louisiana coast. Their intention was to detach Louisiana from the United States.

For the British, the siege of New Orleans was to be a series of blunders in judgment. The first mistake was their decision not to sail up the Mississippi past Fort St. Philip, but rather to approach the city from the rear through Lake Borgne, a shallow arm of the Gulf of Mexico. Here on December 14, 1814, the British, in landing barges, overwhelmed five small American gunboats guarding the city's water approach. During the night of December 22–23 the enemy advanced in small boats to a point just nine miles from New Orleans and occupied several sugar plantations below the city.

General Andrew Jackson, the commander of the military district which included Louisiana, had arrived at New Orleans on December 2. He brought with him his regulars and Tennessee militiamen. Jackson had hardly time to organize his forces when the British were on American soil. When he received that news on December 23, he decided on a bold plan: he would strike the enemy on the very night of their arrival.

Catching the British off guard, he gave them the impression that they were being met by a formidable force. He defeated them in a night battle and then withdrew his men a few miles upstream to the Rodriguez Canal, a ditch forming a boundary between two plantations. Here his men threw up a shoulder-high rampart, using mud, fence rails and posts, kegs, and almost anything they could lay their hands on. This mile-long rampart stretched from the Mississippi River to an almost impenetrable swamp.

On Christmas Day, 1814, General Sir Edward M. Pakenham, brother-in-law of the Duke of Wellington and a seasoned campaigner, arrived to command the British forces. Pakenham ordered an attack on the Americans on December 28, but it was repulsed, as was another on January 1, 1815, when the British big guns, brought up laboriously through the swamps, were silenced by American artillery fire.

Fearing that further delay would demoralize his army, Pakenham decided on a frontal assault. In the half light of dawn, on January 8, his men advanced, only to be mowed down in droves by American cannon and the sharpshooters from Tennessee and Kentucky who were part of Jackson's ragtail army. An attack made by the British on the west bank of the Mississippi was successful at first, but it had to be called off because of the bitter defeat suffered by the main force. During the battle General Pakenham was killed.

In this dreadful battle there were 2,057 British casualties and only 71 American. On January 19 the enemy stole away, leaving their campfires burning. Ironically, two weeks before the final battle at New Orleans, England and the United States had signed a treaty of peace; but the news did not reach Louisiana until the battle was over.

The Battle of New Orleans and the American victory had a profound effect on American history. By increasing the people's confidence in the nation's military power, it encouraged a feeling of unity. It strengthened America's prestige in the world and made a popular hero of Andrew Jackson, who was instrumental in stamping frontier democracy on the American political and social order. The battle ultimately sent Andrew Jackson to the White House. It also marked the last bloodshed between the two great English-speaking nations.

Ten years after the Territory of Orleans became the State of Louisiana its population had reached more than 153,000, double the original figure at the time of the purchase. By 1840 the figure increased to 350,000, approximately half of whom were black. The commerce of the state grew almost magically; the plantation system expanded dramatically, and New Orleans emerged as one of the great ports of the world. The arrival from Pittsburgh in 1812 of the first steamboat, a boat prophetically named *New Orleans,* ushered in the city and state's great pre-Civil War development. Steamboat arrivals, slow at first because of a strangling monopoly on steamboat trade, rose from 21 in 1814 to 1,573 in 1840, and tonnage increased from 67,560 to 537,400 during the 26-year period. How much additional freight came by rafts down the river was never recorded, but by 1840 New Orleans had grown to be the fourth largest city in the nation, and it was second as a port only to New York.

Sugar and cotton were two of the principal reasons for the growth of the state. Planters from neighboring states migrated to Louisiana with their slaves because of the fertile land. Sugar plantations sprang up quickly after Jean-Etienne Boré raised the first successful commercial crop in 1796. By 1803 there were 75 sugar mills in the state, and the annual value of the sugar crop before the Civil War was 25 million dollars. It was a similar story with cotton. By 1809 cotton was the principal crop in the northern part of Louisiana. With the coming of the steamboat, which facilitated transport, plantations along the Mississippi and its tributaries were producing ever-increasing crops. By the 1830's yearly production was one-half million bales, all shipped to New Orleans, which by that time had half a dozen compresses and large warehouses.

A man who had much to do with Louisiana's development was Henry Miller Shreve. A pioneer steamboatman, Shreve cleared the Red River of an immense raft, an accumulation of logs, driftwood, and vegetation. Extending over a distance of more than 150 miles, it had clogged the stream from time immemorial. Shreve also invented the snagboat, making possible the removal of dangerous obstructions to steamboat navigation in the rivers. The new settlement of Shreveport was named for him, although he never visited the place.

In 1835 the Caddo Indians who lived in the northwestern part of the state sold their land to the United States for $80,000. When the Red River was unblocked in 1838, this section of the state was rapidly settled, and the Red River became the state's second most important trade artery, with the resulting growth of Shreveport, Natchitoches, and Alexandria.

By 1845 the state constitution of 1812 had become outmoded, and a constitutional convention was called to revise it. Some radical changes were made, including the election of the governor by direct popular vote instead of by the legislature; the broadening of the franchise by eliminating property qualifications for voting; the creation of the office of lieutenant governor; the establishment of a system of free public schools and the creation of the office of a Superintendent of Public Education. Eight state constitutions have been adopted since 1845; the latest one in 1974.

To defend Louisiana's western frontier from frequent depredations by border ruffians and troublesome riffraff, forts were established— Cantonment Jessup west of Natchitoches in 1822 and Cantonment Atkinson at Lake Charles in 1830. In the 1830's American settlers in Texas were engaged in a struggle with Mexico, and Louisianans, particularly in New Orleans, played an important part in the expansion movement that brought on the Mexican War. Orleanians held mass meetings in support of the Texans and helped them with money and mail service and by sending volunteer fighters.

In 1845, in an attempt to settle grievances which had been brought on by the annexation of Texas, President James K. Polk named John Slidell envoy to Mexico; but his mission proved a failure, and General Zachary Taylor, who commanded Fort Jessup, was ordered to march into Texas. There was great excitement in Louisiana, and nearly five thousand citizens answered the call for volunteers. Most of these were mustered out before serious fighting began, as they had only enlisted for three- and six-month hitches. In the Mexican War General Taylor, a Louisianan by adoption, became a popular hero. The success he achieved led to his election as President of the United States. Young P. G. T. Beauregard, of Civil War fame, won his spurs in this war, and another Louisianan, General Persifor Smith, distinguished himself by his skillful leadership and bravery.

After the Mexican War numerous filibustering expeditions against Cuba and other Latin American countries were formed, to help Latin Americans win their independence or overturn existing governments. Primarily because of its geographical situation, New Orleans became the base of many of these operations. In 1849, 1850, and 1851 Narciso López organized expeditions to overthrow Spanish rule in Cuba. Two of these reached Cuba, but in the last one López and a number of his American leaders were captured and executed. Another filibusterer, William Walker, who once called New Orleans his home, led expeditions into Mexico and Nicaragua in the 1850's. Like López, he ended his career before a firing squad. For years thereafter, though, Louisiana harbored jingoes who schemed and plotted ways to intervene in Central American politics.

Outside of New Orleans, Louisiana in the antebellum period was almost entirely rural. Baton Rouge, the second largest town, had 4,000 inhabitants; only six towns had as many as 1,000 persons. In 1860 only 29 per cent of the population owned slaves, and quite a number of these slaveholders were themselves free people of color.

In the 1840's and 1850's most of Louisiana's plantation homes were built along the rivers and bayous. The Greek Revival style was then in full flower, and these stately columned mansions were the symbols of the wealth which had been wrung from the land in sugar plantations in the South and in the cotton fields of the North. Many of these imposing edifices after years of neglect have been restored with care and taste and stand as memorials to a period of history that has vanished.

The plantation economy produced a new upper class—men who advanced in state affairs through wealth rather than birth. Allied with the planters were the brokers, bankers, factors, steamboat owners, lawyers, and shipping operators; they dominated business in New Orleans. The city's credit facilities for export and import, sales and purchases, and the legal negotiations essential to the economic life of the plantation system depended on this new class. Many of them were Anglo-Americans who had come to the state after the purchase; there were waves of immigrants from foreign countries, too, particularly Germany and Ireland. Eventually the newcomers eclipsed the Creole population. The aristocratic Creoles resented these *parvenus,* and the city of New Orleans was split up into three municipalities named, logically enough, the First, Second, and Third Municipality. The two lower sections were largely Creole, the upper one largely Anglo-American.

The mushroom growth of banks in New Orleans in the 1820's and 1830's, combined with inadequate supervision, the issuance of too much paper money, and an immense speculative movement in lands, resulted in a great financial crash. On May 13, 1837, fourteen New Orleans banks suspended specie payment, and a wave of bankruptcies in commercial houses soon followed. It was not until 1839 that some recovery occurred, although effects of the panic were still being felt as late as 1845.

From 1796 on, almost annually, Louisiana, and particularly New Orleans, was stricken by epidemic diseases, mostly brought by trading ships from Mexico and the West Indies. In 1832 New Orleans was visited by a frightful cholera epidemic, and between 1817 and 1860 there were 23 yellow fever epidemics. During these forty-three years, 28,192 deaths were reported from yellow fever alone. One of the worst outbreaks occurred in 1853, when more than 8,000 died. During the Civil War there were few cases, largely because of the blockade and the cessation of trade with countries in the tropics; but in 1867 a virulent epidemic broke out and more than 3,300 died. In 1870 and again in 1873 there were lesser epidemics, but another violent epidemic struck in 1878, when there were 27,000 cases and more than 4,000 deaths. In that epidemic the fever spread to the surrounding countryside. There were nearly 2,500 cases in Baton Rouge, with 193 deaths, with 65 deaths in Thibodaux, 83 in Donaldsonville, and 109 in Morgan City. No cure was known until 1900, when an intrepid band of scientists of the United States Army Yellow Fever Commission in Cuba proved that the sting of an infected mosquito caused the spread of the disease. Yellow fever visited Louisiana for the last time in 1905, when the disease was finally conquered by the elimination of breeding grounds of the *Aedes aegypti (stegomyia)* mosquito.

The 1850's have been called Louisiana's lush decade. The prosperous agriculture of the state and the burgeoning shipping business of New Orleans combined to make the era one of unlimited promise. But, unfortunately, beneath the glittering surface forces were operating, at the time imperfectly understood, which would soon sound the death knell of Louisiana's slavery-linked plantation system and the prosperity of the port of New Orleans.

The Erie and Ohio canals, built in 1831 and 1832, were to bring new competition to New Orleans. Through these canals commodities from the Ohio Valley could find their way to New York rather than down the Mississippi to New Orleans. This eventually cut into New Orleans's prosperity. Railroad building, too, took its toll. New Orleans had all the business it could handle, so there was no motivation to build railroads. In 1850 the whole state of Louisiana had only 81 miles of tracks. States' rights and the slavery question, recurring more and more in discussion and debate, became vital issues in the 1850's; these ominous signs of trouble to come were ignored. New Orleans still was rich: 2,214,296 bales of cotton came down the river, and exports and imports valued at $185 million passed over its wharves in the season 1859–60. New Orleans banks had $12 million in specie in their vaults and boasted deposits of nearly $20 million, and just before the outbreak of the Civil War the state ranked second in per-capita wealth in the nation. But the clouds of disunion were gathering over the South, and the tides that made Louisiana prosperous and New Orleans a great world port would suddenly recede, not to return for a long, long time. 1861 was the fateful year.

On the eve of the Civil War, Louisiana found itself in a peculiar position. The state, and New Orleans in particular, was bound to the nation by strong economic ties. About half of its agricultural interests and nearly all its commercial interest depended upon its connection with the Union. Louisiana had little cause to withdraw from the United States.

However, by 1860, the sentiments of many Louisiana citizens were changing. The election that year of Abraham Lincoln, who received not a single vote in the whole state, marked the turning point. The feeling was that the day of compromise was past. When a vocal group of secessionists won control of a convention to consider Louisiana's future relations with the Union, an Ordinance of Secession was passed by a large majority. For nine days Louisiana existed as an independent republic; then it joined the newly formed Confederacy.

Wild excitement broke out in New Orleans. Immediate steps were taken to mobilize. The forts below the city were seized, as were the federal mint and the custom house, and soon volunteers by the hundreds were marching off to training camps and to the battlefields of Virginia.

For a year after the outbreak of hostilities, Louisiana remained undisturbed by warfare within its borders, but in 1862 it became apparent to Southern leaders that the Federals intended to get control of the lower Mississippi and cut the Confederacy in half. Under the command of David Glasgow Farragut, a fleet was assembled, and on April 18 a flotilla began the bombardment of Forts St. Philip and Jackson on the lower Mississippi, then New Orleans's chief defenses. After five days of incessant mortar fire the forts still held out and Farragut decided to run his ships past them. Fourteen ships were able to pass in the terrific fight that ensued, and as a result, New Orleans was left practically defenseless. The city fell to the Union forces two days later. On May 1 General Benjamin F. Butler brought in 15,000 troops and began a harsh rule which made him hated not only in Louisiana but throughout the South. For the next fifteen years New Orleans was to be an occupied city.

Continuing up the Mississippi, Farragut took Baton Rouge and Bayou Sara. The Confederates made a desperate attempt to recapture Baton Rouge, which they wanted for use as a base of supplies from the Red River Valley. Their attack, with General John C. Breckenridge leading 3,000 men, failed because of insufficient naval support; the heavily armored *Arkansas,* an iron-clad ram, which they hoped to use to drive off Federal gunboats, had broken down.

Up to the early part of 1863, practically all of Louisiana west of the Mississippi was in Confederate hands, with Opelousas as the state capital. The Confederates, under General Dick Taylor, son of Zachary Taylor, were able to keep Butler bottled up in New Orleans and in the parishes east of the river. But Butler's successor, General Nathaniel P. Banks, was able to force the Confederates out of southern Louisiana as far west as Morgan City. As the Federalists advanced, the capital was moved to Shreveport.

Shortly after Vicksburg fell on July 4, 1863, Louisiana suffered a heavy blow with the loss of Port Hudson. The Federals, 30,000 strong, attacked by river and land, and the Confederates were soon hard pressed for food. Nevertheless, they fought gallantly until their commander, General Frank Gardner, realizing that it was useless to continue to fight since Vicksburg had fallen, surrendered. Now the entire Mississippi was under Federal control.

A Federal attempt in 1864 to take Shreveport and conquer the Red River country was frustrated by Taylor and his little army. Banks sent two forces, one up the Red River and the other up Bayou Teche. These penetrated as far as Mansfield, where Taylor met them in a bloody engagement and drove them back to Alexandria in full retreat. After that, there was little fighting in Louisiana. But time was running out for the Confederacy. Though the war continued until April, 1865, the Confederate army in Louisiana did not surrender until May 26.

There were two governments in Louisiana during the war. The one in Opelousas, and later in Shreveport, was Confederate and under the administration of Thomas O. Moore and Henry Watkins Allen. The other, under the control of the Federals and centered in New Orleans, was administered by a military governor, George Shepley, and later by Michael Hahn, a German-born lawyer. Before the war's end, a constitutional convention in 1864 formally abolished slavery. The new constitution, drawn up by a republican body in occupied Louisiana, was proclaimed a model for "rebel" states. Although it had the support of President Lincoln, it failed to gain the approval of Congress. Still, it continued in use until a Reconstruction constitution was adopted in 1868.

After Lincoln was assassinated on April 14, 1865, the powerful Radical Republicans in Congress wanted to punish the South, to treat it as conquered territory instead of granting the "soft" peace that Lincoln had planned. As a result, Reconstruction and military occupation would last twelve more years and Louisiana would suffer what George W. Cable called "a hideous carnival of political profligacy."

The First Reconstruction Act was passed by Congress in 1867. General Philip Sheridan, who commanded occupation troops in Louisiana, interpreted its terms so harshly that only half the white citizens of the state could vote to elect delegates to a new constitutional convention, though all the Negro males could vote.

The results were foreseeable: the new constitution enfranchised Negroes and granted them full equality in the public schools and in common carriers. The freed Negroes provided Louisiana with one of its most difficult problems. They were beguiled by their new status, and some of them interpreted freedom as freedom from work. With little or no education the ex-slaves became the tools of carpetbaggers and white scalawags who for a time controlled the political and economic lot of Louisiana. After the convention Louisiana was readmitted to the Union.

In 1868 Henry Clay Warmoth, a self-described scalawag, was elected governor, with Oscar J. Dunn, a Negro, as lieutenant governor. Given almost unlimited power by the new constitution, the new governor could appoint registrars, local police, and returning boards. These boards could throw out votes the governor did not want counted. Graft became rampant; there was scandalous bribery, crushing taxation, racial strife, and official plundering.

Hardly had the Warmoth-Dunn regime taken office when the Republicans began to quarrel among themselves. The easy pickings attracted William Pitt Kellogg, a Vermonter, and Stephen B. Packard, a United States marshal who had backing in Congress. In the 1872 election Warmoth and his faction, calling themselves Liberal Republicans, united with the Democrats to support John McEnery against Kellogg, the Radical standard bearer. McEnery apparently won the election by about 9,000 votes, but the corrupt Radical-supported returning board counted him out. Kellogg and C. C. Antoine, a Negro and Kellogg's lieutenant governor, were supported by President Grant and placed in office with the help of federal troops.

Both McEnery and Kellogg were sworn in as governors of Louisiana the same day, January 13, 1873, the former at Lafayette Square in New Orleans and the latter at Mechanics Institute, less than half a mile away, and Louisiana had two regimes. Unfortunately for the McEnery cause, a bloody race riot occurred at Colfax, a small town in Grant Parish, on April 13, 1873, when a group of white men from that and neighboring parishes sought to regain the courthouse and offices taken from them by a Negro uprising. About 70 Negroes and three whites were killed. When other acts of violence followed the Colfax riot, President Grant publicly recognized the Kellogg administration.

By 1874 Louisiana was bankrupt, with a debt of $53 million on which it could not pay the interest, let alone the principal. For nearly a decade the state had endured one corrupt government after another; many citizens had suffered disfranchisement and were forced to pay exorbitant taxes that were stolen or squandered by inept Radical politicians who kept themselves in power by manipulating the Negro vote and by collusion with the federal government whose soldiers were ever present.

Throughout the state, conservatives saw no relief from an intolerable condition except by direct action. White leagues sprang up in the country parishes, their avowed objectives being to declare war on carpetbaggers and scalawags. In New Orleans, General Frederick N. Ogden organized the Crescent City White League which soon had 2,800 men enrolled under a quasimilitary discipline. When another armed confrontation took place at Coushatta, the situation in New Orleans became tense. On September 14, 1874, the White League, which had

pledged itself to get rid of Kellogg and restore self-government, met head-on with Kellogg's Metropolitan Police in a 15-minute battle near the New Orleans riverfront. Twenty-seven men were killed and more than a hundred wounded. The White Leaguers routed the Metropolitans. The next morning the State House was surrendered, and the McEnery officials were formally inducted into office. The victory was short-lived, however, for President Grant by proclamation ordered the White League to disperse and "submit to laws and constituted authorities of the state." McEnery surrendered and the Radicals again resumed control.

In the 1876 election there were again two sets of candidates—each claiming victory. Though the Democrats, who had nominated Francis T. Nicholls, had a clear majority of votes, the corrupt returning board counted the Republicans the winners, and on January 8, 1877, two inaugurations took place. At the St. Louis Hotel, then serving as the State House, Stephen B. Packard, a Maine-born carpetbagger, was inaugurated, and at Lafayette Square 10,000 persons saw General Nicholls take the oath of office. This time the Democrats were determined to rid Louisiana of Radical rule, come what may. The next day the re-formed White League, now called the Continental Guards, under General Ogden, assembled 3,000 strong and marched to the Cabildo, where they took possession of the Supreme Court chambers, the arsenal, and the police station. The Republicans holed up in the State House while Packard tried futilely to get recognition from the White House.

In Washington, Rutherford B. Hayes, a Republican, had won the presidency in an extremely tight election. Though the fraudulent returns from Louisiana had been counted in his favor, Packard did not benefit from them. Most historians believe that some kind of deal was made by Governor Nicholls's representatives in Washington, who explained Louisiana's dire predicament to members of Congress close to Hayes. The new President sent a commission to Louisiana to make an investigation. As a result, President Hayes ordered all federal troops out of New Orleans on April 27, 1877, and Packard surrendered the State House. The period of Reconstruction in Louisiana was over at last!

Louisiana was slow to recover from the political and economic chaos that had prostrated the state during the Civil War and the period of Reconstruction. By the 1870's New Orleans had dropped from second port in the nation to eleventh. During the days of the Civil War, sandbars had built up at the Mississippi's mouth and the large ships then being built had trouble entering and leaving the river or were held up by vessels aground at the passes. Something had to be done. A canal to bypass the mouths of the river was proposed; but another solution was found by James Buchanan Eads, a great self-taught engineer. After studying the situation Eads decided that the proper way to open the river to commerce was by building parallel dikes or jetties at the passes. After much controversy Eads was given a contract to build a jetty at South Pass for $5,250,000. Work started in June, 1875, and after four years of herculean labor, the bar was swept into the gulf and the middle channel measured 30 feet deep. New Orleans regained its importance as a port and has held on to it since.

The Civil War had also caused an almost complete disruption of steamboat traffic on the Mississippi. When the war was over, the finest of New Orleans packets—which had holed up in streams like the Red and Yazoo rivers—were gone forever, sunk in conflict or destroyed by the Confederates themselves to avoid capture. But this was not to be the passing bell of steamboating. In the 70's and 80's bigger and better boats like the *Rob't. E. Lee, Natchez, Richmond, Great Republic, Ruth,* and *Henry Frank* were built, and for a long time steamboats and steamboating seemed to dominate the river. The 1870's also witnessed the expansion of the railroads in the state. The road to the north, the New Orleans and Jackson Railroad (1854–58), and the road to the west, the New Orleans, Opelousas, and Great Western (1853–57), were the only main lines built before the Civil War. The Jackson and Opelousas lines were heavily damaged during the war, but were repaired and put back into service.

In 1870 a road to the east was opened: the New Orleans, Mobile, and Chattanooga, now part of the Louisville and Nashville Railroad. The road to the southwest, the New Orleans Pacific, now part of the Texas-Pacific-Missouri Pacific system, began operations in the late 1870's; and

the road to the southeast, the New Orleans and Northeastern, now part of the Southern Railway System, started up in the early 1880's. The New Orleans and Jackson was eventually absorbed by the Illinois Central Railroad, and the New Orleans, Opelousas, and Great Western became part of the Southern Pacific Lines.

Through train service between New Orleans and Chicago was inaugurated on December 24, 1873. Nearly ten years later, on February 5, 1883, the first through passenger train from New Orleans to San Francisco started over the Southern Pacific Lines, connecting the two cities 2,069 miles apart. In 1884 "The Iron Feeders of Crescent City Commerce" were hauling 1,400,000 tons of freight in and out of the city; by 1899 this had increased to 5,500,000 tons, and New Orleans was beginning to regain some of its former commercial importance. But in the 1890's steamboat traffic had begun to decline, and by the second decade of the present century most of the steamboats had disappeared from the lower Mississippi.

Before 1880 southwest Louisiana was largely rural. There were only three sizable towns—Opelousas, incorporated in 1821; Lake Charles, in 1861; and Lafayette, in 1863. The coming of the Louisiana Western Railroad in the early 1880's, the easing of the state laws covering the incorporation of towns, and the beginning of nationwide urbanization all contributed to the founding and growth of new towns in this sparsely settled section. Promoters induced many Midwestern farmers to move to the region, and rice growing began in earnest. The towns of Jennings, Rayne, and Crowley were built along the line of the railroad, and by the end of the century other towns—Welsh, Sulphur, Abbeville, Breaux Bridge, and Eunice—showed promise of future growth.

The Mississippi, which had brought so much wealth to Louisiana, also brought destruction and suffering when it went on a rampage. To reclaim the land that formed the flood plain of the mighty river the early settlers of Louisiana had built levees or dikes to confine the annual floodwaters. For two centuries the only means of flood control were these earthen embankments. Because these levees were constructed by those who owned land adjoining the river, they were generally deficient in width and height and sometimes inadequately maintained. In the two centuries between 1735 and 1935 there were 38 major floods in the lower river section, and New Orleans was flooded at least nine times. Truly, the Mississippi was one of the most troublesome problems confronting Louisianans!

From 1870 on, the work of strengthening and rebuilding the levees proceeded vigorously. In 1879 the Mississippi River Commission was formed, and the job of construction and maintenance of the levee system was assigned to the United States Army Corps of Engineers. However, nature took a hand; in 1882 a great flood occurred which created 284 crevasses and melted away 56 miles of levees. That year at Baton Rouge a gathering of representatives of the federal government and all states concerned resolved to pool their efforts and resources and start a concerted effort to control the river.

Despite steady improvements in the levee system, heavy rains in 1922 caused three levee breaks in Louisiana—one of which occurred at Poydras just 14 miles below New Orleans. In 1927 an even bigger flood came down the Mississippi, and breaks in the levee flooded New Iberia, located over a hundred miles from the river. New Orleans itself was seriously threatened. In the emergency the War Department gave permission to cut the levee at Caernarvon in St. Bernard Parish, and as the water flowed through the breach the river above the city began to drop. In the 1927 flood 1,112,200 acres of crop lands in Louisiana alone were covered and thousands of persons made homeless.

By this time it became apparent that the federal government should assume the responsibility for controlling floods originating in distant states, and the Flood Control Act of May 15, 1928, was passed. This resulted in the building of the Morganza floodway, the Bonnet Carré spillway 23 miles above New Orleans, and a series of cutoffs to hasten the flow of the river to the gulf. Tested by floods in 1936 and 1937, all the levees below Cairo, Illinois, held, and the danger of serious floods in Louisiana seems to have been removed for good.

The 1890's witnessed the finish of the Louisiana Republican party as a functioning political entity. The party was split between the Black-and-Tans, successors to the Radical wing which insisted on full Negro suffrage, and the Lily-Whites, which excluded Negroes and which included sugar planters who favored high tariffs. Defeated in 1892 by the Democrats, the Republicans united again in 1896, but they were "counted out" and a Democrat was elected again. After that, the Republican party in Louisiana ceased to exist except in name until 1964, when it was reactivated. The result was a one-party system. Political campaigns were generally marked by clashes between two or more Democratic factions. Nomination by the Democratic party became tantamount to election.

A gradual buildup of sentiment against blacks by whites in Louisiana resulted in separate-but-equal segregated schools and in laws which provided for segregated trains and waiting rooms in railway depots. Alarmed by the exceedingly high Negro vote in the election of 1896, and favored by the Supreme Court's ruling on the separate-but-equal doctrine, many whites determined to eliminate the Negro politically. A constitutional convention called in 1898 adopted the so-called Grandfather Clause, which meant essentially that any male over twenty years of age, whose father or grandfather could vote before January 1, 1867, could register without having to meet certain prescribed educational and property tests.

The Grandfather Clause was eminently successful in barring blacks from politics—at the time of the convention there were 130,344 Negroes registered to vote in Louisiana, and two years later their number had dwindled to only 5,320, despite the fact that about half the population of Louisiana was black. When the United States Supreme Court killed the Grandfather Clause in 1915, other means were sought to continue the disfranchisement of Negroes. The constitutional convention of 1921 wrote into the state's tenth constitution the Understanding Clause and the poll tax proviso. The Understanding Clause required an applicant for registration to be able to read "any clause in this Constitution or the Constitution of the United States and give a reasonable interpretation thereof." By 1940, these devices were so effective in keeping the blacks away from the all-white Democratic primaries that there were only 897 registered Negro voters in Louisiana.

In 1944 the Supreme Court struck down the Understanding Clause as unconstitutional. Thereafter Negro registration in Louisiana rose rapidly, increasing to 239,573 in 1966. In 1954 the Supreme Court handed down the momentous decision in the case of *Brown* v. *Board of Education of Topeka* revising the separate-but-equal doctrine. Denouncing the Supreme Court, the Louisiana legislature set about at once to circumvent the decision. Altogether, over a period of seven years the legislature passed no fewer than 64 acts and 17 resolutions aimed at preserving segregated education, and the Orleans Parish School Board filed no less than 37 delaying motions. But in the end all were voided by the federal courts. On November, 14, 1961, four little Negro girls, accompanied by U.S. marshals, entered New Orleans public schools to the jeering of white parents who watched the proceedings. Segregation was ended in the Catholic parochial schools in 1962. With the segregation barrier broken down in New Orleans, it became only a matter of time before the entire state of Louisiana recognized that integration was here to stay.

The 1890's were marked by several notable events in Louisiana. The first, in 1890–91, was the assassination of New Orleans's able chief of police David C. Hennessey. Members of a gang of immigrant Sicilians were accused of the crime. They were acquitted, but eleven of them were subsequently lynched by a mob of armed men who thought there had been a real miscarriage of justice.

In 1897 the city council of New Orleans passed an ordinance introduced by Alderman Sidney Story to set aside an area near the French quarter where prostitution was to be permitted in order to control what had become a real civic nuisance. This 38-block red-light section became one of the most amazing spectacles in America. To Alderman Story's disgust, the section became known as Storyville, and it operated full blast for twenty years until the federal government closed it as a war measure in 1917.

During the post-Reconstruction years Louisiana politics had generally been controlled by men who had been Civil War leaders and those of the upper classes such as bankers, lawyers, physicians, merchants, and business executives—in short, conservatives who decided who could run for office and who dictated policies after their candidates were elected. After 1900, when most of the Civil War crop of leaders had passed from the political scene, this group of

conservatives still retained power, and together with the potent New Orleans politicians shaped the destinies of the state through their governors and legislators. Reforms were badly needed; they were promised but little was done for the masses of poor whites and Negroes who made up a large segment of the population. The state continued to lag behind the rest of the Union in highways, educational facilities, social welfare, and the proper use of natural resources.

John M. Parker, who was elected governor in 1920, has been termed a "conscientious fighter for honesty and decency in government . . . who never let the prospects of profits interfere with his political convictions . . . [Parker] had great faith in the future of Louisiana and the South, and pioneered in the development of their limitless resources. More than any other man of his time, he gave his people enlightened business and political leadership in Louisiana." Parker's administration was marked by the tenth constitutional convention, held in 1921, by the freeing of the New Orleans Port Commission and other state agencies from the stranglehold of machine politics, by the laying of the foundation of the highway system, and by reforms in civil service. His term of office ended in 1924.

Henry L. Fuqua (1924–26) won the nomination (and election) over two opponents, one of whom, Huey P. Long, was making his first bid for the big time. Governor Fuqua died in office and was succeeded by Oramel H. Simpson (1926–28), his lieutenant governor. During their administrations legislation was enacted to curb the activities of the anti-Negro and anti-Catholic Ku Klux Klan, which was then very powerful; the Chef Menteur-Rigolets free bridges were started to provide toll-free access to the Florida parishes, and amid the hysterical fears that New Orleans would be destroyed by high water of the great flood of 1927, Governor Simpson signed a "public emergency" proclamation giving permission to dynamite the levee below the city at Caernarvon.

Huey Long's amazing career began when he was elected to the Louisiana Railroad Commission at the age of twenty-five. Using his office as a stepping stone, he ran for governor in 1924, but was defeated. Running again in 1928, with heavy support from rural districts, he was elected governor and soon gained notoriety by his erratic and picturesque conduct. But he secured large appropriations for highway construction, had the legislature enact a free textbook law for elementary schools and high schools, increased the appropriations for the State University, gave voters the right to vote without payment of poll taxes, and fathered other reforms.

To get appropriations for his ambitious programs, Long introduced bills to increase the severance tax on oil, gas, timber, and other natural resources. The giant Standard Oil Company was one of his favorite targets. Long ran roughshod over the 1928 legislature in order to secure the passage of his bills, and when that body met in 1929, his uncouth tactics and personal lobbying from the floor of the House aroused so much resentment that he was expelled. Led by the *Times-Picayune,* a campaign to impeach the governor grew, and the House of Representatives brought impeachment charges against him. The Senate was to try him, but Long cleverly outmaneuvered his enemies by getting 15 of its members to sign a round robin to the effect that they refused to hear evidence against him. A round robin, of course, was a document with signatures written in a circle so that no one could tell who signed first. The trial collapsed.

Huey Long's abortive impeachment trial received nationwide publicity—mostly unfavorable. People outside the state considered the governor an unscrupulous demagogue and a clown. But the trial had an effect on Long. He swaggered around the state after the round robin affair and from that time on became ruthless in his efforts to gain power. Swiftly he won control over one state agency after another. Because the newspapers of the state fought him, he founded his own paper, the *Louisiana Progress,* and he used the radio to influence public opinion. Rewarding those who went along with him, he set out to destroy those who opposed him.

With two years of his term of governor yet to run, Long was elected United States Senator in 1930. But because he hated his successor, lieutenant governor Paul Cyr, he refused to take his new office. Cyr made the mistake of getting himself sworn in as governor, whereupon Long declared that he was no longer lieutenant governor. Long appointed one of his friends, Alvin O. King, president of the state senate and thus the succeeding governor and departed for Washington to take his seat in the United States Senate.

In the Senate Long advocated the redistribution of wealth, a theme on which he harped constantly. His philosophy of trying to help the masses to a better life eventually culminated in his national Share Our Wealth program, a scheme halted only by his death.

In 1932 the mild and amiable Oscar K. Allen, a longtime friend and protégé of Long's, was elected governor of Louisiana. But the real boss of the state was still Huey Long, the "Kingfish." Long consolidated his control by having the legislature called in numerous special sessions to enact laws which abolished self-government, giving him control of the appointment of policemen, firemen, and school teachers. He also secured the command of the judiciary, of election officials and tax assessors, and of the state militia. At one time, because of his enmity with Mayor T. Semmes Walmsley of New Orleans and the New Orleans regular Democrats organization, he had laws passed which gave the state control of the city's police, fire, sewerage, and water departments and which took away its power to assess taxes. New Orleans was virtually insolvent; Long had beaten a great city to its knees so that he could enforce his will.

Louisiana had not witnessed such a bitter period of personal politics since the days of the carpetbaggers. Though Long was idolized by the masses for the good roads, the free bridges, the free schoolbooks, and other benefits that had arrived under his leadership, his enemies were legion. He was constantly under the protection of bodyguards, but this availed him nothing. On the night of September 8, 1935, he was shot and fatally wounded in one of the corridors of the State Capitol—allegedly by Dr. Carl A. Weiss, a Baton Rouge physician. On September 10 Long died from the effects of his wounds.

Governor Allen died suddenly on January 28, 1936, and for a few months James A. Noe served as governor. The Long organization continued its attack on the city government until one by one the city politicians surrendered and Mayor Walmsley was forced to resign. Robert S. Maestri, a staunch Long supporter, was certified by the Democratic parish committee as the only candidate, and became mayor. The Long regular forces, now working together, moved on to bigger things. By 1940, twenty-seven new taxes, including a sales tax of 2 per cent, were levied under the governorship of Richard Leche, and the machine continued to exact "deducts," or contributions, from the pay of state employees. Flagrant graft and the plundering of the state's mineral resources went on unabated.

The editor of the *New Orleans States,* James Evans Crown, sponsored an investigation. On June 7, 1939, a reporter and photographer, acting on a tip, found evidence that millwork was being manufactured for a private individual at state expense. The resulting public disclosure of this fact inaugurated investigation of what came to be known as the Louisiana Scandals. Under fire, the president of Louisiana State University resigned, and on June 26, 1939, Leche followed suit. A federal grand jury began an investigation which resulted in the return of 49 indictments involving 145 individuals and 42 firms or organizations. The charges involved income-tax evasion, cash kickbacks, stolen oil, conspiracy to defraud, and mail fraud. As a result, many of the top leaders of the state administration, contractors, slot-machine operators, political fixers, and the former governor himself were convicted. Leche, charged with defrauding the state of $31,000 on a truck sales deal, was given a stiff 10-year sentence. His lieutenant governor, Earl Long, Huey Long's brother, became governor.

Sam Houston Jones was elected governor on a reform ticket in 1940. He had the task of cleaning an Augean stable. During his administration the New Orleans Board of Port Commissioners, or Dock Board, was depoliticized, a civil service law passed, and many other reforms carried out. When his term ended in 1944, he was succeeded by a protégé of Jones, Jimmie Davis, one-time teacher, hillbilly singer, and composer. (His most famous song is "You Are My Sunshine.") Davis' record in office was good; it was largely attributable to the high quality of the legislature which was elected with him.

However, there was a Long in the wings waiting for his cue. The cue came in 1948, when Earl Long won his way to victory by promising free lunches to school children, a pay raise for teachers, a bonus for veterans, and higher old-

age pensions. When he was elected with 65 per cent of the vote, he immediately resorted to the same tactics that his brother had practiced before him. He killed the civil service law and manipulated the legislature. Dissension arose in the legislature over Long's tactics, and some of his leaders began to desert him because they felt he had gone too far.

In the election of 1952 Robert F. Kennon, a reform candidate, brought about a businesslike administration, one of the best in many years. Kennon initiated important reforms, making civil service a part of the state constitution, requiring the ratification by a two-thirds majority in the legislature of all bills increasing taxes or levying new ones, and inaugurating boards of citizens to control highways, welfare, and other institutions. Kennon was not a master politician, however, like Earl Long, and in 1956 Earl ran again and was swept to victory.

The third administration of "Ole Earl," as he called himself, was an incredible farrago— Long was a sick man, and before his term was up his antics made headlines everywhere. He was committed to a hospital in Texas, and when he returned, his public utterances before the legislature and in speeches outside were so wild, incoherent, and vindictive that he was again committed to a mental hospital. By sheer will power (and with the help of some of his friends in the administration) he had himself released. More weird attempts to secure his renomination as governor followed. After his term expired he ran as a candidate for Congress from his home district and defeated the incumbent, but a stroke suffered a few days after his victory caused his death.

The industrialization of Louisiana, which began in the early years of this century, had reached respectable proportions by the time of the Huey P. Long era. In 1930 the leading industries were oil refining, sugar refining, making of lumber and timber products, rice processing, cottonseed oil and cake processing, paper and alcohol manufacturing. Shipping and financial enterprises, centered principally around New Orleans, and railroads, electric, gas, and telephone utilities probably accounted for as much income as industrial activities did. Population, slowly changing from rural to urban, increased from 1,381,000 in 1900 to 2,101,000 in 1930, and New Orleans had close to half a million persons.

Then came the Depression, bank failures, and unemployment. By 1934, 227,388 persons, or 11 per cent of the state's population, were on relief, and the federal government spent $102 million between 1933 and 1939 to ease the distress. It was an era most Louisianans would like to forget!

After World II Louisiana witnessed an industrial boom. Oil and gas, once Huey Long's favorite scapegoats, came into their own as the backbone of Louisiana's industrial complex. Thousands of oil and gas wells, many offshore, produced a mineral output in 1968 of $4.3 billion; Louisiana was first in the nation in the production of salt and sulphur, and second only to Texas in oil production. Farm receipts in 1968 were more than $400 million, and livestock receipts amounted to $230 million. Today, from Baton Rouge to below New Orleans on the banks of the Mississippi, great oil refineries, petrochemical, aluminum, and electric plants, and one of the largest shipbuilding operations in the world have risen in what were formerly cane fields. By 1972 more than $5 billion had been invested in new plants or in the expansion of old ones, and Louisiana had reached an era of industrialization and prosperity undreamed of half a century earlier. In 1970 the state had a population of 3,641,306. Although the population of Orleans Parish, which is the city of New Orleans proper, had shrunk slightly, the figures for the metropolitan area rose from 907,123 to 1,045,809. Louisiana's five largest cities, excluding New Orleans, had populations of 950,388: Shreveport, 294,703; Baton Rouge, 285,167; Lake Charles, 145,415; Monroe, 115,387; and Lafayette, 109,716.

Today, two and three-quarter centuries since the French first came to Louisiana, the state is a realm so rich that John Law in his wildest dreams could not have imagined it. From forests and farmlands, from the rivers and the sea, from the bowels of the earth and from the skills and ingenuity of its inhabitants have come the good life which Law so freely promised early settlers to induce them to come to Louisiana.

A Pictorial History

Early Louisiana

3

Dioramas at the Indian Museum at Louisiana State University show the life of the state's earliest inhabitants. Sometime between 500 B.C. and A.D. 300 the Tchefuncte Indians camped in simple huts along a bayou in the marsh country of southern Louisiana (1). Farther north, the Marksville Indians interred their dead in earthwork mounds raised above the surrounding countryside (2). Between A.D. 900 and A.D. 1500 imposing temples were constructed, with a wooden framework and a broad flight of steps leading up to them (3). At the time when the Europeans first came to Louisiana, the Indians of the southern part of the state lived in thatched-roof huts, set with a protective stockade made of wooden palings (4). The pottery vessel shown at top opposite (5), with a human face depicted on it, was made around A.D. 1400. Around a thousand years earlier, the Marksville Indians made the pottery below it (6); the size of the vessels can be judged by comparison with the hand shown holding one of them.

4

5

6

27

The First Inhabitants

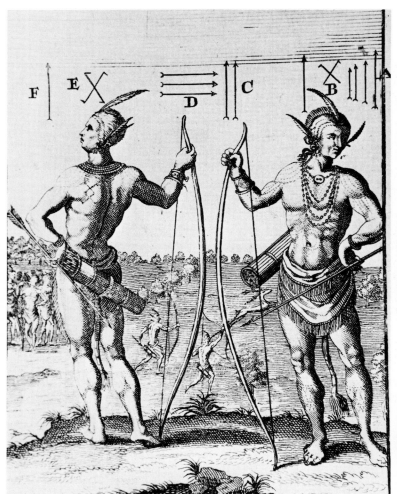

Dance générale.

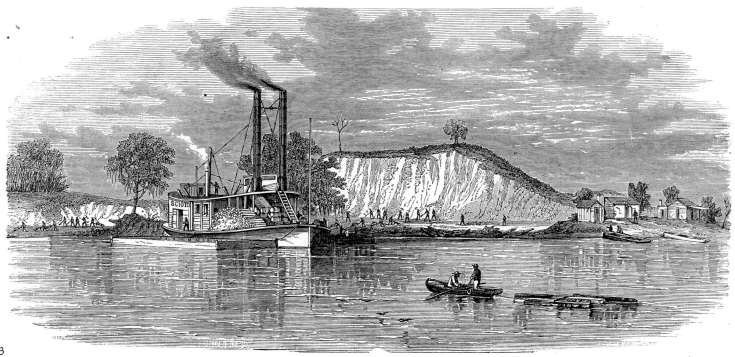

Marche du Calumet de Paix

European views of Louisiana Indians show two braves armed with bow and arrow (1), and various rituals: a circle dance (2); another dance in which tribesmen offer a peace pipe to visitors (4); and a human sacrifice in which certain individuals committed suicide (6) (the building in the picture is a sort of open-air tomb). Long before these Indians inhabited Louisiana, the region was home to one of the oldest Indian cultures in North America, that of the Poverty Point Mound Builders, who constructed mounds like those visible as ridges in the aerial view at upper right (5). When Louisiana was settled by whites, Indian mounds made of clam shell were mined to provide shells for paving the streets of New Orleans (3).

2

The "Savages"

1

The first Frenchmen to come to Louisiana called the Indians savages and remarked on the primitive way of life which the natives led. The Indians lived in villages (1) consisting of rudimentary huts furnished only with beds. A French immigrant wrote of huts like the chief's seen at top (2): "They are made of mud and are round in shape like windmills; the roofs of the houses are made mainly from the bark of trees." The Indian "temple" (3), above, was located in a village of the Colapissa Indians on the shore of Lake Pontchartrain. Twenty-two feet long and 14 feet wide, it was roofed with mats woven of cane and ornamented with crudely sculpted but brightly painted figures that represented turkeys. This temple also served as a burial vault for chiefs. Opposite, Indians are shown on the warpath (4) and working to hollow out a canoe with fire (5). The tribesman seen striking a pole (6) is performing a ritual that was supposed to consecrate a vow.

4

5

6

1

2

The first European to set foot in Louisiana was a member of the party of the Spanish explorer Hernando De Soto, who discovered the Mississippi in 1541. De Soto died on the soil of Louisiana and was buried in the river that he had discovered. No contemporary portrait of the explorer exists; this romanticized lithograph (1) depicting his burial was made in 1850. The first European to travel along most of the length of the Mississippi was René-Robert Cavelier, sieur de La Salle (2), who was accompanied on his journey by an Italian adventurer, Henri de Tonty (3). La Salle knew the Mississippi River as the River Colbert, for the French had given it that name in honor of Jean Baptiste Colbert (4), who served as minister of state to Louis XIV. In 1682 La Salle traveled all the way down the "River Colbert" to its mouth past the site of New Orleans. A contemporary engraving (5) shows him at the place where the river empties into the Gulf of Mexico; the artist has imaginatively embellished the scene with a background of mountains. A map made in 1684 from information provided by La Salle on his return to Canada shows the mouth of the "Fleuve Colbert" or "Mississippi" (6).

3

5

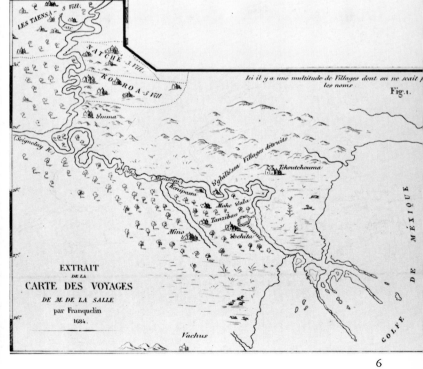

EXTRAIT
DE LA
CARTE DES VOYAGES
DE M. DE LA SALLE
par Franquelin
1684.

4

6

33

One French Canadian family played a major role in the exploration and colonization of Louisiana—the Le Moynes, sons of a Norman innkeeper who had amassed a fortune in Canada and been ennobled by the king. Four of his 12 sons were important in Louisiana history. Pierre le Moyne, sieur d'Iberville (1), led an expedition to settle Louisiana in 1699. He was accompanied by his brother, Jean-Baptiste, sieur de Bienville (2), who founded New Orleans in 1718. Two other brothers—Antoine, sieur de Chateaugay (3), and Joseph, sieur de Serigny (4)—were also leaders in the colony. (The brothers took their titles from places in Normandy near their father's birthplace.) Iberville traveled to the Gulf Coast in a three-masted sailing ship characteristic of those (5) used by the French during the period. A fanciful eighteenth-century engraving (6) shows him in 1699 supposedly finding the arms of France that La Salle had erected at the mouth of the Mississippi 17 years earlier.

5

DECOUVERTE DU COURS DU MISSISSIPI ET DE LA LOUISIANE 1699.

30.

35

The Domain of the King

Louisiana was named after the long-lived king Louis XIV who ruled France for seventy-two years. A contemporary painting (1), owned by the city of New Orleans, shows Louis's mother, Anne of Austria, proudly exhibiting her son's portrait (along with her own shapely, sandal-clad leg) to the French people. Louis's minister of marine was the Comte de Pontchartrain (2); it was in his honor that Iberville named Louisiana's largest lake. Pontchartrain's son and successor as minister of marine was the Comte de Maurepas (3). It was under his direction that the work of establishing French settlements in Louisiana was carried out by Iberville. Iberville named a small lake next to Lake Pontchartrain after Maurepas and also gave his name to the first French fort in the region, Fort Maurepas, whose plan (5) is shown opposite. A marble tablet (4) was found at the site of the fort marked with the name of Pierre Le Moyne. In 1712 Louis XIV granted Antoine Crozat (6) exclusive trading rights in Louisiana. This made him virtual master of a territory that was many times the size of France. A contemporary map (7) shows Crozat's grant. Eventually Crozat's scheme of establishing plantations and discovering gold and silver mines collapsed, and he had to surrender his grant.

4

6

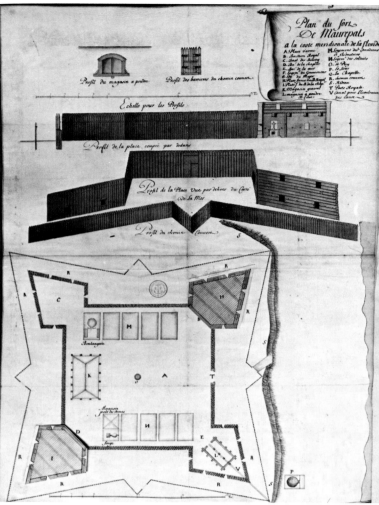

5

7

1

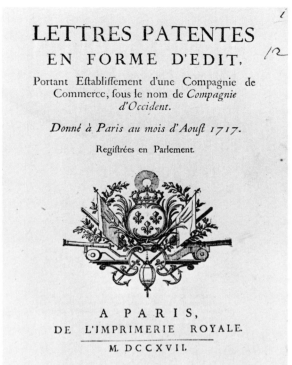

2

LETTRES PATENTES
EN FORME D'EDIT,

Portant Establissement d'une Compagnie de
Commerce, sous le nom de *Compagnie
d'Occident.*

Donné à Paris au mois d'Aoust 1717.

Registrées en Parlement.

A PARIS,
DE L'IMPRIMERIE ROYALE.
M. DCCXVII.

3

When Antoine Crozat surrendered his grant to
colonize Louisiana in 1717, the Scottish financier,
John Law (1), received a royal patent (2) to
establish the Company of the West to colonize
and exploit Louisiana. The coat of arms of the
Company of the West (3), at left, showed a river
flowing from a golden horn of plenty, flanked by
the figures of two Indians and surmounted by a
crown. Law's agents founded New Orleans, naming
it after the Duke of Orleans (4), the prince who
ruled France for 8 years as regent for the young
Louis XV. Law eventually managed to merge
his private bank with the royal treasury, issuing
his own banknotes (5). His Company of the
West spread promises of quick wealth, and its
stock was eagerly bought by French speculators. A
1720 cartoon (6) satirizes the gullibility of those
who invested in Law's schemes. It shows "Fortune"
riding on a chariot, while above her another
figure, "Folly," showers speculators with meaning-
less papers and prizes and the devil in a cloud
blows soap bubbles, symbolizing the fragility of
Law's schemes.

4

N.o 596185   *Cent livres Tournois.*

LA BANQUE promet payer au Porteur à vüe Cent livres Tournois en Especes d'Argent, valeur reçeüe. A Paris le premier Janvier mil sept cens vingt.

Vû p.r le S.r Fenellon.   Signé p.r le S.r Bourgeois.

     Controllé p.r le S.r Durevest.

1

A print (1) distributed by John Law's agents to promote investment in his company and emigration to Louisiana shows Frenchmen and Indians trading at the mouth of the Mississippi. The picture was accompanied by a caption that promised investors and immigrants great wealth. "The farms and vineyards . . . yield large amounts of wheat and wine. . . . Since gold and silver are so common, the savages . . . change pieces of gold and silver for European merchandise. . . ." Pamphlets (2) promoting emigration to Louisiana were distributed in Germany. John Law's concession near the present-day site of Biloxi is shown in a contemporary view (4). The settlers lived in tents, but there was also a palm-thatched infirmary and surgeon's office and a large wooden warehouse. In 1720 the Royal Council of State issued a series of pamphlets, one of which appears here (3), attempting to clarify the tangled financial affairs of the Company of the West. That same year Law lost his influence at court and his office, and he had to flee the country.

Ausführliche
Historische und Geographische
Beschreibung
Des an dem grossen Flusse
MISSISSIPI
in Nord-America gelegenen herrlichen Landes
LOUISIANA;
In welches
die neu-aufgerichtete Frantzösische grosse
Indianische Compagnie
Colonien zu schicken angefangen;
Worbey zugleich
einige Reflexionen über die weit-hinaus-
sehende Desseins gedachter Compagnie,
Und
des darüber entstandenen
Actien = Handels
eröffnet werden.
Andere Auflage.
Mit neuen Beylagen und Anmerckungen
vermehret.
Leipzig bey J. Fried. Gleditschens seel. Sohn,
1720.

2

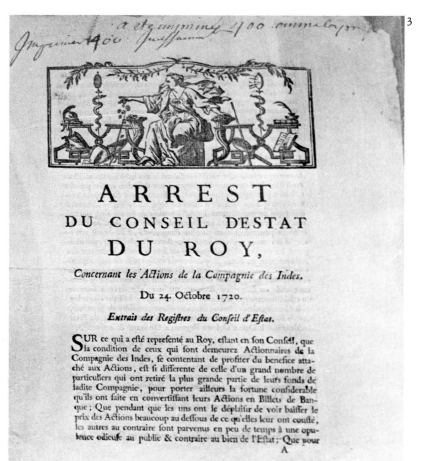

a et imprimé 1700 ommeloyon

Imprimé 1700 Juillant

ARREST
DU CONSEIL DESTAT
DU ROY,

Concernant les Actions de la Compagnie des Indes.

Du 24 Octobre 1720.

Extrait des Registres du Conseil d'Estat.

SUR ce qui a esté representé au Roy, estant en son Conseil, que la condition de ceux qui sont demeurez Actionnaires de la Compagnie des Indes, se contentant de profiter du benefice attaché aux Actions, est si differente de celle d'un grand nombre de particuliers qui ont retiré la plus grande partie de leurs fonds de ladite Compagnie, pour porter ailleurs la fortune considerable qu'ils ont faite en convertissant leurs Actions en Billets de Banque ; Que pendant que les uns ont le déplaisir de voir baisser le prix des Actions beaucoup au dessous de ce qu'elles leur ont cousté, les autres au contraire sont parvenus en peu de temps à une opulence odieuse au public & contraire au bien de l'Estat ; Que pour

A

1

2

In 1720 New Orleans consisted of little more than a cluster of houses overlooking the Mississippi (1). By 1726, when the watercolor view opposite (2) was made, the church, visible at the center of the little settlement, had been constructed. The 1723 plan at right (3) shows the streets that would eventually be built, although only the area shown in white had been cleared for settlement. Another map (4), drawn two years later, shows the first cemetery, a canal that was never finished, the principal buildings (most of which were then merely projected), and the narrow streets neatly laid out in the wilderness by skilled military engineers. A later plan of the city (5), dated 1732, shows that the Place d'Armes was fenced off; another fence kept vehicles from driving along the levee and weakening it.

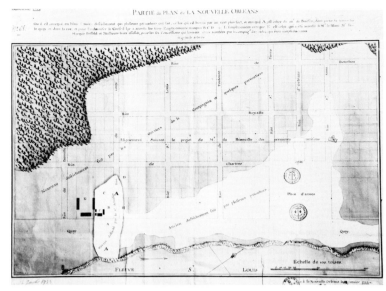

3

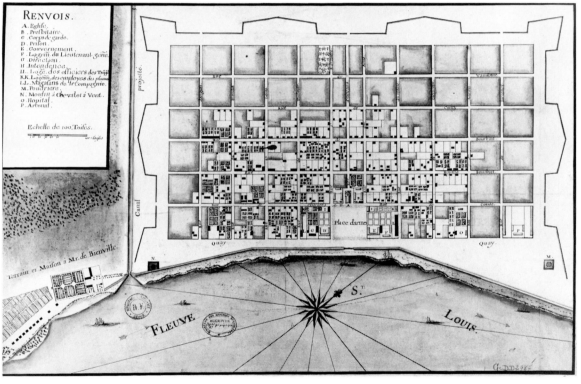

4

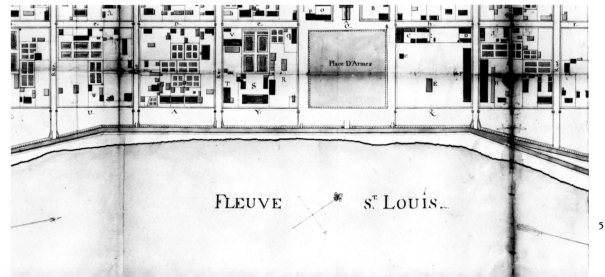

5

Architecture

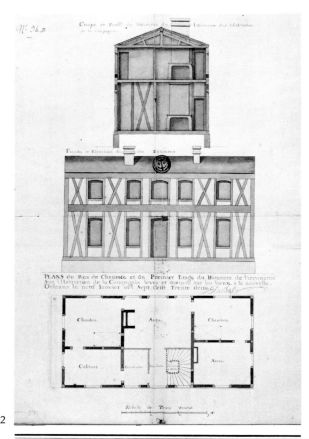

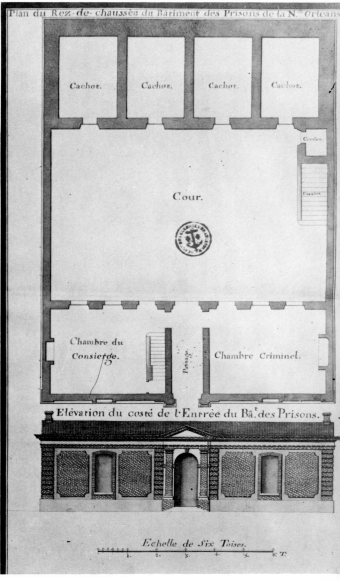

One of the first pictures of New Orleans (1), drawn by the surveyor Jean-Pierre Lassus in 1726, shows the infant city in great detail, its scattered houses set between the river and a dense forest. The French brought well-trained engineer-architects to Louisiana, among them Alexandre de Batz, who depicted many of the buildings of New Orleans as part of an inventory of the property of the Company of the Indies. His drawings show: the dwelling of the plantation manager of the company (2), the New Orleans prison (3), and an imposing house on Dumaine Street (4, 5) used as a residence and astronomical observatory. Picture number 4 shows the front of the house; number 5, the imposing entrance gate with a small kitchen building to its left. The French found that the marshy soil of southern Louisiana made wooden houses that were built directly on the ground deteriorate and heavy brick houses subside. So they developed a combination: a brick basement above ground supporting a wooden upper story. They soon discovered that broad galleries, such as the one on the 1788 house (6), still standing on Dumaine Street in New Orleans, protected the buildings and let the breeze in.

44

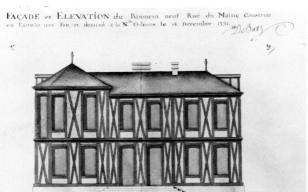

FAÇADE et ELEVATION du Bâtiment neuf Ruë du Maine Construit en l'année 1730. Fait et dessiné a la N.elle Orleans le 14 Decembre 1731.

Echelle de Trois Toises.

4

FAÇADE et ELEVATION de la Porte d'Entrée du Bâtiment neuf Ruë du Maine Construit en l'année 1730. Fait et dessiné a la N.elle Orleans le 14 Decembre 1731.

Echelle de Trois Toises.

5

The Church in Louisiana

1

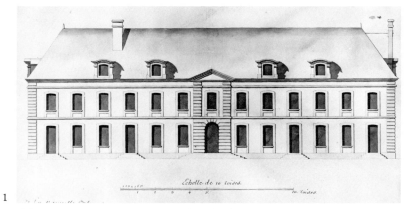

3

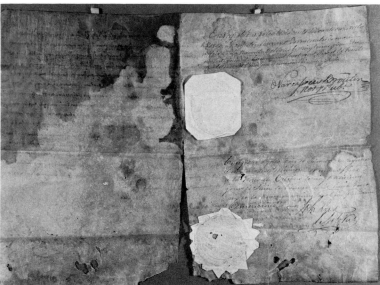

Louisiana's oldest building, dating from 1745–50, is the Ursuline convent in New Orleans, shown in an architect's drawing (1), a photograph (2), and in a site plan (4) dating from the end of the eighteenth century. The king of France encouraged religious life with a charter (3) giving the Ursulines the right to establish a convent at New Orleans. Soon after New Orleans was established, a church (5) was built. The churches of Louisiana and the Ursuline convent contain many religious treasures, such as this wooden statue of the Virgin and Child (6), a wrought-iron crown for a religious statue (7), and a marble baptismal font (8), donated by Louis XVI to the church at St. Martinville.

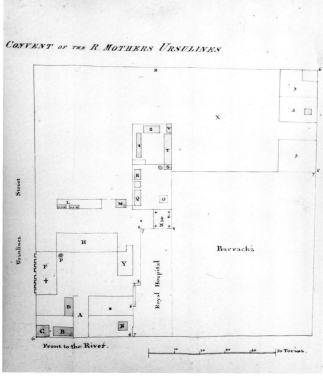

CONVENT OF THE R. MOTHERS URSULINES

4

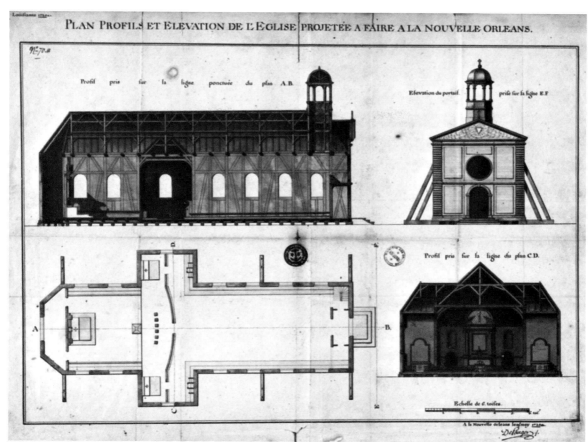

PLAN PROFILS ET ELEVATION DE L'EGLISE PROJETÉE A FAIRE A LA NOUVELLE ORLEANS.

5

6

7

8

1

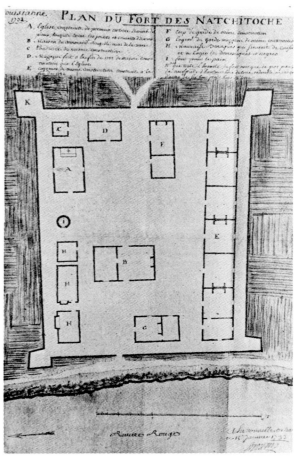

PLAN DU FORT DES NATCHITOCHE

3

2

4

Settlements grew up outside New Orleans as the French built plantations and villages along the rivers and bayous, dividing up the land in long plots stretching back from the water (1) so that each landowner could have the advantages of river frontage. The oldest town in Louisiana was Natchitoches, where a fort, shown in a proposed reconstruction (2) and a plan (3), was built as early as 1714. The first school in Natchitoches was the Roque house (4), now a historical museum. The town of Opelousas, founded in French times, grew to be a substantial settlement; its fort was under the command of the sieur de la Morandière (5). Perhaps the oldest remaining house in Opelousas is Ringrose (6), built around 1770. About the same time that the infant city of New Orleans was being laid out, word came from France to mark the entrance of the Mississippi "by two small towers on which fires can be made at night." A beacon called the Balize was established; it can be seen on the left in the nautical scene opposite (7). Plans were made for building a stone tower (8) and a barracks for troops (9), but these buildings were never constructed.

5

6

7

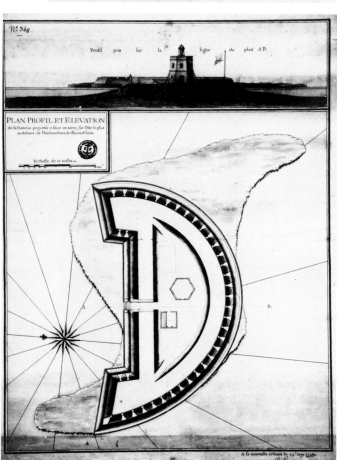

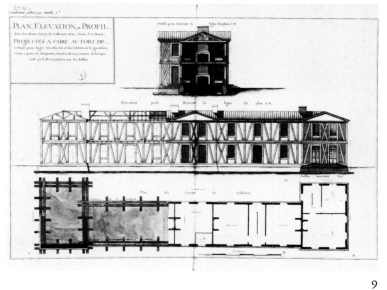

8

9

49

1

2

3

4

The fine furniture made in early Louisiana shows many resemblances to furniture manufactured in France during the same period. But the Louisiana products were much less ornate. In Louisiana furniture was manufactured by local cabinetmakers who had learned their skills in Europe, and sometimes by black slaves who worked alongside them. The open-doored armoire (1) shown opposite was made around 1825. The drawers inside had richly decorated drawer pulls, partly of porcelain (2). Another armoire, made of cypress wood (3), is similar to pieces from French Canada. The small table opposite (4) comes from the Ursuline convent in New Orleans. Almost all of its parts are fitted together—either pegged or joined and glued. Only one nail was used in the entire piece, inside the drawer. The two chairs shown here (5, 6) are made with rush seats. The one with arms is full size. The other is smaller, made especially for a child. The small chest of drawers above (7) was probably used as a bedside table.

A Varied Population

The population of eighteenth-century Louisiana was varied. Immigrants from France and Germany mingled with native Indians, black slaves brought in from Africa or the West Indies, Acadian refugees, and, later, Spaniards. A de Batz drawing (1), done in 1735, shows Indians "of several nations" in New Orleans. The nations include the Illinois and the Atakapas; an Indian slave and a black are also shown. One of the packages on the ground contains "bear grease," which pioneers used to smooth down their hair. It was on a slave ship, such as the one depicted here (2), that the first blacks came to Louisiana in 1720. Soon more than one in three people in New Orleans was black. The Code Noir (3) or Black Code was introduced in 1724 to regulate the treatment of slaves and guard against excessive cruelty. In the city of New Orleans, a prosperous upper-class family, such as Dr. Joseph Montegut's, shown in a group portrait (4) painted a few years before the end of the century, had the leisure and culture to enjoy a flute and harpsichord concert.

2

LE CODE NOIR

OU

EDIT DU ROY,

SERVANT DE REGLEMENT

POUR

Le Gouvernement & l'Administration de la Justice, Police,
Discipline & le Commerce des Esclaves Negres, dans
la Province & Colonie de la Loüisianne.

Donné à Versailles au mois de Mars 1724.

LOUIS PAR LA GRACE DE DIEU, ROY DE
FRANCE ET DE NAVARRE : A tous presens &
à venir, SALUT. Les Directeurs de la Compagnie
des Indes Nous ayant representé que la Province
& Colonie de la Loüisianne est considerablement
establie par un grand nombre de nos Sujets, lesquels se servent
d'Esclaves Negres pour la culture des terres ; Nous avons jugé
qu'il estoit de nostre authorité & de nostre Justice, pour la
conservation de cette Colonie, d'y establir une loy & des regles
certaines, pour y maintenir la discipline de l'Eglise Catholique,

A

3

4

1

Politics and Trade

3

2

The king of France and its colonies during most of the eighteenth century was Louis XV (1), who ruled from 1715 to 1774. From its inception in 1699 to 1743, Louisiana had 9 changes of governor. Four times Bienville filled the office, when lesser men were recalled or died. When Bienville retired to France in 1743 he had spent more than 30 years in the colony. He was succeeded by the Marquis de Vaudreuil (2), who governed for the next 10 years; and the Chevalier de Kerlérec (3), who followed him. Vaudreuil and Kerlérec were accompanied by their wives. The Marquise de Vaudreuil (4) captivated Louisiana with her elegant manners and elaborate entertainments. Kerlérec and his wife (5) had less peace of mind for entertainment, for Kerlérec's regime was marked by difficulties with the Indians. The French continually placated the Indians with gifts; occasionally, to flatter their chiefs, they sent illuminated commissions, such as this one (6), given by Kerlérec to a Cherokee chief in 1761, showing an Indian and a Frenchman together. The colony was enriched by goods carried in ships, like the *Amitié* (7). Sometimes playing cards (8) were used as scrip, exchangeable for bread at a storehouse or bakery.

54

4

6

7

5

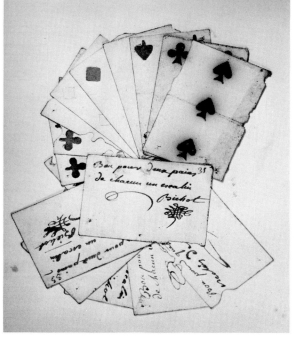

8

55

1

EXTRAIT
DE LA LETTRE DU ROI,
A M. D'ABBADIE, DIRECTEUR GÉNÉRAL, COMMANDANT POUR SA MAJESTÉ, A LA LOUISIANNE.

MONS. D'ABBADIE; Par un Acte particulier, passé à Fontainebleau le 3. Novembre 1762. ayant Cédé de ma pleine volonté à mon Très-Cher & Très-Amé Cousin le Roi d'Espagne, & à ses Successeurs & Héritiers, en toute propriété, purement & simplement & sans aucune exception, tout le Pays connu sous le nom de la Loüisianne, ainsi que la Nouvelle Orléans & l'Isle dans laquelle cette Ville est située; & par un autre Acte passé à l'Escurial signé du Roi d'Espagne le 13. Novembre de la même Année, S. M. Catholique ayant accepté la Cession dudit Pays de la Loüisianne & de la Ville & Isle de la Nouvelle Orléans, conformément à la Copie desdits Actes que vous trouverez ci-joints: Je vous fais cette Lettre, pour vous dire que mon intention est, qu'à la reception de la Présente & des Copies y jointes, soit qu'elle vous parvienne par les Officiers de S. M. Catholique, ou en droiture par les Bâtimens Français qui en seront chargés, vous ayez à remettre entre les mains du Gouverneur, ou Officier à ce préposé par le Roi d'Espagne, ledit Pays & Colonie de la Loüisianne & Postes en dépendants, ensemble la Ville & Isle de la Nouvelle Orléans, telles qu'elles se trouveront au jour de ladite Cession: Voulant qu'à l'avenir elles appartiennent à S. M. Catholique, pour être Gouvernées & Administrées par ses Gouverneurs & Officiers, comme lui appartenant en toute propriété & sans aucune exception. J'espère en même-tems pour l'avantage & la tranquilité des Habitans de la Colonie de la Loüisianne, & je me promets en consequence de l'amitié & affection de S. M. Catholique, qu'elle voudra bien donner des ordres à son Gouverneur & à tous autres Officiers employés à son Service, dans ladite Colonie & Ville de la Nouvelle Orléans, pour que les Ecclésiastiques & Maisons Religieuses qui Desservent les Cures & les Missions, y continuent leurs Fonctions, & y joüissent des Droits, Priviléges & exemptions qui leur ont été attribués par les Titres de leurs établissemens: Que les Juges Ordinaires continuent, ainsi que le Conseil Supérieur, à rendre la Justice suivant les Loix, Formes, & Usages de la Colonie: Que les Habitans y soient gardés & maintenus dans leurs Possessions: Qu'ils soient confirmés dans les propriétés de leurs Biens suivant les Concessions qui en ont été faites par les Gouverneurs & Ordonnateurs de la Colonie, & que lesdittes Concessions soient censées & reputées confirmées par S. M. Catholique, quoiqu'elles ne l'eussent pas encore été par Moi. Espérant au surplus que S. M. voudra bien donner à ses nouveaux Sujets de la Loüisianne, les mêmes marques de Protection & de bienveillance qu'ils ont éprouvés sous ma Domination, & dont les seuls malheurs de la Guerre les ont empêchés de ressentir de plus grands effets. Je vous ordonne de faire Enregistrer ma présente Lettre au Conseil Supérieur de la Nouvelle Orléans, afin que les différens Etats de la Colonie soient informés de son contenu, & qu'ils puissent y avoir recours au besoin. Et la Présente n'étant à autres fins; Je prie Dieu, Mons. D'Abbadie, qu'il vous ait en sa Sainte garde. Ecrit à Versailles, le 21. Avril 1764. Signé LOUIS & plus bas, LE DUC DE CHOISEUL.

De l'Imprimerie de DENIS BRAUD, Imprimeur du Roi.

DON ALESSANDRO O'REILLY

3

DE PAR LE ROI,
DON ALEXANDRE Ô REILLY
Commandeur de Benfayan dans l'Ordre de Alcantara, Lieutenant-Général & Inspecteur-Général des Armées de Sa Majesté Catholique, Capitaine-Général & Gouverneur de la Province de la Louisianne.

EN vertu des Ordres & Pouvoirs, dont Nous sommes muni de Sa Majesté Catholique, déclarons à tous les Habitans de la Province de la Louisianne, que quelque juste sujet que les Evénemens passés ayent donnés à Sa Majesté de leur faire sentir son indignation, Elle ne veut écouter aujourd'hui que sa Clémence envers le Public, persuadée qu'il n'a péché, que pour s'être laissé séduire par les intrigues de Gens Ambitieux, Fanatiques & mal intentionnés, qui ont témérairement abusé de son ignorance & trop de crédulité; ceux-ci seuls répondront de leurs crimes & seront jugés selon les Loix.
Un Acte aussi généreux doit assurer Sa Majesté, que ses nouveaux Sujets s'efforceront chaque jour de leur vie de mériter par leur fidélité, zéle, & obéissance la Grace qu'elle leur fait, & la Protection qu'elle leur accorde dès ce moment.

A la Nouvelle Orléans, le vingt-un Aoust mil sept cens soixante-neuf.

Alexandre ô Reilly

4

5

6

7

8

In 1764 Louisianans were startled by the publication of a broadside (2) informing them that their colony had been ceded to Spain. The first Spanish governor, Antonio de Ulloa (1), was unable to gain control and was expelled by the Louisianans. Spain then sent Alexander O'Reilly (3) with troops to arrest the ringleaders of the revolt. Posting a broadside (4), O'Reilly executed the ringleaders and pardoned those who had signed a petition to expel Ulloa. Later governors were the Baron de Carondelet (5) and Don Estevan Miro (6). During Carondelet's tenure, from 1792 to 1797, New Orleans saw its first theatre opened and published its first newspaper. The streets were lit by eight street lamps, and a small force of night watchmen was formed to protect citizens. Carondelet followed the French custom of presenting gifts to the Indians. A detail of a presentation certificate (7) shows the awarding of a medal to an Osage Indian named Little Bird. In 1777 Louisiana's first poet, Julien Poydras, published his earliest work: "The Epistle to Don Bernardo de Galvez" (8). It was a laudatory poem in honor of another Spanish governor.

1

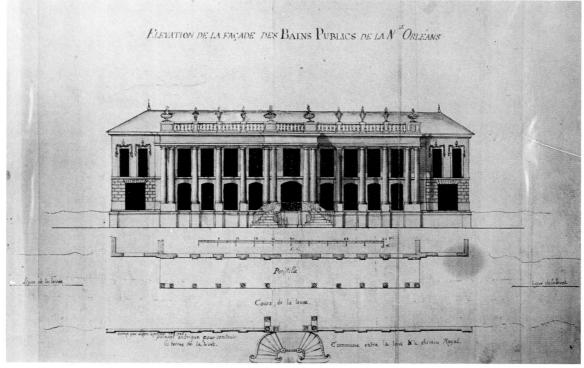

RELATION

DE l'Incendie qu'a éprouvé la ville de la Nouvelle-Orléans, le 21 mars 1788.

VERS une heure & demie après-midi, le feu s'est déclaré à peu près au centre de la Ville. Le vent du sud, qui souffloit pour lors avec une grande violence, l'a animé à un tel point, qu'auffitôt il s'est manifesté en plufieurs endroits à la fois. Toute la vigilance des Chefs, & les prompts fecours qu'ils ont fait apporter, font devenus inutiles, même les pompes, dont quelques-unes ont été brûlées par l'ardeur des flammes, qui fe portoient à une diftance incroyable. Dans un péril fi imminent, chacun craignant pour foi, s'est retiré pour voir s'il étoit poffible de fauver quelques effets; la frayeur des plus proches voifins du danger leur a fait perdre le peu d'inftants qui leur reftoient, & la confiance de ceux qui étoient plus éloignés & qui cherchoient à foulager les autres, les a jeté dans le même

2

3

ELEVATION DE LA FAÇADE DES BAINS PUBLICS DE LA N.le ORLEANS

4

N°. 26.

MONITEUR
DE LA
LOUISIANE.

Bombalio, Clangor, Stridor, Taratantara, Murmur

Lundi 25 Août de l'année Commune 1794.

AVIS DIVERS.

Wm. Butler, à l'honneur de prévenir le public, qu'un américain nommé Comfort Joy, ayant négocié à un certain Thomas, un billet signé *William Lesby & comp.* de St. Augustin, en datte du 12 Mars 1791, pour la somme de 1042 Piastres : comme il est très probable que le dit billet a été payé, je préviens toutes les personnes auxquelles il pourroit être présenté, de ne pas le recevoir en payement, ni d'en donner la valeur de quelque maniere que ce soit, sans être préalablement adressé à moi.

Le soussigné a pris le parti de donner cet avis, parcequ'il a appris que le susdit Comfort Joy, avoit paru en ville, & avoit propos é de négocier le billet dont il s'agit.

La Maison de Mrs. Liauteau, Fabre & Engelin, ayant en le malheur de perdre un des associés, Mr. Fabre, décédé le 7 du courant ; il est de toute nécessité de dissoudre la société ; en conséquence il prévient toutes les personnes qui peuvent avoir quelque relation d'affaires ou comptes à régler, de se présenter dans la quinzaine. Par procuration de Mr. Angelin. A. Bonnabel.

A VENDRE , deux arpens de terre cultivable, sur 8 de profondeur, attenant à l'habitation des Demoiselles

Deverges, près de la ville dans le chemin du Bayou. Celui qui voudra en faire l'acquisition , s'adressera aux dites Dlles. qui feront crédit jusqu'à la fin de cette année.

Id. m. une habitation à un quart de lieue de la ville ci - devant au Sieur Duff sne. Il faut s'adresser à Mr. Paul Assani.

Nlle. ORLÉANS, 21 AOUT.

Par des lettres dignes de foi, nous apprenons que l'armée des alliés a engagé le 26 Avril une action des plus vive; qui s'est terminée à son avantage, mais dont on ignore encore les détails. La perte des Conventionistes est des plus conséquente, & celle des alliés monte à dix mille hommes tant tués que blessés.

Le 17 Mai, les alliés devoient attaquer derechef, l'armée de la Convention ; ce qui fait croire que le plan proposé par le Roi de Prusse , de marcher en droiture à Paris , & de faire une guerre de campagne sans s'arrêter à former des siéges , a été adopté : au reste les seules places de Cambrai & Peronne que les alliés ont encore devant eux, pouvant se tourner, & leur garnison rester bloquées par un corps de Cavalerie après la défaite de la grande armée du Nord ; il est certain que rien ne pourroit empêcher

Two major New Orleans buildings that survive from Spanish times are the Cabildo and the Presbytère, which can be seen flanking the cathedral overlooking Jackson Square (1). Under the Spaniards, New Orleans suffered two great fires, which destroyed almost all of the city's buildings. The first, in 1788, is described in a pamphlet (3); according to the report the fire was fanned to great intensity by the south wind. The extent of the second fire is shown in the lighter area of a contemporary map (2). Within a few years the town had risen from the ashes; a contemporary drawing (4) shows the columned façade of the proposed public baths building. The first bishop of Louisiana, Luis Peñalver y Cardenas (5), was appointed in 1795. His arrival elevated the Church of St. Louis to the status of a cathedral. Accompanying the bishop was Père Antoine (6), who remained a prominent figure in Louisiana for many decades. Along with the religious life of New Orleans, cultural life flourished, with the opening of the city's first theatre and the publication of its first newspaper, the *Moniteur de la Louisiane* (7).

7

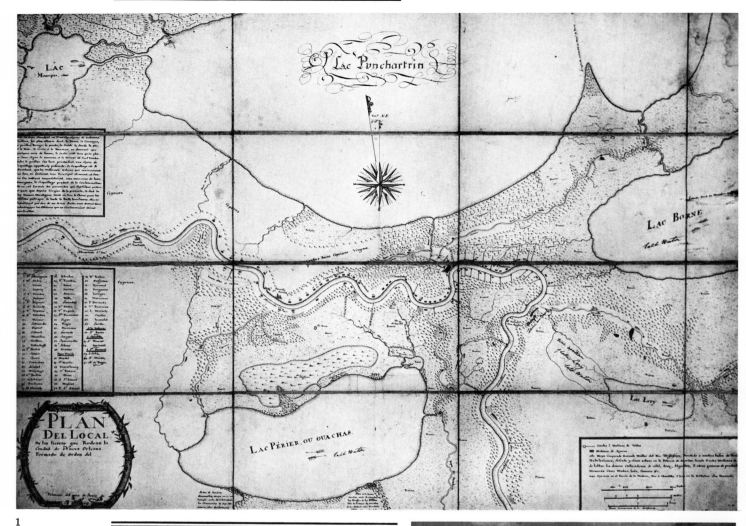

1

An 1803 map (1), made by a Spanish engineer, shows the location of 69 plantations along the Mississippi near New Orleans. Distinguished Louisianans—many of them plantation owners—included Nicholas D'Aunoy (2) (shown with his son), who became a lieutenant general in the Spanish army; Pierre Marigny (3), whose plantation appears on the map just outside the city of New Orleans; Andres Almonester y Roxas (4), an immensely wealthy speculator in real estate, who loaned the government money for the building of the Cabildo. Marie de Reggio Ducros (5) was the wife of a Spanish official and the aunt of the famous Civil War general Pierre G. T. Beauregard. Don José de Hoa y Cacho (6), like Señora Ducros's husband, was an official of the Spanish treasury.

3

4

5

6

Early Plantation Houses

1

3

4

Few eighteenth-century plantation houses survive in Louisiana. One of the most famous is Ormond (2), built around 1790. (The wings are a later addition.) Less imposing is Voisin (1), which was built around 1785 near Laplace and demolished in 1974. Homeplace (3), in St. Charles Parish, dates from around 1790. It contains fourteen rooms, including a dining room with a marble floor. A plantation house now within the city limits of New Orleans on Bayou St. John is the so-called Spanish Custom House (4) constructed around 1784. This was a plantation dwelling and not a custom house, as is often claimed. All four of the buildings illustrated have the characteristic second-story gallery.

Overleaf: Whitehall plantation, shown in a contemporary painting, was in its time the most impressive building in Louisiana. The building, designed in the Italian style, was painted to resemble marble. The artist, who portrayed himself sketching on the opposite bank of the Mississippi, took the liberty of reducing the river's width.

The American Revolution

In 1772, when this map of West Florida (1) appeared in London, the British held the territory east of the Mississippi above New Orleans. Another map below (2), dating from a few years earlier, shows the distribution of British troops in America in 1765, with black squares marking the areas where troops were concentrated; a large force was stationed in West Florida to guard against the French in Louisiana. The Stamp Act was levied to force Britain's American colonists to pay for the upkeep of these troops; but its taxes were levied without the consent of the colonists, inspiring them to rebel. When the revolution finally broke out, the Spanish governor of Louisiana, Bernardo de Galvez (3), whose equestrian portrait combines oil painting and calligraphy, supplied arms and ammunition to the American colonists.

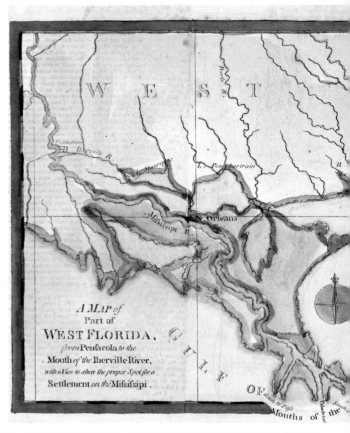

A MAP of Part of WEST FLORIDA, from Penfacola to the Mouth of the Iberville River, with a View to shew the proper Spot for a Settlement on the Mifsifsipi.

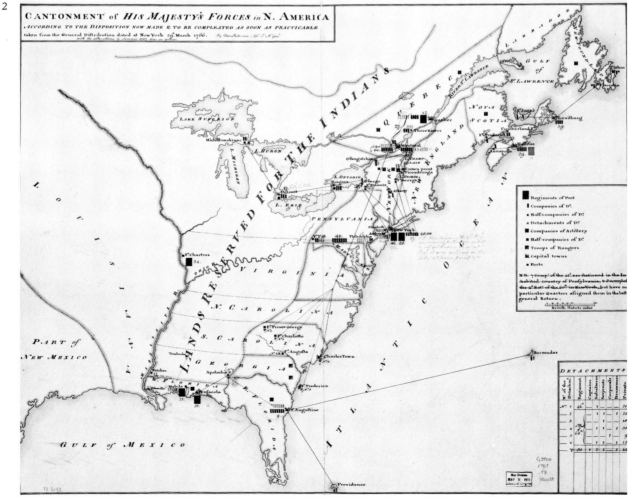

CANTONMENT of HIS MAJESTY'S FORCES in N. AMERICA. ACCORDING TO THE DISPOSITION NOW MADE & TO BE COMPLEATED AS SOON AS PRACTICABLE taken from the General Diftribution dated at New York 29 March 1766.

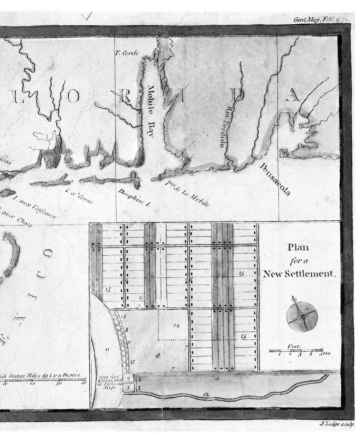

1

2

Since 1795 Americans had enjoyed the right to trade through New Orleans. However, in 1802, a Spanish official closed the port to them. To regain trading rights, Americans resolved to buy New Orleans. Negotiations were begun with Napoleon, since the French, in the meantime, had taken over Louisiana again. The French sent Clement de Laussat (1) to Louisiana as prefect, and he issued a proclamation (2) informing Louisianans of the change of masters. Laussat's official stamp is at left (3). Napoleon sold Louisiana because he feared the English would seize it and because an expedition, dispatched to take over the colony, had been defeated trying to put down a revolt in another colony, the Caribbean island of Saint Domingue. The Saint Domingue uprising (4) sent many refugees to Louisiana, including James Pitot, whose New Orleans house is shown in a drawing made in the 1820's (5).

3

Vorstellung der auf der Französchen Colonie St: Domingo von denen schwartzen Sclaven eingebildete
Französchen democratische Freÿheit, welche selbige durch unerhörte Grausamkeit zu erwerben gedachten. Sie ruinirten viele
hundert Coffe- und Zucker Plantagen und verbranten die Mühlen, sie metzelden auch ohne Unterschied alle Weise die
in ihre Hände fielen, dabeÿ ihnen ein weises Kind zur Fahne diente, schändelen Frauen und schlepten sie in elende Gefangen-
schaft, 1791. allein ihr Vorhaben wurde zu nichte.

1

2

3

4

Barbé Marbois.

5

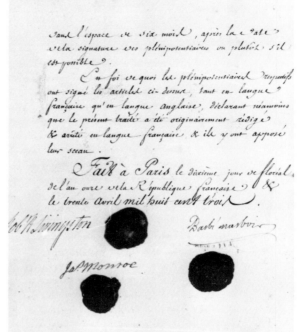

6

The American era in Louisiana began when Thomas Jefferson (1) sent James Monroe (2) to France to negotiate the purchase of the territory. Monroe and the American minister to France, Robert Livingston (3), arranged the sale with two French officials, the duc de Talleyrand (4) and François Barbé-Marbois (5). Napoleon's decision to sell Louisiana was made on April 30, 1803, but the document of sale (6) was actually signed a few days later. Napoleon (7), who had acquired Louisiana from Spain in exchange for the Italian duchy of Parma, had held on to it for only three years. The transfer of sovereignty from France to the United States took place in the room called the Sala Capitular in the New Orleans Cabildo (8) just before Christmas in 1803.

7

8

UNDER ★ MY ★ WINGS

The Louisiana Purchase

A contemporary painting celebrating the Louisiana Purchase shows the American eagle flying triumphantly over the busy port of New Orleans.

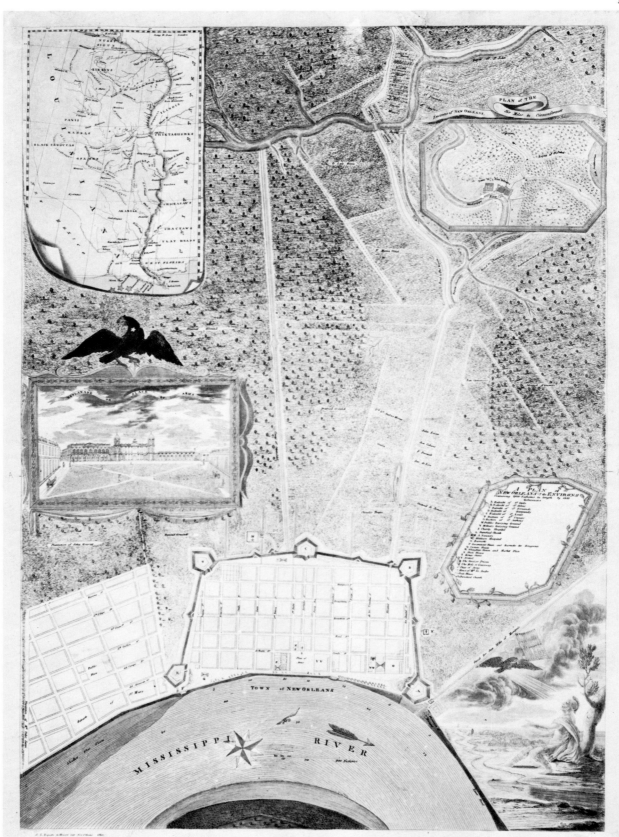

A PLAN OF NEW ORLEANS

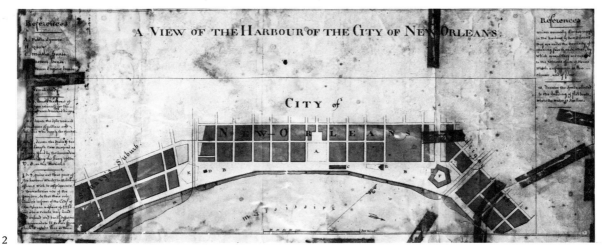

CITY of

NEW ORLEANS

2

3

A DIGEST

OF THE

CIVIL LAWS

NOW IN FORCE

IN THE

TERRITORY OF ORLEANS,

WITH

ALTERATIONS AND AMENDMENTS

ADAPTED TO ITS

PRESENT SYSTEM OF GOVERNMENT.

By Authority.

NEW-ORLEANS:

PRINTED BY BRADFORD & ANDERSON, PRINTERS TO THE TERRITORY.

1808.

4

5

A map (1), probably made in 1803, shows the new American city of New Orleans and, in insets, the entire Louisiana Territory (upper left) and the city's main square, the Place d'Armes (left center). The map of New Orleans harbor (2) dates from a few years later. William C. C. Claiborne (3) was the first American governor of the new territory of Louisiana. French laws prevailed in the territory and later in the state (4), even after Louisiana entered the union in the year 1812. One of the state's most prominent English-speaking citizens was Edward Livingston (5), a New Yorker and the brother of the man who had originally negotiated the purchase of Louisiana. Livingston moved to New Orleans, married into a French family, and later served his adopted state as a representative in Congress.

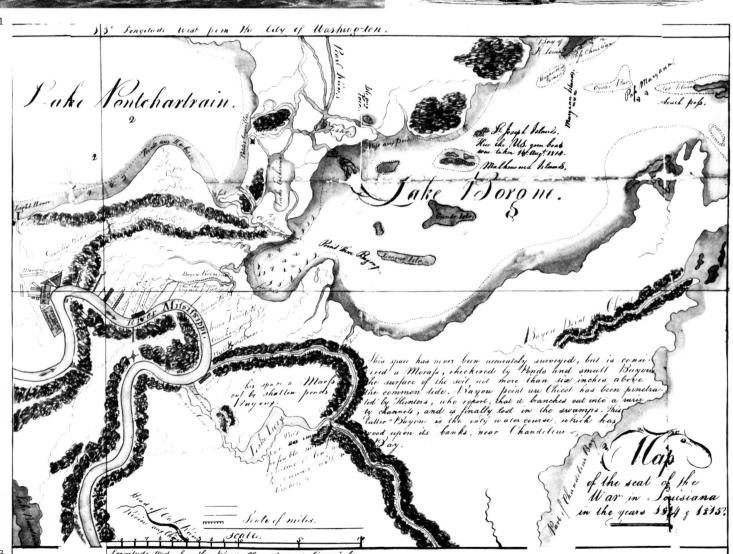

The final action of the War of 1812 saw the British attempting to capture New Orleans. The first engagement of the siege was an unsuccessful effort to prevent the British from landing; a troop of 1,000 British armed sailors and marines captured an American flotilla (1) on Lake Borgne and were able to come ashore. That same day, December 14, 1814, a steamboat, the *Enterprise* (2), arrived in New Orleans with a cargo of military supplies—the first time in history that a steamboat had taken part in a military operation. Fort St. Charles (4) was the only fort guarding New Orleans, but it was in a decayed state. To defend the city, the Americans stationed themselves at a plantation 7 miles below the city, at a position just above the words "River Mississippi" on the contemporary map (3) opposite. Another map (5) shows the American defense lines more closely. Andrew Jackson (6) was in command of the American forces and Sir Edward Pakenham (7) was in command of the English.

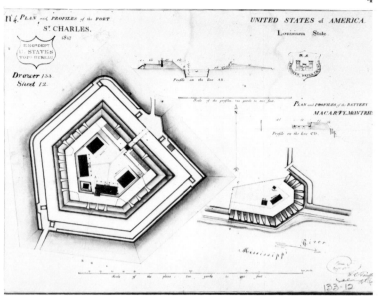

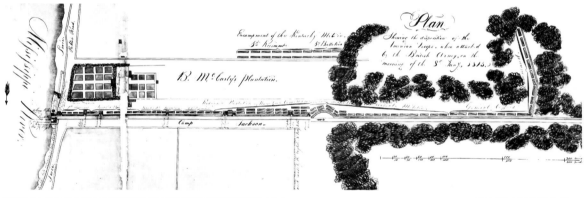

5

6

7

PEACE.

CONNECTICUT MIRROR, EXTRA. February 13, 1815.

By the mail this morning we have received an extra sheet issued yesterday morning from the office of the New-York Commercial Advertiser, from which we have extracted the following

GLORIOUS NEWS!!

2

1

3

6

7

Newspapers and broadsides reported the signing of a peace between the Americans and British at Ghent on December 24, 1814 (1), but news of it didn't reach New Orleans until after the armies had joined in battle on January 8. Numerous depictions of the famous battle were made in the years after 1815, most of them inaccurate. The primitive woodcut opposite at top (2) is highly imaginative; the broad-ranging view below it (3) is closer to the actuality. Above are two depictions (6,7) of the death of General Pakenham in the battle. The scene of the battle today is marked by an embankment and cannon (4) and a marble obelisk (5) erected in 1855.

New Orleans Grows

1

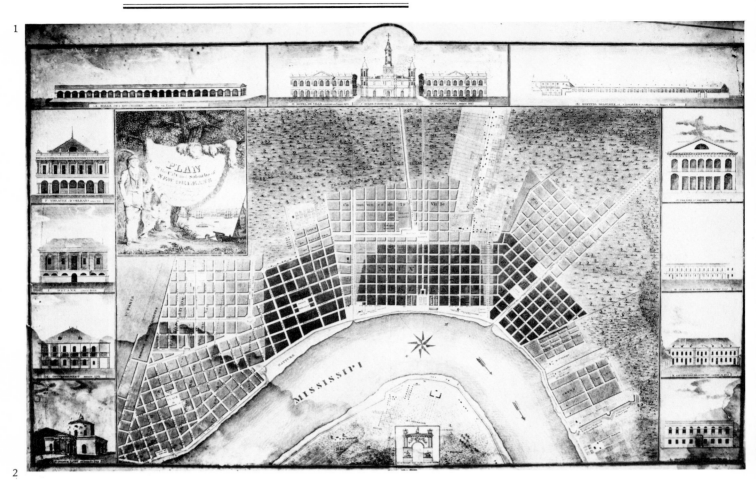

2

An 1815 plan of New Orleans and its suburbs (1) also depicts some of the most important buildings of the city, including (top left) the meat market and (top right) the hospital. A riverfront view of the city (2) shows the Place d'Armes, which can also be seen at the top center of the map. Prominent citizens of New Orleans were Etienne Boré (3), the first mayor and the first Louisianan to produce sugar in commercial quantities, and, somewhat less respectable, the Lafitte brothers Jean and Pierre, privateers and at times pirates, who are shown reveling in a contemporary painting below (4). Jean is the man holding up a drinking glass; his brother Pierre stands at the center.

3

1

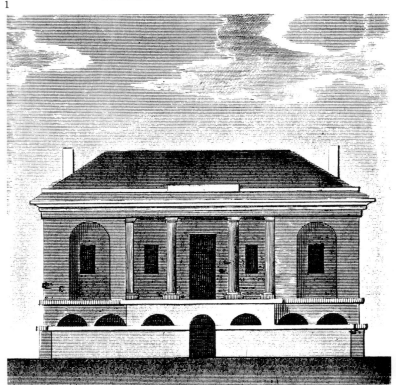

2

3

4

The architect Benjamin Henry Latrobe (2) came to New Orleans in 1819 and was responsible for designing the Custom House (1), the water-works (3), and the Louisiana State Bank (4). Several years later his son, John H. B. Latrobe, visited New Orleans and made several sketches of the city. Shown above are the St. Louis cemetery No. 1 (5) and a street scene (6), both of them by John Latrobe.

1

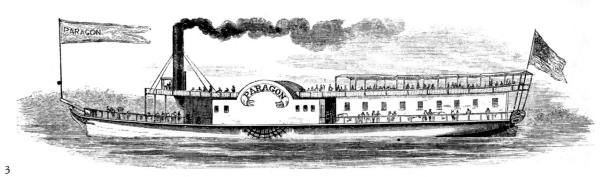

2

3

4

6

Its thriving port was the basis of New Orleans's great prosperity. An 1827 sketch (1), opposite, shows the city's bustling waterfront. One New Orleans merchant, Maunsell White, was part owner of the *Paragon* (3), a steamboat which was built in 1819. Another early steamboat, the *John Randolph,* is shown in the vignette (2) on a check issued by the Louisiana State Bank; it sank at Carrollton in 1841. At the mouth of the Mississippi was the pilot's station, the Balize, shown above in an 1822 view (4); below it is a pilot's receipt (5). Louisiana's second major waterway, the Red River, was impassable to steamboats until the 1830's, blocked by a great "raft"—a mass of logs and river-borne debris that extended for 150 miles. Captain Henry Miller Shreve (6), after whom Shreveport is named, broke up this barrier with his snagboats, making navigation possible.

1

2

3

4

6

5

At the time of the purchase, Louisiana had a polyglot population of French, Spanish, Creoles, Negroes, Americans, Germans, and Indians. Blacks, both slave and free, made up a little more than half of the total population of New Orleans. As Louisiana grew, the population remained cosmopolitan. In New Orleans itself, a varied crowd strolled through the streets. A view of the public square in front of the cathedral (1), engraved around 1845, shows a troop of soldiers drilling before an audience of interested citizens. In a lithograph dating from the 1820's (2), a dandy, shaded from the sun by a parasol, walks through a suburban street, while fettered slaves clean the gutters. New Orleans's mixed population included: Bernard de Marigny (3), the scion of an important Louisiana family and a friend of King Louis Philippe of France (de Marigny dissipated his large fortune through gambling and high living); a dignified though unnamed black woman (4) wearing a *tignon*, a typical Negro headdress; General Jean-Robert-Marie Humbert (6), who fought with Jackson at the battle of New Orleans; and Louis Philippe de Roffignac (5), a French count who served in the Louisiana legislature, became mayor of New Orleans, and eventually returned to live out his days in France.

Overleaf: Many Indians still lived in the back country, and Indians were often seen in New Orleans. This 1847 painting shows an Indian family walking along a bayou.

1

Audubon

3

2

4

John J. Audubon, the famous naturalist, first arrived in New Orleans in 1821 where he earned a precarious living sketching "phizzes" as he called them—portrait sketches at $25 a head—and teaching drawing. He combed the New Orleans markets or hunted in the nearby swamps for new specimens of birds for his slowly growing portfolio which was eventually to become *The Birds of America.* Practically penniless most of the time, Audubon lived for a while in a keelboat moored near the market. In 1837, after the publication of his famous work, he returned to New Orleans for a short time, renewed old acquaintances, and was royally treated by distinguished citizens. At left is an engraving portraying Audubon (1). Among the birds painted by Audubon in Louisiana were Louisiana's state bird, the brown pelican (2), the indigo bird (3), the green-winged teal (4), the ring-necked duck (5), the common gallinule (6) and, probably, the little blue heron (7).

5

6

7

As New Orleans grew, the countryside along the Mississippi and the other Louisiana waterways became populated with settlers. An 1820 watercolor (1) shows a rude pioneer cottage along the banks of the Mississippi above New Orleans. Three wash drawings, done by the artist Samuel M. Lee in the vicinity of the Acadian town of St. Martinville, show a boarding house (2); the St. Martinville church, built by Acadian refugees in 1765 (3); and a landscape above the Bayou Teche (4). Another view of the Teche, in an engraving published some decades later, depicts a columned house with a path leading down to the river (5). One of the few remaining eighteenth-century houses in central Louisiana is Kent House (6) built near Alexandria sometime around 1795.

3

4

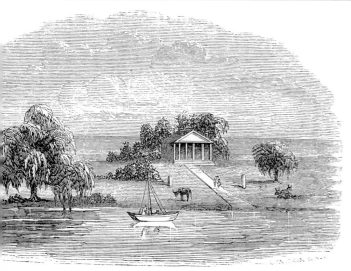

5

6

3

Belle Helene (1), formerly called Ashland and built in 1841, lies along the banks of the Mississippi near Darrow. It is noted for its massive 30-foot-high, 4-foot-square columns and is one of the state's most famous plantations. Equally imposing in its heyday was the plantation house called Uncle Sam (2). Construction of the house began in 1841; about a century later the building was destroyed. Directly across the river from Uncle Sam, in St. John the Baptist Parish, was Evergreen (3) with its beautiful curving stairways. Unlike Uncle Sam, Evergreen has been restored and is in fine condition today. The White Plantation house (4) on Bayou Lafourche is a simple raised cottage, with three dormers and windows at the front; it was the home of one of Louisiana's governors, who held office in the 1830's, and of Chief Justice of the United States Edward Douglass White, who was born there in 1845.

4

The Great Plantations

1

2

One of the most beautiful and ostentatious plantation houses in the South was Belle Grove (3) in Iberville Parish; it survived as a decaying, picturesque ruin for many years, until it was finally destroyed by fire in 1952. A great many early Louisiana plantation houses were of immense size —among them the Sarpy house (1) in Jefferson Parish, photographed from the top of a neighboring levee. A pencil-and-watercolor drawing, by a visiting Italian artist, done about 1854, shows a typical plantation in southern Louisiana (2). The substantially built main house and 9 out-buildings are shown with the stacks of a sugar mill in the distant background.

3

98

Along the Great River

2

An 1858 chart (1), designed by the immigrant French artist Adrien Persac, shows the plantations bordering the lower Mississippi between Natchez and New Orleans. Of great historical value, the chart documents the location, ownership, and size of every one of the plantations along the riverbank. Vignettes in the four corners show the cities of Baton Rouge and New Orleans (bottom) and depict a cotton plantation (at upper left) and a sugar plantation, Belle Grove (at upper right). Belle Grove can also be seen in the photograph on page 97. Persac painted many Louisiana scenes, including the Isle Copal plantation (2) with its slave quarters separated from the columned big house by two fences; and a peaceful business establishment overlooking a duck pond: John Dominique's general store (3), located on the outskirts of New Orleans.

1
2

3

4

In the backwoods the typical pioneer lived in a so-called dogtrot house (1), a log or plank cabin, raised on piers, with a central hallway and a long front porch. The interior of these houses was simple. Typical interiors are seen opposite (2,3). Above is a reconstruction of an old blacksmith shop (4) with an iron anvil resting atop the brick forge. Most backwoods settlements were accessible by water. The little town of Vidalia (5), opposite Natchez, was easily reached by Mississippi riverboat.

1

2

3

4

Cotton was the mainstay of the plantation economy. A lithograph from the 1850's done by an American traveler, Henry Lewis, shows a cotton plantation, with slaves bringing in the crop (1). The cotton was carried to the gin house (2) where it went through the gin (3) so that the seeds could be removed. Then the cotton was pressed into bales (4) and the bales were transported (5) to market. Eventually much of the cotton ended up at presses such as the Orleans Cotton Press (6), where up to 25,000 bales could be stored while awaiting shipment.

5

6

1

3

Sugar was an even more important crop than cotton in southern Louisiana. Engravings from *Harper's Magazine* published in 1853 show a sugarcane field (1), slaves gathering the cane (2), sugar being crushed in a mill (3), and the interior of a sugar house (4), with the syrup being boiled. Below is a riverside sugar refinery (5), with barrels being loaded by stevedores onto a ship.

1

THART SLAVES

2

The economy of Louisiana was largely built on slavery. In 1850, there were some 240,000 slaves in the state and about 270,000 free inhabitants. New Orleans had an active trade in slaves and slave auctions were common. An 1842 engraving above (1) shows blacks being auctioned in the St. Louis Hotel Rotunda along with household goods. In another engraving (2), from 1860, well-dressed slaves are lined up for sale. Slave sale notices (3) appeared in the newspapers, along with notices of runaway slaves (4). In the countryside, most slaves lived in rows of shacks. The slave quarters at Evergreen Plantation (5) were made more pleasant by being located along an avenue of moss-hung live oaks. Field slaves spent long hours working in the heat of the outdoors. An Austrian traveler sketched a group of slaves, harvesting sugar cane under the supervision of an overseer or their owner, who can be seen on horseback (6).

BY TRICOU DOMINGON & CANONGE.

WILL be sold on Saturday. 2d April next, at 12 o'clock at Hewlett's Exchange the following valuable Slaves:

Sprice,	aged about	40 years,	overseer of slaves
Lever,	"	30 "	sawyer and driver
Isaac,	'	45 "	blacksmith
Louis	"	15 "	ploughman
Antoine,	"	20 "	do
Charles,	"	30 "	do
Henry,	"	25 "	do
James,	"	30 "	field hand
Brown,	"	45 "	excellent gardener
Scipion,	"	40 "	ploughman & carman
Ode,	"	12 "	} orphans
Andrews,	"	8 "	
Kitty,	"	28 "	mul. wench, field hand
Maria,	"	24 "	do house servant
Haga,	"	18 "	field hand
Suckey,	"	24 "	do
Thérésé,	"	18 "	do
Charlotte,	"	85 "	house serv't, seam'ress
Françoise,	"	25 "	do do
Betty,	"	15 "	spinster
Betty,	"	18 "	and her child
Louisa	"	25 "	and her child, 8 years
Mary,	"	28 "	and Rebecca 11 do
Nancy,	"	35 "	field hand
Mulaker	"	36 "	do
Piny,	"	45 "	do
Josephine,	"	45	good house servant and

good sick nurse. These slaves are only guaranteed free from all vices and diseases prescribed by law.

Terms—1 and 2 years credit, for approved endorsed notes and mortgage until final payment.

Acts of sale before F Grima, Esq, notary public, at the expense of the purchaser.　　　　m 17-5t

---

Runaway Slave—Runaway from the subscriber No 221 Magazine three weeks ago the negro woman slave named SOPHIA, aged 27 years, about 5 ft high, marked with the small pox, crooked feet; big lips, wants some teeth before, was dressed when she started with a blue spotted domestic frock, she is well known in suburb St Mary is a washer by the day, and is supposed to have been harboured in said suburb.

Ten dollars reward will be given for the apprehension and delivery to the subscriber of said slave or for lodging the same in the jail of New Orleans.
m 31-3t　　　　　　　　P. SHIELD.

FIFTEEN DOLLARS REWARD.

Run away from the subscriber, Esplanade corner of Rampart street, on the 28th inst, the negro girl SARAH, 19 years, 5 feet 2 inches high, she has a sulky look when spoken to; when she left was dressed in a light purple and spotted calico frock. She has a large scar between her shoulders. The above reward will be paid to whomsoever will will apprehend said slave and lodge her in the parish jail of New Orleans.
mar 31　　　　　　　JAMES FINLAY.

NOTICE—Detained in the jail of the parish of Jefferson, a negro boy who calls himself John, is about 12 years old, and says he belongs to Mr Williams. Also a mullatto boy called, Anfield, 14 years old who says he belongs to Mr Bouligny. The owners are requested to claim them in conformity with the law.　　J. CHARBONNET,
m 29　　　　　Sheriff of the parish of Jefferson.

Slavery

Overleaf: This moving painting of the burial of a slave was done in the 1850's by John Antrobus. The mourners pray over the simple wooden coffin in a grove of trees while the plantation owners, at the right, watch from a distance.

Education

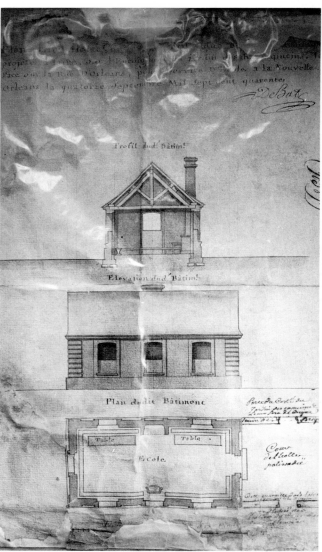

Louisiana's first school was founded in 1725. An architect's drawing (2), dating from a few years later, shows the plan for another school at New Orleans that was never built. In 1812 the College d'Orléans (1) was established. Centenary College was built at Jackson in 1825. The nearly ruined but still imposing building below (3), a famous relic of the original campus, eventually had to be demolished. Jefferson College (4) was established in St. James Parish in 1834 to educate the sons of planters. The present building, now the property of the Jesuit Order, dates from the 1840's. At Minden, near Shreveport, a placid-looking academy for young ladies (5) was incorporated in 1854, although it had already been in existence as an educational establishment for many years.

1

2

3

4

Early nineteenth-century New Orleans had many newspapers; by the year 1837, 6 were being published in the city, 5 in English and 1 in French. The *Picayune,* which still survives, began publication in January, 1837. An issue of October 20 (1) boasts that the newspaper gets there first with the news—ahead of other papers, including the French-language *L'Abeille* or "The Bee" (5) whose logo was adorned with a picture of a beehive. The *Daily Delta* (6) displayed advertisements on its front page. Illustrations from the 1857 *New Orleans City Directory* show the buildings which housed the "Bee" (2), the *Delta* (3) and the *Picayune* (4), which the city directory misspelled as "Pacayune."

L'ABEILLE.

JOURNAL POLITIQUE. COMMERCIAL & LITTERAIRE.

Imprimé par F. DELAUP, et publié tous les jours, rue St.-Pierre No. 94, entre Royale et Bourbon.

NOUVELLE-ORLEANS, MARDI, 27 JANVIER 1829.

Extrait de la Gazette de France, du 3 Mai, 1828.

COMPARAISON DES PIANOS FRANÇAIS ET DES PIANOS ANGLAIS.

NOUS eûmes occasion, il y a peu de temps, de mettre en parallèle les Pianos de Londres et ceux de Vienne. Les artistes, disions-nous, et les amateurs les plus distingués, en reconnaissant aux premiers une belle qualité de son, leur reprochent d'avoir des Claviers généralement fort durs, ils reconnaissent au second, au contraire, des claviers faciles ; mais ils leur reprochent de manquer de son. Un artiste allemand, M. Charles Schunke, élève du célèbre Hummel, nous adresse aujourd'hui une lettre que nos lecteurs trouveront d'autant plus digne de leur intérêt, qu'elle concerne une branche importante de l'industrie française.

"Monsieur,

"Comme il pourrait paraître extraordinaire que je n'eusse pas adopté dans les concerts les pianos de M. M. Erard, mon opinion sur la supériorité de ces instrumens étant bien connue, je dois à la vérité de déclarer que, si je ne m'ai pas fait

LOTERIE
De l'Eglise Catholique
DE L'ETAT DE LA LOUISIANE—3ème. classe
Autorisée par l'Etat de la Louisiane au profit de l'Eglise Catholique des Natchitoches.

Le Tirage aura positivement lieu à la Nlle. Orléans, le 4 Février 1829.

— PROSPECTUS :—

1	prix	de	$6,000	$6,000
1	"	"	5,000	5,000
1	"	"	4,500	4,500
1	"	"	4,000	4,000
1	"	"	3,540	3,540
1	"	"	3,000	3,000
6	"	"	1,000	6,000
12	"	"	250	3,000
156	"	"	100	15,600

Vente par le Marshal.

Le Maire, les Aldermen et habitants de la ville de la Nouvelle-Orléans,

contre L'EMPLACEMENT N°. un, dans l'ilet N°. vingt-six, faubourg Lacourse, dont le propriétaire est inconnu.

Les memes *contre* l'emplacement N°. deux, dans l'ilet N°. vingt-six, faubourg Lacourse, dont le propriétaire est inconnu.

Les memes *contre* l'emplacement N°. un, dans l'ilet N°. trente-six, faubourg Lacourse, dont propriétaire est inconnu.

Les memes *contre* l'emplacement N°. deux, dans l'ilet N°. trente-six, faubourg Lacourse, dont le propriétaire est inconnu.

Les memes *contre* l'emplacement N°. sept, dans l'ilet N°. trente-six, faubourg Lacourse, dont le propriétaire est inconnu.

Les memes *contre* l'emplacement N°. un, dans l'ilet N°. soixante-neuf, faubourg Lacourse, dont le propriétaire est inconnu.

Les memes *contre* l'emplacement N°. cinq dans l'ilet N°. 74, faubourg Lacourse, dont le propriétaire est inconnu.

Les memes *contre* l'emplacement N°. six, dans l'ilet N°. soixante-quatorze, faubourg Lacourse, dont le propriétaire est inconnu.

Les memes *contre* l'emplacement N°. sept, dans l'ilet N°. soixante-quatorze, dont le propriétaire est inconnu.

Les memes *contre* l'emplacement N°. quatre, dans l'ilet No. quatre-vingt-cinq, faubourg

Vente par le Marshal.

Stephen Cockran vs. Brown, propriétaires du bateau à vapeur

EN vertu d'un writ de fi. fa. sé. par l'hon. P. F. S... la Cour de Cité, j'exposerai Janvier 1829, à midi, au Caf...

Le bateau avec ses ammeubl... tisfaire a... dans l'affaire ci-dessus.

30 Déc.   L. D...

Vente par le...

Ralf Marsh contre Jes... juge président de la ... poserai en vente, Mardi 27e... Bureau du Marshal, rue St... après-midi, un Cabriolet av... tre paires de Roues de char... Cidre ; saisis dans l'affaire ...

16 Janvier   L.

VR. ROUMAGE o... ticles suivants en d... navires Henry Astor et ... deaux : Eau-de-vie en pipes ...

The Daily Delta.

VOLUME I.]   **NEW ORLEANS, FRIDAY MORNING, NOVEMBER 28, 1845.**   [NUMBER 42.

Colleges and Schools.

N. Orleans High School for Young Ladies

REMOVED

L. HITCHCOCK respectfully informs his patrons and the public, that he has removed his Seminary to APOLLO STREET, No. 10, near Triton Walk, where, in addition to his present number, a few Young Ladies will be received, either as Day or Boarding Pupils. For day pupils he has reduced his charges *materially*. A Circular, containing terms, &c., may be had at the School, or at any of the Camp-street Bookstores. o12

ACADEMY FOR YOUNG LADIES.

HIGH SCHOOL FOR YOUNG LADIES, as Boarders or Day Pupils, *Carondelet street, near St. Joseph street,*

Under the superintendence of the MISS ALLISONS.

In this institution the most competent Instructors are employed in every department essential to a highly finished education. Particular care is bestowed on the formation of the manners of the Young Ladies, and the most unwearied attention is devoted to their mental improvement. The mode of discipline pursued by the Miss Allisons is one of uniform gentleness, as calculated to produce the happiest effects upon all dispositions, and to create a truly feminine and ladylike deportment and character.

The study of the French Language forms a part of the daily employment of all the pupils, under the superintendence of a Professor from Paris, and is included in the terms of tuition : all other Languages with the accomplishments of Music, Singing, Drawing and Dancing, are the separate charges of the teachers and masters engaged in the institution.

The Miss Allisons refer to—

W. Freret, Esq.,	Rev. Dr. Wheaton,
S J. Peters Esq.,	Judge Rawle,
H C. Cammack, Esq.,	W. P. Converse, Esq.,
Theodore Shute, Esq.,	A. Lanfear, Esq.,
H. Palfrey, Esq.,	L. C. Duncan, Esq.,
H. Lockett, Esq.,	o12

SPANISH LANGUAGE.—Evening Class.

No. 42 CUSTOMHOUSE STREET.

DON E. GOMEZ, Professor of Spanish Literature, has the honor to inform the public that he will open

Fashionable Clothing.

REMOVAL.

JOSEPH FALZUN, Wholesale and Retail Dealer in CLOTHING, HATS, BOOTS, SHOES and DRY GOODS, has removed to *No. 30 New Levee, corner of Poydras street.* o12

BOOTS AND SHOES.

MICHAEL FLOOD, *Dealer in Boots and Shoes,* of the best quality, at the lowest prices, 132 *NEW LEVEE, corner of DELORD street,* New Orleans. Making and Repairing also done to order. n1-tf

INDIA RUBBER GOODS AND CLOTHING—Long Capes and Ponchos, Leggins for Riding, Pillows, Life Jackets and Preservers ; Cloth by the yard or piece ; also, a general assortment of Ready Made Clothing, of the latest mode ; Boys' and Children's Clothing ; Trunks and Carpet Bags, &c.   FOLGER & BLAKE,

n9   17 Old Levee, corner of Customhouse st.

CLOTHING!—CLOTHING!!

At No. 34 NEW LEVEE.

THE best selected and cheapest stock in New Orleans. Also, a large assortment of DRY GOODS, of the latest and newest styles, and a complete assortment of HATS, BOOTS and SHOES, for sale low at the store of JAMES CORLIS, 34 New Levee,

n1 6m—n8   A few doors above Poydras st.

He has now with him in the store, Mr. J. CONNOLLY, who will use his utmost endeavors to give satisfaction to the customers of the house.

S. M. BON,

Corner CARONDELET AND COMMON STREETS,

RESPECTFULLY informs his friends and the public that he is now prepared to make New Garments out of Old, by thoroughly renovating and cleaning them ; also to DYE Gentlemen's and Ladies' Garments ANY COLOR, at the shortest notice.

TAILORING—Civil and Military.—The strictest attention will be paid to this branch of the business ; and those favoring me with their custom, can be assured that their work will be done to their satisfaction, in a thorough workmanlike manner. n12-6m

TAILOR AND MILITARY WORKMAN

JAMES MANAHAN, Tailor and Military

Fancy and Dry Goods.

FRENCH MILLINERY, &c.

MRS. BANISTER, *Importer of French Millinery and English Straw Bonnets, No. 66 ROYAL STREET, corner of Bienville,* has just received her Fall Stock of WINTER BONNETS. Also, a select assortment of Ribbons, Flowers, Caps, Plumes, Veils, Corsets, Gloves, Ladies' and Infants' Embroidered Robes, Collars, Handkerchiefs and Fancy Goods. n15 tf

NOTICE OF REMOVAL.

MICHAEL KERNAN, late 66 Royal st., begs to inform the Ladies of New Orleans and his Country friends, that he has removed to No. 30 CHARTRES street, corner of Customhouse, where he is now opening the most extensive and elegant Stock of rich French FANCY DRY GOODS, that have ever been imported into this city ; he flatters himself from his well known reputation for keeping fashionable and GOOD GOODS, to merit a continuance of public patronage heretofore so liberally bestowed. n1

NEW STOCK OF DRY GOODS.

JUST now receiving and of direct importation, a large assortment of the latest and newest styles of Foreign and Domestic Dry Goods. For sale low at NOLAN'S, cor. Chartres and Canal sts.

N. B.—CARPETS, viz : Brussels, Venitian, 3 ply, and ingrain of all qualities.

Wilton and Turkey Rugs ; Blankets and Flannels, &c., in great variety, at

o12 tf   NOLAN'S 34 Canal street.

Coal.

COAL! COAL!!

W. L. THOMPSON & CO., *Dealers in Coal, corner of Julia and Commerce streets, and No. 143 St. Louis street.* Orders left at the yards, or at the store of B. Brower & Co., No. 17 Camp street, will be promptly attended to. n6-3m

COAL! COAL!! COAL!!!

FARRELL & WICKERSHAM—*Office in the yard,*

Hotels & Boarding-Houses.

PRIVATE BOARDING.

FAMILIES AND SINGLE GENTLEMEN can be accommodated with BOARD, and very pleasant ROOMS, within a few minutes walk of the Saint Charles Exchange. Inquire at this office. n8tf

BOARDING.

MRS. J. H. WILSON, 27 *BIENVILLE STREET,* is now ready to receive gentlemen, for permanent or transient Boarding, on the most reasonable terms. o28 tf

BOARDING.

MRS. ROSENDALE, 134 *MAGAZINE ST.,* is now ready to receive families and single gentlemen, for permanent or transient Boarding, on the most reasonable terms. o25 1y

BOARDING---REMOVAL.

MRS. MILLIKEN has REMOVED *from No. 73 Canal street to No. 120 POYDRAS STREET,* (one door below St. Charles,) where she is now prepared to receive families and single gentlemen, either as permanent or transient boarders. o23 1y

FAMILY BOARDING-HOUSE.

MRS. E. OVIATT, *No. 9 CANAL STREET,* having leased the adjoining building, is now able to accommodate from twenty to thirty families. Families visiting the South, will find it one of the most desirable and healthy locations in the city. A continuation of the liberal patronage that she has received, is most respectfully solicited. o23-6m

BOARDING HOUSE.

MRS. HINSDELL has fitted up the pleasant and commodious house No. 5 *DIMOND'S ROW,* in *Tchoupitoulas street, between St. Joseph and Delord streets,* for a BOARDING HOUSE, and is now ready to receive Boarders. Her rooms are large and pleasant, her table will be well supplied, and her terms moderate. N. B.—A small family can be accommodated with Board and Rooms on very reasonable terms. n11

BOARDING.

MRS. PROCTOR informs her friends and the public that her house has been thoroughly refitted and arranged for the coming season. She is now ready to receive boarders, and trusts that her central

1

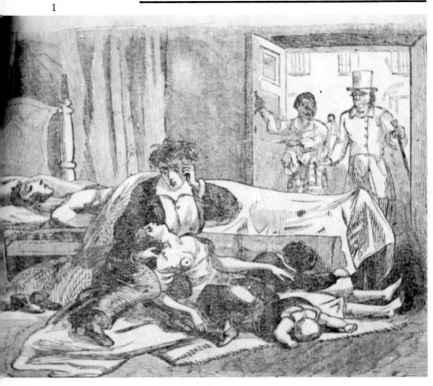

2

From 1796 on, Louisiana, and particularly the closely built city of New Orleans, was stricken by epidemic diseases—cholera and yellow fever. New Orleans was a dirty and unhealthy city with imperfect drainage and no sewage system. It depended on unscreened wooden cisterns to catch rain for drinking water. Such an environment naturally engendered the spread of diseases. Yellow fever was by far the worst pestilence. In New Orleans between 1817 and 1860 there were 23 yellow fever epidemics and, as a result, 28,192 deaths were recorded. A victim of the disease is shown in an 1853 engraving (1), which comes from a book describing one of the worst of the epidemics. Those stricken by this and other diseases were carried to the Charity Hospital (2), built in 1832, to recuperate in a private room or in one of the wards (3). New Orleans's doctors were not above advertising their services, as Dr. Mullen of Exchange Alley did (4). Those who failed to survive the doctors' attentions ended up in one of the city's cemeteries, generally built above ground because the city's soil was too marshy for interments. Characteristic New Orleans tombs appear in the photograph opposite (5).

3

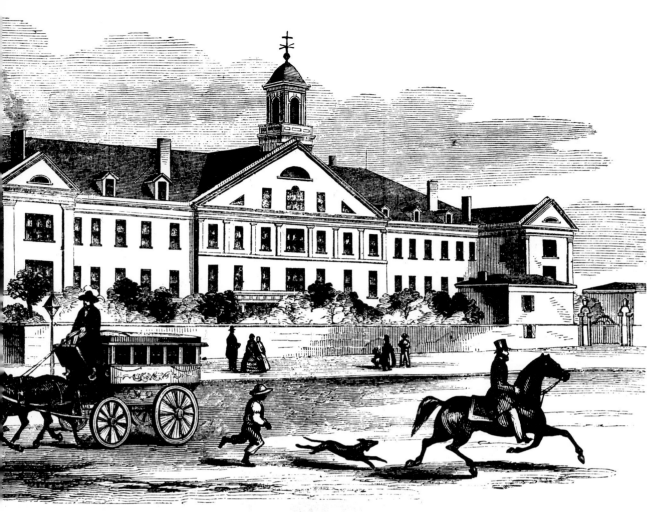

4

5

Sonntags=Blatt
der
New Orleans Deutschen Presse.
Geschäfts-Lokal: No. 48 Bienville Straße, nahe Chartres.

No. 7.   Sonntag den 3. Mai 1868.   Jahrgang 1.

Louisiana's French- and English-speaking population was swollen during the nineteenth century by many immigrants, particularly by arrivals from Germany and Ireland. The Germans established their own newspaper (1) and built their own churches. The German Catholic Church of St. Mary's Assumption recalled the old country in both its exterior (2) and interior (3). One group of Germans, led by Count Maximilian Leon, established a religious settlement along the Red River, making certain to situate their colony at about the same latitude as Jerusalem. Eventually Leon died and his widow, Countess Leon (4), established a new settlement near Minden. Her simple cabin (5) is still standing. Opposite is the gravestone (6) of an Irish immigrant, a native of County Cavan, Ireland, who died in New Orleans in 1858. Despite the presence of newcomers, French remained the principal language of the southern rural districts and election notices, such as this one (7), appeared in two languages.

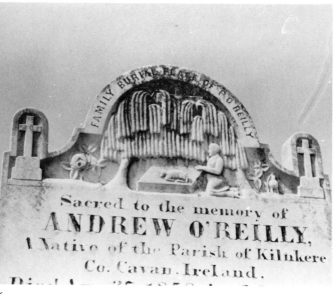

6

AVIS D'ELECTION.

ÉTAT DE LA LOUISIANE.

Paroisse St. Jean-Baptiste.

QU'IL soit notoire aux Electeurs de la paroisse St. Jean-Baptiste, que conformément à la loi, l'Election annuelle par la voie du scrutin, aura lieu dans chacun des arrondissements de cette paroisse, le LUNDI 14 MAI 1860, depuis 9 heures du matin jusqu'à 3 heures de l'après-midi, à l'effet de pourvoir au remplacement des Membres du Juri de Police, dont les fonctions seront expirées, et qui seront ci-après denommés ; la dite Election sera tenue aux lieux suivants et sous la surveillance des commissaires ci-après nommés, savoir :

RIVE DROITE.

MEMBRES ENCORE EN FONCTIONS POUR UN AN.

1er Arrond.—Cyprien Songy.
2nd   "   —Damien Haydel.
3me   "   —Emile Mericq.

RIVE GAUCHE.

MEMBRES ENCORE EN FONCTIONS POUR UN AN.

1er Arrond.—Cyprien Chauff.
2nd   "   —Adolphe Boudousquie.
3me   "   —Jean-Baptiste Baudry.

RIVE DROITE.

MEMBRES A REMPLACER A CETTE ELECTION.

1er Arrond.—Jean F. Burcard.
2nd   "   —Eugène Landaiche.
3me   "   —P. A. Becnel.

RIVE GAUCHE.

MEMBRES A REMPLACER A CETTE ELECTION.

1er Arrond.—Edouard Montz.
2nd   "   —Louis Trègre.
3me   "   —Eugène Chenet Sr.
Les dites Elections seront tenues comme suit :

RIVE DROITE

1er Arrond.—A la Grocerie de Jean Martin, sous la surveillance d'Ernest Perret et Valcourt Songy, Commissaires par moi nommés à cet effet.
2nd. Arrond.—Au Billard de M. G. Chaband, sous la surveillance d'Armand Périlliat et Valcourt Bossier, Commissaires par moi nommés à cet effet.
3me Arrond.—Au domicile de Mme Mericq sous l'inspection de l'Hon. F. Crozet, Juge de paix,

RIVE GAUCHE.

1er Arrond.—Au Billard d'Onésime Bossier, sous l'inspection de l'Hon. Théodore Fortineau, Juge de paix.
2nd Arrond.—Au Café d'Antoine Vicknair, sous l'inspection de l'Hon. Léo Elfer, Juge de paix.
3me Arrond.—A la Grocerie d'Eugène Chenet Sr., sous la surveillance de Drauzin Trépagner et d'Eugène Chenet Sr., Commissaires, par moi nommés à cet effet.
Les Commissaires des dites Elections sont priés de faires parvenir leurs procès-verbaux dans le plus bref délai au soussigné.
P. A. BECNEL,
Président du Juri de Police.
Paroisse St. Jean-Baptiste, ce 7 avril, 1860.

ELECTION NOTICE.

STATE OF LOUISIANA.

Parish of St. John the Baptist.

BE it known to the Electors of the parish of St. John the Baptist, that according to law, the annual Election by ballot shall be opened in each of the wards of this parish, on MONDAY the 14th day of MAY 1860, from 9 o'clock, A. M., until 3 o'clock P. M. for members to the Police Jury in lieu of those whose time of Office, shall be expired and who shall be hereinafter named Commissioners, to wit :

RIGHT BANK.

MEMBERS YET REMAINING IN OFFICE FOR ONE YEAR.

1st Ward.—Cyprien Songy.
2nd   "   —Damien Haydel.
3rd   "   —Emile Mericq.

LEFT BANK.

MEMBERS YET REMAINING IN OFFICE FOR ONE YEAR.

1st Ward—Cyprien Chauff.
2nd   "   —Adolphe Boudousquie.
3rd   "   —Jean-Baptiste Baudry.

RIGHT BANK.

MEMBERS WHOSE TIME OF OFFICE SHALL BE EXPIRED

1st Ward.—Jean F. Burcard.
2nd   "   —Eugène Landaiche.
3rd   "   —P. A. Becnel.

LEFT BANK.

MEMBERS WHOSE TIME OF OFFICE SHALL BE EXPIRED

1st Ward.—Edouard Montz.
2nd   "   —Louis Trègre.
3rd   "   —Eugène Chenet Sr.
The said Election shall be held as follows :

RIGHT BANK.

1st Ward.—At the Grocery of Jean Martin, under the superintendence of Ernest Perret and Valcourt Songy, Commissioners by me appointed to that purpose.
2nd Ward.—At the Billiard-room of Mr. G. Chaband, under the superintendence of Armand Periliat and Valcourt Bossier, Commissioners by me appointed to that purpose.
3rd Ward.—At the domicile of Mme Mericq under the inspection of the Hon. F. Crozet, Justice of the Peace.

LEFT BANK.

1st Ward.—At the Billiard-room of Onésime Bossier, under the inspection of the Hon. Theodore Fortineau Justice of the Peace.
2nd Ward.—At the Coffee-house of Mr. Antoine Vicknair, under the inspection of the Hon. Léo Elfer, Justice of the Peace.
3rd Ward.—At the Grocery Store of Eugène Chenet Sr., under the superintendence of Drauzin Trépagner and Eugène Chenet Sr., Commissioners, by me appointed to that purpose.
The Sundry Commissioners will please send their proces-verbal to the undersigned without delay.
P. A. BECNEL,
President of the Police Jury.
Parish of St. John the Baptist, April 7th 1860.

Principal Front.

Façade Principale

3

Religious Life

2

St. Louis Cathedral (1) in New Orleans was built between 1789 and 1794 and was the gift of a wealthy philanthropist, Don Andres Almonester y Roxas, who donated money after the previous New Orleans church had been destroyed by fire. The cathedral, which was served for a time by Archbishop Blanc (2), survived until 1849, when its walls were found to be in such poor condition that the entire building had to be reconstructed. Plans for the rebuilding called for a central steeple of wood and iron tracery (3), but this proved impractical and the church steeple (4) was eventually enclosed in a weatherproof covering of slate. The oldest church in Louisiana in continued use is the Mortuary Chapel (6) of St. Anthony on Rampart Street. It was built in 1826 when the law forbade holding funeral services in the cathedral, because of the fear of yellow-fever contagion. New Orleans churches served all classes of the population. Opposite, a devout young girl stands on tiptoe to reach the holy-water font (5).

1

118

4

5

6

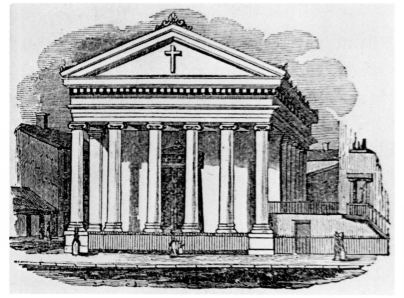

With the influx of Americans after the Louisiana Purchase, Protestant congregations began to appear in Louisiana. The first Protestant church in New Orleans was Christ Church, an Episcopal church founded in 1805; its second structure (1), an imposing columned building, was erected in 1835. Other Protestant churches in New Orleans by that time were the Congregational church (2), the Methodist church (3), and the Presbyterian church (4). The Christ Episcopal church building shown above was in use for only little more than a decade. A new Gothic style church (6) was built to replace it; the architect's perspective view appears opposite (5). The original church was sold to a Jewish congregation which used it as a synagogue. Later another Jewish congregation built the imposing Temple Sinai (7), with its mixture of architectural styles.

1

2

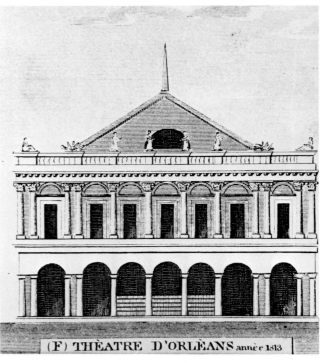

(F) THÈATRE D'ORLÉANS annèe 1813

SAINT CHARLES THEATRE, NEW ORLEANS

LUDLOW & SMITH PROPRIETORS & MANAGERS

3

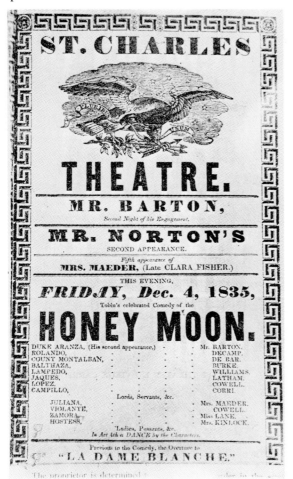

Theatrical and operatic performances made New Orleans and exciting metropolis. The Théâtre d'Orléans (2) was the city's third theatre. After the Louisiana Purchase, plays were occasionally produced in English, but it was not until the early 1820's that an American theatre (1) was built. The American theatre soon became known for excellent entertainment, and almost every notable actor and actress of the day appeared there. St. Charles Theatre, built in 1835, cost $350,000 and could seat 4,100. It burned in 1842 and was richly rebuilt (3). Shortly after it first opened, *The Honey Moon* was performed there, announced by the playbill at left (4). Another playbill (5) announces an 1827 performance of the French-language melodrama *Jocko,* or *The Brazilian Monkey* by a New Orleans troupe appearing in New York. Louisiana musical life was active, and the state was especially proud of a native son, Louis Moreau Gottschalk, a pianist and composer who based many of his works on native folk tunes. Above are engravings of the gold medal (6, 7) presented to him in 1853 by his proud fellow citizens. Another, somewhat less cultural diversion was provided by New Orleans's many barrooms. The engraving of one below (8) appeared in France before the Civil War.

1

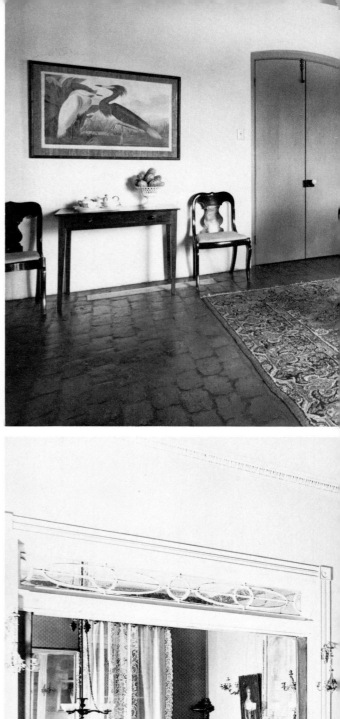

Louisiana furniture-making maintained a French tradition long after the region was incorporated into the United States. This can be seen in the bedroom of the Pontalba House in New Orleans (1), where, though the quilted bedspread is typically American, the armoire seems French. One of the most notable New Orleans cabinetmakers was François Seignouret, who may have made the chairs in the dining room (2) in the Pitot House in New Orleans. Another New Orleans house, the Puig House (3), was filled with more typically American furniture. One of the biggest furniture stores in New Orleans (4) was the establishment of the Montgomery family where prosperous citizens could purchase both new furniture—American and imported—and antiques.

124

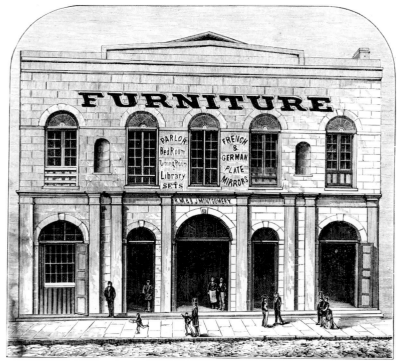

3

1

2

3

Cast-iron work was a feature of much nineteenth-century American architecture, but nowhere did it flourish with such exuberance as in Louisiana, and especially in New Orleans. Varied examples of New Orleans iron work, opposite, all dating from the middle years of the nineteenth century, show: characteristic New Orleans cast-iron balconies, on the La Branche buildings at the corner of St. Peter and Royal streets in the French Quarter (1); a detail of a wrought iron fence (2); one of New Orleans's two existing "corn-stalk" fences (3). This fence, made in 1859, is on the grounds of a house in the Garden District. Grace Church Cemetery in St. Francisville contains some fine examples of cast-iron work; on this page are shown an iron cherub (4), gateways (5, 6), and a fence made with a latticework design and adorned with spiked finials (7).

Louisiana enjoyed a flourishing artistic and intellectual life in the years before the Civil War. Julien Poydras (2) was Louisiana's earliest poet, and a congressman and businessman as well. Another Louisiana artist of note was the plantation owner Pierre Joseph Landry. His most famous sculpture is *The Wheel of Life* (1), which represents the various stages of human development. A detail at right (3) portrays the joys of youth. Another Landry sculpture (4), showing a man and woman under two trees, is designed so that the space between the trees depicts Napoleon Bonaparte in silhouette; the sculpture was made to commemorate Napoleon's death in 1826. Pauline Boyer (5), a French immigrant, settled in New Orleans in 1832 and taught young Louisianans to play the harp. *Immortelles,* 6 of which appear opposite (6), were pictures on glass and zinc to be attached to tombstones to serve as commemorative plaques. They were not made in Louisiana but were imported from France.

4

5

6

Nineteenth-century portraits show Louisiana's women, young and old, black and white: the child Lee Hattie Kit, painted by Henry Hilary Byrd, 1860, holding her doll and dressed in a lacy frock (1); a bespectacled young lady, Mrs. A. J. Rouzan, painted in 1839 by J. J. Vaudechamp (2); a miniature of a black woman, by A. Alauz, anonymous but elegantly attired (3); a nun, Mother Seraphine, painted around 1850 (4); another child, this one quite serious, Mary Ellen Byrnes, by Paul Poincy (5); a stern-visaged elderly woman, Mrs. Cantrelle, painted around 1860 by Francisco Bernard (6).

4

5

6

131

1

2

3

Baton Rouge became the capital of Louisiana in 1849. Built on a high bluff commanding the Mississippi, it had a long history as a settlement and fort. The Pentagon buildings (1) were constructed there about 1820 to house United States troops. One of the earliest known views of the city (2), a lithograph made around 1853, shows the Mississippi crowded with steamboats and the newly constructed state capitol dominating the town. The capitol (3) was built between 1847 and 1850, in the Gothic style with a crenellated roof line. Burned during the Civil War, it was reconstructed in 1882. The building is notable for its central colored-glass dome (4) supported by a single iron column.

4

The Coming of the Railroad

RAIL ROAD NOTICE !

From and after this date, until further notice, the train of cars on the West Feliciana Rail Rroad will run regularly on

Mondays, Wednesdays, and Satu days,

leaving Woodville and Bayou Sara at the usual hours. Thanking the people of Louisiana for their former kindness we take pleasure in informing them that we shall carry freight and passengers, especially the former. at prices to suit the hard times.

J. Burruss McGehee,
Pres. W. F. R R. C.

1

One of the first railroads in Louisiana was the West Feliciana Railroad (1), which was built in 1835 and operated from St. Francisville to Woodville, Mississippi. At first horses or mules pulled the cars, but in 1836 a locomotive arrived to do the task. Like most early Louisiana railroads it was constructed to transport cotton from plantations to the river. By about 1840 railroads were used in combination with steam packets and post coaches from New Orleans to the eastern United States. An advertisement (2) for the Great Mobile & New Orleans Mail describes the route. The Carrollton Hotel (3) served as ticket office for the short New Orleans and Carrollton line; in the drawing a steam locomotive is shown waiting outside the hotel. Another New Orleans station, that of the Pontchartrain line, is visible at the left in a view of the New Orleans riverfront (5); it is little more than a shed to shelter passengers. The New Orleans, Opelousas, and Great Western Railroad, whose advertisement appears on the opposite page (4), carried passengers to Texas.

2

134

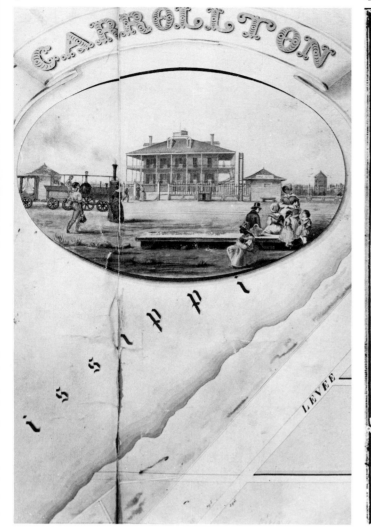

TEXAS
AND
NEW ORLEANS
GREAT SOUTHWESTERN
PASSENGER ROUTE!
CONVEYING THE
CONFEDERATE STATES MAIL
AND
SOUTHWESTERN EXPRESS!

Train leaves Depot of N. O., O. & G. W. R. R., at Algiers, daily, at 8 o'clock, A. M. Passengers leave the Hotels at 7 o'clock, connecting at the Opelousas Landing with the Ferry Boat leaving at half-past 7 o'clock.

Connecting with fast Mail Passenger Packets

CRICKET AND ST. MARY,
AT
BERWICK'S BAY!

The First Steamboats Arrive

New Orleans's prosperity was based on the steamboat. By 1850 boats had reached a high degree of perfection in design and practicality, and the steamboat was making New Orleans a world port. In 1850 there were 2,784 steamboat arrivals at New Orleans. Perhaps the most famous steamboat painting was done 3 years later by the French artist Hippolyte Sebron; his painting, at left, shows an afternoon scene at New Orleans when the five o'clock departure of steamboats made the levee an exciting scene.

Overleaf: The Belle Creole and *The Music* are shown tied up along the New Orleans waterfront.

1

2

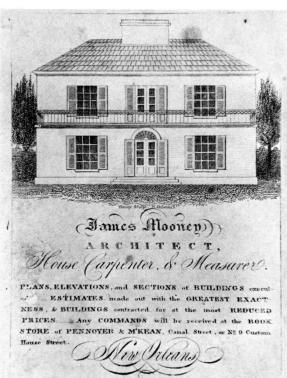

A lithograph done about 1830 shows the cobble-stoned Canal Street (1), which was to become New Orleans's main thoroughfare. Not far away was the suburban Faubourg Marigny, shown in a view made about 1821 (2). In the foreground behind a picket fence is the large house of Bernard de Marigny. An Indian family is seen crossing the street in front of the house. Typical of the elegant New Orleans houses of the time was the Charbonnet house (3), built around 1810 and set in a large garden. An advertisement (4) from the *New Orleans City Directory* shows the work of the architect and carpenter James Mooney, who was responsible for building many New Orleans houses. In 1830 the visiting French artist Charles Alexandre Le Sueur sketched pleasure boats on the Bayou St. John (5) and the characteristic New Orleans street lights of the time—oil lamps suspended between two posts. Another Le Sueur sketch depicts the French Market (6) in New Orleans.

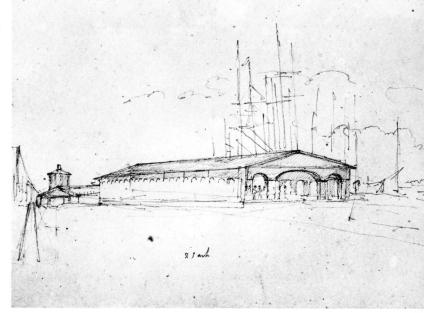

1

2

Two magazine engravings dating from a decade or so before the Civil War show children playing and well-dressed gentry strolling in Lafayette Square in New Orleans (1) and a top-hatted horseman riding along a street in front of St. Augustine's Church (2). An omnibus can be seen at the corner. Canal Street, which was built along a route originally planned for a canal though the canal was never built, became inundated by one of the periodic floods that overwhelmed New Orleans. An 1849 watercolor (3) shows a street flooded, after part of the levee above the city collapsed. The citizens of New Orleans adapted to the floods by traveling by boat. Monplaisir (4), an old house by the banks of the Mississippi, inhabited by the prominent New Orleans philanthropist John McDonogh, is shown in an 1850 lithograph.

1

3

2

144

4

As New Orleans's population grew, buildings became more imposing. In 1855, the four-story-high commercial structure called the Touro Buildings (1) was constructed on Canal Street. On St. Charles Street, the elegant St. Charles Hotel (2) was built by the Anglo-Americans in 1842. Its rival, just as elegant, the City Exchange (St. Louis Hotel), built by the Creoles in 1836–40, was at the end of Exchange Place (3). Its dome can be seen in this lithograph by Adrien Persac. Exchange Place (or Alley) held Persac's office, and his sign is faintly visible at the left. Persac also painted the pictures of plantation life on page 99. One of the city's finest buildings was Gallier Hall (4), erected between 1845 and 1850 and used as the city hall until 1957. Designed in the Greek revival style, its pediment (5) shows figures representing Justice, blindfolded and holding scales; Liberty, displaying a shield with stars and stripes; and Commerce seated beside a bale of cotton and a barrel of sugar.

5

The Building of the Custom House

Commerce played a major role in New Orleans life and the Custom House was one of the city's most important buildings. In the 1850's a new Custom House (1) was built under the supervision of several architects, including Thomas Wharton, a Northerner who became a prominent New Orleans citizen. The working drawings (2) for the marble work of the general business room show the carved Corinthian columns (3) that adorned the room. Wharton's own drawings depict a marble cutter at work (4) and the construction of the building (5).

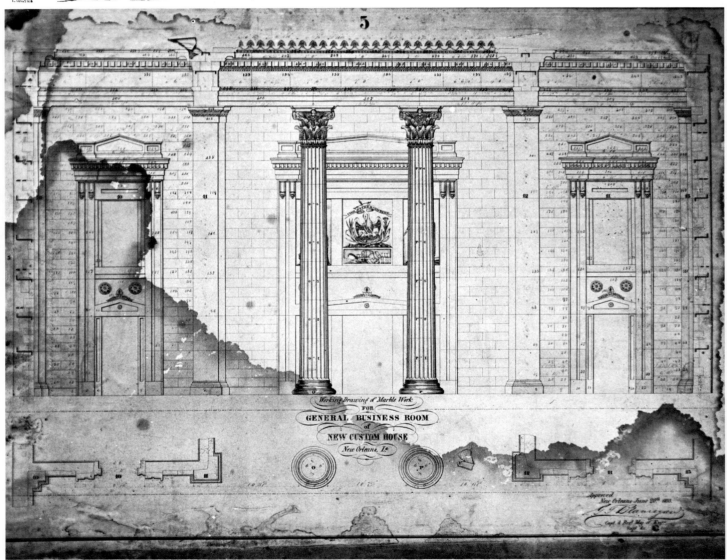

Working Drawing of Marble Work
FOR
GENERAL BUSINESS ROOM
of
NEW CUSTOM HOUSE
New Orleans, La.

3

4

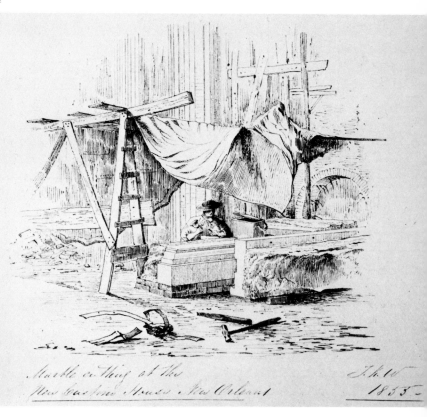

Marble co ing at the
New Custom House New Orleans

J. h. 10
1855

Interior of
Vestibule Canal Street Front
New Custom House New Orleans

J. K. Wharton
March 1. 1855

5

The Metropolis of the South

2

By 1850 New Orleans had grown into the handsome and busy city shown in the famous Smith lithograph (1). The city's influence was now felt in the West, as well as in the rest of the South. Deeply involved in the Mexican War, New Orleans sent volunteers to Texas (their flag (2) appears above); and the war hero Zachary Taylor, later president of the United States, was welcomed with a triumphal arch (3) when he returned from Mexico in 1847. Within New Orleans life remained peaceful. A painting by Richard Clague shows a French Market coffee stand (4).

3

4

1

THE LEVEE AT NEW ORLEANS.

2

New Orleans's wealth stemmed from its port, shown in an engraving (1) dated about 1841. A busy levee scene appears below it (2). During the financial panic of 1837, New Orleans had to issue its own bonds (3) to raise money; but prosperity, based largely on the cotton trade, soon returned. A view from the 1840's shows one of the city's cotton presses (4). These presses were always susceptible to fire. In 1853 the city's Alabama Cotton Press burned (5), causing almost a million dollars' worth of damage.

4

5

1

2

3

4

5

6

7

8

In the decade before the Civil War, feeling for states' rights in Louisiana was never as strong as it was in neighboring states. New Orleans had strong economic and social ties with the rest of the nation, and Louisiana's sugar industry was protected by federal tariff. The election of Abraham Lincoln marked a turning point, and a fiery sermon by Dr. Benjamin Morgan Palmer (1), a Presbyterian minister, on Thanksgiving Day in 1860, seems to have crystallized a major change in public thinking. By January, 1861, the state passed an Ordinance of Secession and soon joined with other Southern states in forming the Confederacy. Governor Thomas Overton Moore (3) ordered the Louisiana militia to seize federal military posts and garrisons in the state, a step that was bound to lead to civil war. Later, after the fall of New Orleans, Governor Moore transferred the capital to Opelousas, and still later to Shreveport where his term ended in 1864. Distinguished Louisianans during the Civil War era were General Henry Watkins Allen (2), who later became governor of Louisiana; Alfred Mouton (4) and Bishop Leonidas Polk (5), both of whom became Confederate generals and lost their lives in battle; Pierre Soulé (6) and John Slidell (7), two distinguished Confederate statesmen; and Judah P. Benjamin (8), who was secretary of state of the Confederacy. The Confederacy issued its own paper money and stamps, and sometimes even individual municipalities and organizations printed currency and stamps. One of the rarest postage stamps ever issued is this provisional 5-cent stamp (9) made by the postmaster of Mt. Lebanon, Louisiana; through an error the stamp was printed in reverse. Paper money put out by the state of Louisiana (10, 11), a New Orleans railroad company (12), and the Parish of Pointe Coupée (13) was used when there was a shortage of regular currency.

10

11

12

13

9

1

2

One of the foremost heroes of the Confederacy was Pierre Gustave Toutant Beauregard (1), a West Point graduate who became a dashing Confederate general. At his command the first guns of the Civil War were fired at Fort Sumter. Beauregard led the Southern armies throughout the war and fought at Bull Run and Shiloh. In the early days of the war New Orleans was gripped with war fever, with companies drilling and uniformed men marching on parade grounds. Thousands of men trained for the Confederate army at Camp Moore (2) in the piney woods near Tangipahoa, about 80 miles north of New Orleans. The war had a profound effect on civilian life. Centenary College in Jackson was forced to suspend classes. Someone scribbled a brief note in the minutes book of the faculty meetings (3): "Students have all gone to war, College suspended, and God help the right."

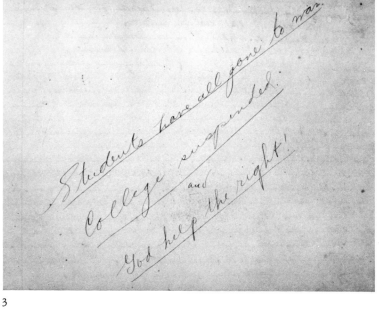

3

The Attack on New Orleans

Confederate leaders, not sure at first whether New Orleans would be invaded from upriver or from the sea, moved with what now seems incredible slowness to defend their most important city. It was not until the fall of 1861, when they sent General Mansfield Lovell to New Orleans, that real defense preparations began. Nearby Forts Livingston, Macomb, and Pike were garrisoned and armed, and New Orleans's main defenses, Forts Jackson and St. Philip, were repaired. Almost 1,000 men were sent to man their 115 guns, and a chain barrier across the Mississippi near the forts was strengthened. The man chosen by the Federal Command to take New Orleans was Captain David G. Farragut (1). With a fleet of 20 mortar boats and 17 warships he entered the Mississippi (2), attacked the forts (3), and eventually cut the chain barrier. Though his attempts to soften the defenders in the forts with mortar fire failed, he boldly got most of his fleet past the forts despite terrific resistance, which included attacks on his ships by Confederate rams (4). This enabled him to sail upriver toward New Orleans, which was now virtually undefended.

4

The Surrender of New Orleans

1

After the Yankee ships had passed the forts below New Orleans, the news was telegraphed to the city, and the populace awakened by the tolling of bells became almost frantic (1). Shops and businesses were closed; transportation stopped; and cotton, corn, sugar, and rice were sent to the levee to be burned. The Federal fleet dropped anchor in New Orleans harbor on April 25, 1862 (2), and Farragut immediately sent emissaries to demand the city's surrender (3). With no means to combat so formidable a force, the Confederate General Lovell evacuated his troops.

2

3

The Fall of Baton Rouge

It was inevitable that once New Orleans was occupied, Baton Rouge, about a hundred miles upriver, would also fall, since it had no real defense. The city was taken without a struggle on May 8, 1862, and General Benjamin F. Butler sent a force of 4,500 men to occupy it. A photograph (1) shows their camp on the outskirts of the city. On August 5 the Confederates under General John C. Breckinridge attacked the occupying forces with 3,000 troops. But after a fierce fight (2) the Federals still held Baton Rouge, though they would evacuate the town 2 weeks later because Butler feared an attack on New Orleans and decided to consolidate his forces. In December, 1862, Baton Rouge was reoccupied by Federal troops, and the half-ruined town was plundered again. On the night of December 28 the Gothic state capitol was set afire by careless soldiers (3). Despite efforts to save the building, it was only a blackened shell by morning.

1

2

The occupying forces, under Generals Ben Butler (1) and Nathanial P. Banks, tried to return the territory under their control to normal life. A new governor, Michael Hahn (2), was elected to administer the occupied portions of the state. A new mayor, Brigadier General George F. Shepley (3), was appointed for New Orleans. At the city's market, Yankee soldiers in uniform enlivened an already lively scene (4). The railroad to Kenner began operation again (5) and, after the Emancipation Proclamation, freed slaves were put to work repairing levees along the Mississippi (6).

4

5

6

Resistance

1

2

3

4

5

Even though the North controlled much of Louisiana, Southerners continued their resistance. Rebel guerrillas attacked shipping on the river (1), and Admiral Farragut retaliated by destroying plantations. In 1864 a spectacular fire, attributed to Rebel saboteurs, broke out along the New Orleans riverfront (2) destroying eight boats, valued at $300,000. In New Orleans, citizens who seemed too zealous in the cause of the Confederacy were imprisoned in Fort St. Philip on the river below New Orleans and forced to perform manual labor (3). The women of New Orleans harassed Union soldiers by spitting at them and insulting them. General Butler issued a proclamation (4) threatening with punishment any woman who so annoyed a Federal soldier. A Northern cartoon (5) purports to show the behavior of the ladies before and after the General's proclamation. Some women of the city—those who had lost a husband or father in the war—had more serious concerns. A group of bereaved women is shown below dressed in mourning and visiting a graveyard (6).

"I do order and declare that all persons held as slaves within . . . designated states or parts of states, are, and henceforth shall be free." Thus read the beginning of the Emancipation Proclama-

tion, which President Lincoln published on January 1, 1863. When the news reached Louisiana, many slaves left the plantations on which they had labored and flocked to join Federal troops.

1

2

The fort of Port Hudson, overlooking the Mississippi, gave the Confederates control of the river for more than 150 miles and protected the mouth of the Red River, along which much-needed supplies came from western Louisiana, Texas, and even Mexico. The fort was under the command of Major General Franklin Gardner with about 7,000 ragged Confederates. In March, 1863, 13,000 Federals under General Nathaniel P. Banks advanced upon Port Hudson (1), aided by mortar boats and gunboats under Admiral Farragut. During the night of March 14, Farragut led his squadron past the Confederate batteries of Port Hudson. They were discovered by the Confederates, who poured deadly accurate fire onto the Union ships (2, 3). One of the ships ran aground, was abandoned, and was blown up; several others were damaged and had to drop back, but Admiral Farragut's flagship, the *Hartford,* along with one other ship, passed the batteries. A rare photograph (4) shows a soldier standing atop the Port Hudson fortifications.

3

The siege of Port Hudson lasted 45 days, and there was constant fighting on 21 of those days. One Federal attack (1) on May 27, 1863, was repelled by the Confederates, with the terrible Union loss of 1,995 casualties. (The Confederates lost only 235 men.) Port Hudson was also subjected to constant bombardment by the naval forces on the river. A 100-pound gun on the decks of the Union vessel *Richmond* is shown attacking the fort (3). Though they had resisted all efforts by much superior forces, the Confederates finally surrendered on July 9, after learning of the fall of Vicksburg on July 4, 1863 (2). The Mississippi was now open to traffic for its full course, to the cheers of those favoring the Union cause (4).

4

1

2

3

Northeast Louisiana was invaded by General U. S. Grant in his movement to capture Vicksburg. While the region was spared much of the fighting that took place in other sections of the state, it suffered greatly from destruction of property. One Federal soldier wrote, "Where we marched were smouldering ruins, and for miles ahead we could see smoke and flames." Lake Providence in Carroll Parish (1) was occupied by the Seventeenth Army Corps, and for a while it served as a sort of rest camp for Union soldiers. Alexandria had the misfortune to be occupied twice by Federal forces under General Banks. The first time was in May, 1863 (2), when a flotilla of gunboats arrived, followed by Banks's army. Brashear City, now Morgan City, was the gathering point for the cotton, sugar, and livestock that Banks's men had taken in their campaign in the spring of 1863.

4

"In round numbers," Banks wrote, "I may say that 20,000 beeves, mules and horses have been forwarded to Brashear City, with 5,000 bales of cotton and many hogsheads of sugar." A contemporary engraving (3) shows cotton being unloaded at Brashear City.

The Teche country became the scene of land and naval battles. On January 13, 1863, the *J. A. Cotton*, a Rebel steamer partially armored with railroad iron and cannon, fought off 4 light-draft gunboats and an overwhelming enemy force on each side of the bayou near Pattersonville (4). The battle of Irish Bend (5) near Franklin, was one of a series of battles fought during Banks's Bayou Teche Campaign in April, 1863. Outnumbered, Confederate General Dick Taylor showed superb generalship during this campaign, his small army fighting successful rearguard actions against a superior enemy force.

Rebel Cotton

COTTON HOARDS IN THE SWAMPS.

1

Cotton became a scarce commodity in the North and in England during the Civil War. The Federal blockade of Southern ports kept it from its normal market and loyal Louisianans either burned their bales or hid them in the swamps (1). General Butler, in his first Red River campaign, confiscated all the cotton he and his men could find, and some of his staff officers were accused of paying more attention to getting possession of cotton for personal profit than to soldiering. General Banks had heard of large quantities of baled cotton in Louisiana, Arkansas, and Texas belonging to the Confederates and this had influenced his plans to take Shreveport. Accordingly, Rear Admiral David Porter assembled a large fleet of gunboats at the mouth of the Red River in early March, 1864, and with 10,000 soldiers in transports began the ascent of the Red. They were to be joined by more forces under Banks a little later. Alexandria was again occupied, and so sure of victory were the Federals that when artist C. E. H. Bonwill sketched the view shown in the engraving at right (2), he gave it the caption "Banks's Army, in advance on Shreveport, Crossing Cane River, March 31, 1864." However, the battles of Mansfield and Pleasant Hill prevented Banks's army from ever reaching Shreveport. Instead he was forced to retreat ignominiously to New Orleans.

2

174

The Battle of Mansfield

1

2

3

Lieutenant General Richard "Dick" Taylor (1) was one of the South's finest fighting generals. Despite two invasions of Louisiana west of the Mississippi, the Federals were unable to crush Taylor and the Confederates, though their armies wreaked much destruction on the countryside. During the second Federal campaign on the Red River, the two armies met at Mansfield, about 40 miles from Shreveport, in one of the bloodiest battles ever fought in Louisiana (2). The Federals were routed and the Federal cavalry wagon train attempted to turn back; some of the wagons became mired in a creek. The fleeing artillery became entangled with the wagons (3), adding to the demoralization of the Union forces. The next day the Confederates chased after them. Although the Rebels were pushed back (4), the Northern army finally retreated and gave up its attempt to capture Shreveport. The campaign, culminating in Mansfield, was the last major action in Louisiana.

4

1

2

Although Banks failed to capture Shreveport, his army succeeded in dealing a devastating blow to the people of central Louisiana by the indiscriminate destruction of property of all kinds. The line of march, said a contemporary, could be traced by burned houses, cabins, and cotton gins, and by animals scattered along the road (1). In a contemporary cartoon Banks's soldiers are shown seeking hidden arms in a Louisiana house (2). Two restrain an old man from entering a room, while an officer triumphantly holds up a tiny Confederate flag which he has discovered. After the disaster at Mansfield, Banks's army and Union gunboats and transports headed down the Red River to Alexandria. The boats were constantly harassed by the Confederates, and the Federal gunboat *Covington* (3) was blown up by her own men after being disabled. The *Warner* drifted aground after she was riddled with Confederate bullets (4). Before the battle of Mansfield, Banks had had his headquarters in the town of Alexandria, and his army retreated there after the battle (5).

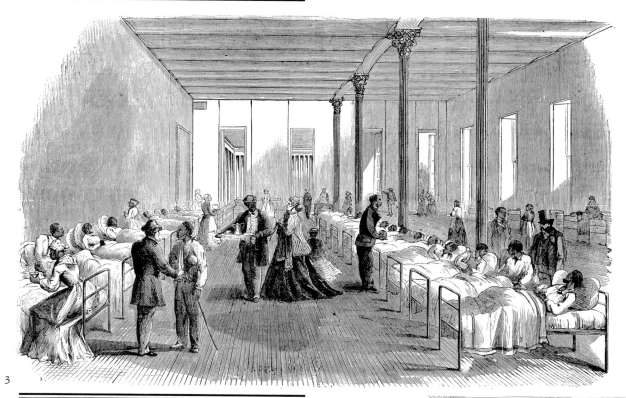

3

One of the last thrilling episodes of the Civil War was the Confederate ram *William H. Webb*'s dash for the open sea from the Red River. Starting at Shreveport on April 16, 1865, the *Webb* steamed into the Mississippi on April 23. Although telegraph wires to New Orleans had been cut, a message got through and the Federal fleet was on the lookout. Even so, the *Webb* passed New Orleans almost unnoticed (1). When she was 25 miles below the city, she was recognized by someone on the U.S.S. *Hollyhock;* a broadside forced her back to the bank, where she was destroyed by her crew who fled into the swamp. In 1865, for a short time, ex-Confederates regained political control of Louisiana; the Radical Republicans determined to reconvene a constitutional convention in New Orleans to oust them. When the convention attempted to meet on July 30, 1866, a riot (2) ensued, in which 38 persons, mostly Negroes, were killed and 147 injured. The wounded were treated at Marine Hospital (3) and, later, witnesses were questioned by a military commission investigating the riot (4).

4

The Freed Slaves

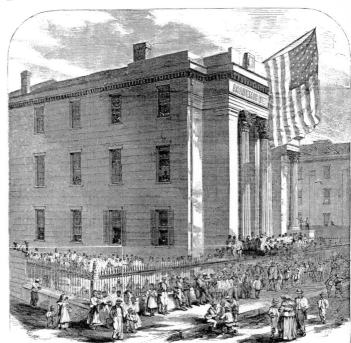

Even before the war ended, freed slaves flocked to New Orleans from the plantations. Many were rounded up by the Federal troops (1) and employed on government work, being paid a salary for the first time in their lives. Efforts were made to inaugurate a school system for the now-free black children. One building of the University of Louisiana in New Orleans became, for a few years, the Abraham Lincoln School for freedmen (2). Some black students are shown in the engraving opposite (3); some of them are almost white skinned, though they had been slaves. In the upper left-hand corner an older ex-slave appears with the initials of his former owner seemingly branded on his forehead. Most likely the initials were placed in the picture as anti-slavery propaganda. The freed slaves received the vote, while their former masters were disenfranchised. Blacks campaigned for office (4), and black policemen along with the Federal soldiers guarded the polls (5). The radical changes that came with emancipation often brought racial tension to the boiling point, and violence was common. One of the worst outbreaks occurred at Colfax in Grant Parish when a pitched battle between blacks and whites occurred. An 1873 engraving shows a group of blacks mourning one of the victims (6).

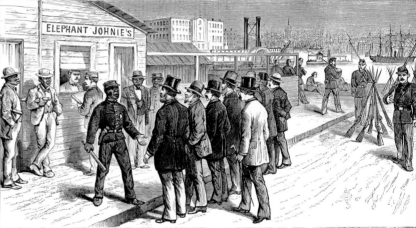

2

3

4

5

In an 1868 lithograph, adorned with the American eagle and the guns and cannon of the recent war (1), Louisiana's black office holders are depicted. An 1880 engraving shows the Louisiana legislature in session, with a black speaker holding the floor (2). Louisiana's postwar politics were marked by racial strife and shameless corruption, in which carpetbaggers, scalawags, and blacks participated. One of the worst offenders was Henry Clay Warmoth (3), who became governor at the age of 26 in 1868. Warmoth was impeached and driven from office to be succeeded for a brief time by Louisiana's only black governor, P. B. S. Pinchback (4). John F. McEnery (5) was the winner of the next election, but dishonest vote-counting kept him from office and gave the governorship to another Northerner, William Pitt Kellogg (6), who was kept in office only by the United States Army. The last carpetbagger governor of the state was Stephen B. Packard (7).

6

7

1

2

The Turmoil of Reconstruction

By 1874 Louisiana was bankrupt after 9 years of corrupt government. Leagues of white citizens, which declared war on carpetbaggers, scalawags, and "non-cooperating" whites, were formed. These leagues armed themselves and attempted to force Governor Kellogg out of office after he had ordered the seizure of the leagues' arms and ammunition. In September, 1874, there was a battle (1) with the White Leaguers forcing the New Orleans Metropolitan Police to retreat, even though the police were armed with cannon. President Grant sent in troops and 3 warships to put down the uprising. In the state legislature, strong-arm tactics were common. An 1875 engraving (2) shows five Democratic members of the House of Representatives being escorted out of the hall by Federal troops after having been ejected by the Republicans. Cartoonists were kept busy satirizing the situation. A Northern cartoon (3) which appeared after the September, 1874, riot shows a misshapen, half-grown chick hatched by the rebellion of the White League, a failure, like the rebellion itself. A cartoonist with Southern sympathies took the opposite point of view and showed Governor Kellogg sacrificing Louisiana on the bloody altar of radicalism, plucking the heart out of the state (4).

3

4

The End of Reconstruction

1   2

The doughty Francis T. Nicholls (1), who rose from captain of his company during the Civil War to brigadier general and who had lost his left arm at Winchester and a foot at Chancellorsville, was nominated for governor in 1876 by the Democrats in a final effort to achieve home rule. The corrupt Returning Board threw out several thousand votes and declared his Republican opponent, Stephen B. Packard, elected. Not discouraged, the Nicholls forces swore their man in as governor at St. Patricks' Hall (6), while Republicans swore in Packard in the St. Louis Hotel, then being used as the state house. Led by General Fred N. Ogden (2), Nicholls's supporters organized themselves into military battalions (3) and took possession of the Supreme Court (4), which was in the Cabildo at that time. Packard forces holed up in the St. Louis Hotel and for 4 months Ogden's men patrolled the streets to keep them bottled up. Federal troop support of the Packard administration was restricted "to protect property from mob violence." With the inauguration of President Hayes, a commission was sent to Louisiana to investigate. This commission decided that the Nicholls government should be permanently established and urged Packard to give up. On April 27, 1877, President Hayes ordered all federal troops in Louisiana withdrawn (5) and Packard surrendered the state house. The era of Reconstruction was over.

4

An Age of Renewal

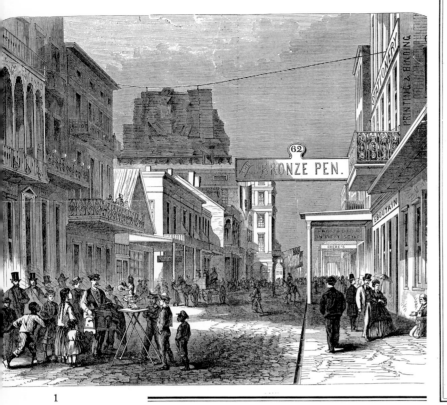

1

New buildings, new businesses, and new houses sprang up in New Orleans with the end of the Civil War. In the French Quarter, crowds, then as now, thronged Bourbon Street (1). In this lively view made in 1868 entertainment was provided by an organ grinder and his monkey who had been trained to play the cymbals. The luxury trade was catered to by various firms including the Gonzales Brothers (2), who imported fine cigars from Cuba; the firm of Schmidt and Ziegler (3), who imported fine wines and wholesale groceries; the ornate establishment of A. B. Griswold & Company (4), which provided wealthy Louisianans with jewelry and silver. Esplanade Avenue and the Garden District were being built up with such fine homes as the Schmidt residence (5), paid for by W. B. Schmidt's profits from his grocery business; the Slocomb residence (6); and the Ellison residence (7). Many commercial establishments had their offices in fine new buildings, like the cast-iron Moresque building (8) at the corner of Poydras and Camp streets.

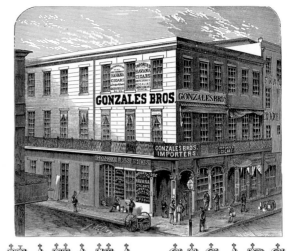

4

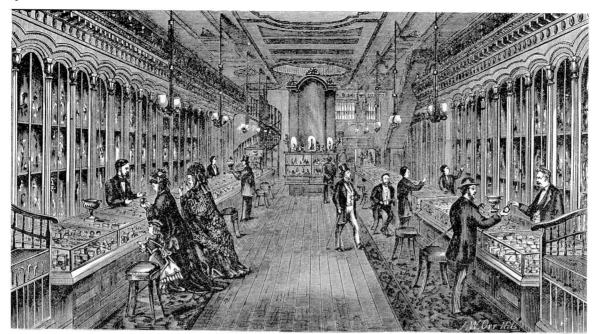

5

6

7

8

The City's Inhabitants

The richness and variety of New Orleans's post-Civil War population is captured in an engraving entitled "Sketches of character in New Orleans" (1) from a drawing by the artist A. R. Waud, who made many pictures of Louisiana life in the period. Dozens of the city's inhabitants appear in the picture displaying the cosmopolitanism that has always been characteristic of Louisiana's metropolis. Two 1876 watercolors by Leon J. Frémaux show Choctaw women selling herbs in the French Market (2) and a black coffee vender at the market (3). Other New Orleans scenes depict a flower girl (4) and some loungers overlooking the levee at the corner of Jackson Square (5).

2

3

4

5

Experiments in Agriculture

1

2
3

5

After the Civil War new crops were introduced to Louisiana farms. There was a rapid increase in rice acreage along the Mississippi, and rice-growing became of major importance on the prairies in the southwestern part of the state. Three 1876 engravings show field workers harvesting the crop (1), a rice threshing mill (2), and a steamboat tied up at a Mississippi River levee loading sacks of rice (3). There were many orange groves around New Orleans (4), and orange crops still provide a valuable part of the state's agricultural income. There were also fields of banana trees (5), but bananas produced in so northern a latitude as Louisiana lacked the flavor of those grown in the tropics and could not find a ready market. Attempts were made to grow ramie (6), a fiber plant, which, it was hoped, would some day rival cotton in importance, but the crop proved unprofitable. Spanish moss (7) was another crop of minor importance. Moss gatherers harvested it in the swamps and sold it for use as stuffing in mattresses and cushions.

6
7

The Artist's View

1

2

In the years around the Civil War many artists worked painting the landscape and people of Louisiana. One of the most active was William Buck, whose work often shows characteristic Louisiana bayous (1), moss-hung cypresses, and rural cabins. The painting of the top-hatted coachman with a horse and dog at left (2) was made by the artist T. Moise in 1859. "Landscape with Plantation House and Cabin" (3) is by Marshall J. Smith. John Genin painted a placid view of the Lake Pontchartrain shorefront (4), and the bucolic Louisiana road scene (5) is by Charles Giroux.

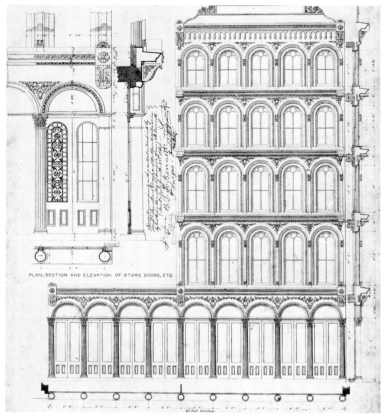

JEWELL'S CRESCENT CITY ILLUSTRATED.

Accommodation Bank of Louisiana,

MASONIC HALL.

E. B. BENTON, PRESIDENT.   R. H. WOOD, CASHIER.

INCORPORATED 1868.

CAPITAL, $200,000.

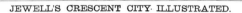

THIS BANK ALLOWS LIBERAL INTEREST ON DEPOSITS,

And advances MONEY in sums to suit on every species of Personal Property, Warehouse Receipts, Stocks, Bonds, Warrants, Gold, Silver, Diamonds, Furniture, Pianos, Merchandise, and Valuables of every description.   Has large Warehouse and Store-rooms attached to the Bank.

The decades following the Civil War saw Louisiana recover much of the prosperity that it had enjoyed before the war. The New Orleans levee was as busy as it had ever been, as can be seen in this 1881 view (2), which shows hundreds of barrels of sugar and bales of cotton and dozens of boats and wagons to transport them. At lower left a banana vender can be seen offering fruit for sale. Many new buildings were constructed in New Orleans and throughout the state; an architect's drawing shows the elevation of a bank building (1) constructed in 1866 in the then fashionable cast-iron style. New banks and factories were founded, among them the Accommodation Bank of Louisiana (3), incorporated in 1868. Factories busily turned out machinery to accommodate the growing economy. The mills of H. Dudley Coleman & Brother (5), shown in an 1875 view, turned out machinery and presses for cotton and sugar plantations. Another well-known firm, Leeds & Company, manufactured cast-iron articles, including cannon for the Confederacy. One of their bills of sale (4) appears here.

4

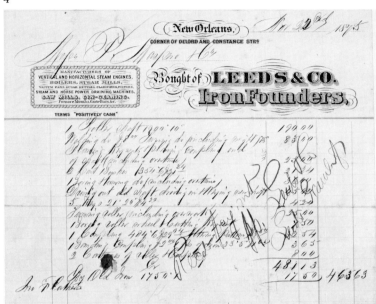

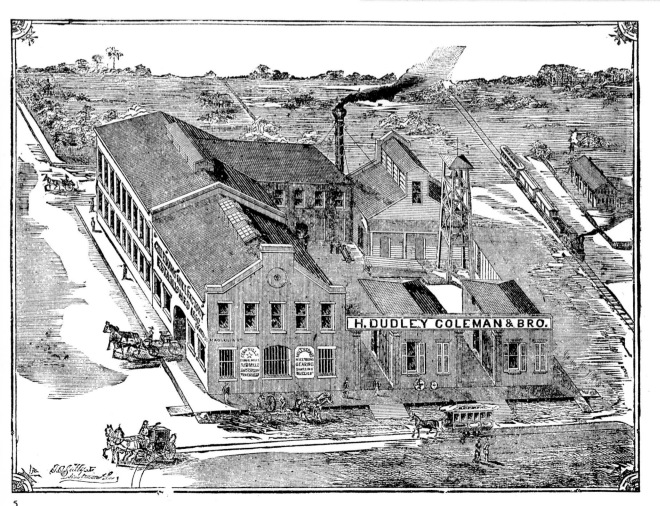

5

In the summer of 1883 *Harper's Weekly* sent a staff artist, J. O. Davidson, to the South and in two issues of the magazine published engravings of his sketches which illustrated the process of cotton culture from planting to marketing. The illustration on page 200 shows: The cotton plant (1). Hoeing cotton (2). Picking the crop (3 and 4). Transporting one bale in an ox-cart (5). Acadian planters bringing cotton to the gin (6). Ginning (7). The cotton after ginning (8). An

old-fashioned press (9). Baling (10). At center a steamboat is being loaded with bales. Page 201: A cotton steamer being unloaded (1). A cotton yard and sheds (2). Weighing and sampling the cotton (3). A steam press (4). A train carrying cotton (5). The sampling room (6). Baling (7). At center is a scene on the New Orleans Cotton Levee.

2

Samples taken from the baled cotton were customarily displayed at the cotton merchant's sample room for examination by prospective buyers. Shown at left is the office of a New Orleans cotton firm (1)—that of the Degas brothers, Achille and René, at 185 Common Street. The scene was painted in 1873 by the famous French artist Edgar Degas while he was on a visit to his brothers in New Orleans. Highly skilled "cotton classers" were employed by cotton commission merchants to test a sample from each bale that was consigned to a merchant. A cut was made into the bale and a sample taken, which was scrutinized for grade, condition, and length of staple; these samples were then wrapped in paper and taken to the merchant's display room for examination by possible purchasers. The cotton classer of the 1870's (2), always a gentleman, affected a white linen shirt with wing collar and bow tie and protected his neatly tailored clothes from cotton lint by donning an apron made of heavy paper.

1

2

3

By 1860 Louisiana was producing nearly 800,000 bales of cotton annually, and New Orleans had developed into one of the world's greatest cotton markets. In the days before the formation of the New Orleans Cotton Exchange, business had often been handled in saloons, which called themselves "exchanges." If the weather was good, cotton merchants left the saloons and transacted their business in the open air on Carondelet Street. In 1871 a group representing cotton interests formed the New Orleans Cotton Exchange, and by the end of the year the exchange had a membership of 258 cotton dealers. Meetings were held in a rented building. By 1881 the membership had expanded to 510 and the exchange had outgrown its headquarters. A new and, for its time, magnificent exchange building was erected in 1882–83 (1). A contemporary engraving (2) shows the cornerstone of the new building being laid under the auspices of the machinery firm of H. Dudley Coleman, whose own factory is shown on page 199. On April 2, 1881, the *Henry Frank* (3), a sternwheeler, carried 9,226 bales of cotton to New Orleans—a record shipment, the largest ever carried to the city by one steamboat. In order to save money on charges for ocean freight, country-ginned bales were recompressed in New Orleans by means of huge steam-operated presses; these reduced the size of each bale by one-third. One such cotton press, the Morse press (5), weighed 400,000 pounds. In 1869 the Louisiana Cotton Manufactory (4) was founded to spin and weave locally grown cotton. The factory demonstrated how much cheaper it was to produce cotton goods close to where cotton was grown.

1

2

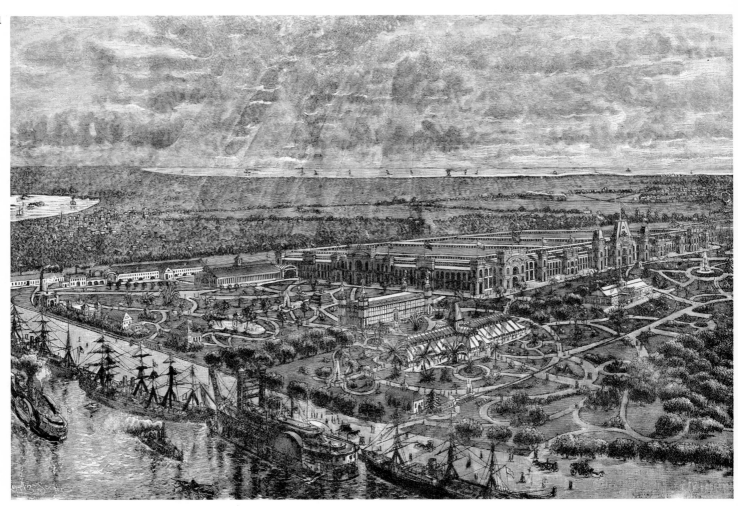

The Great Exposition

5

In 1884 the hundredth anniversary of the first shipment of American cotton to England was celebrated with a World's Fair at New Orleans. Fairgrounds were laid out in a city park and an exposition hall (1) was built; the largest building constructed until then in modern times, it covered 33 acres under a single roof. This building was surrounded by others displaying the products and cultures of various nations. The Japanese exhibit appears opposite (2). An enormous glass-roofed horticultural hall (3) was also built, and many unfamiliar plants were seen for the first time in Louisiana, including the water hyacinth (5), which later spread so widely through the state's bayous that it got out of control and now clogs the waterways. Visitors to the exposition were entertained not just by the exhibits but by military drills, which they could observe while standing on the parade ground or seated in a grandstand (4).

Overleaf: The exhibit of the United States.

DRILLING IN FRONT OF GRAND STAND

INTERIOR OF GLOBE. U.S. DEPT. OF STATE.

The Production of Sugar

For many years around 300,000 tons of sugar were produced in Louisiana annually; nearly half a million people depended on the sugar industry for a livelihood. Photographs from the end of the nineteenth century show a partially harvested sugar-cane field (1) and cane being transported to the mill in carts (2). In 1886, the artist E. W. Kemble did a series of sketches for *Century Magazine* of life on Bellaire, a sugar plantation below New Orleans. His illustrations show a group of field hands returning home from the fields (3), the planter (4), and the gang driver or foreman (5). Two photographs, dating from around the same period, show the cane shed at Bellaire (6) and the sugar house (7), in which the sugar was extracted from the cane.

7

1

2

3

In the early 1870's about 2,000 Chinese laborers were brought to Louisiana to work in the cane fields (1). The sugar industry was expanding, and barrels of sugar filled New Orleans's sugar sheds (2). At New Orleans brokers and weighers (3) examined the sugar, sampling each hogshead for quality. A photograph, dating from around 1885, shows a sugar weigher at work on the New Orleans levee in front of the sugar sheds (4). The expert is taking a sample from a barrel; nearby is a portable scale on which a barrel of sugar is being weighed. A view of the trading floor of the New Orleans sugar exchange (5), made around 1900, shows sugar brokers trading their stock, samples of which can be seen atop tables waiting for buyers to examine them.

5

Lumbering

Louisiana was blessed with about 22 million acres of forested land. The timber in the forests was virtually untouched until the last years of the nineteenth century, when Northern lumbermen acquired large tracts of timberland for as little as 25¢ an acre. Modern sawmills were erected and railroads were constructed through the forests to connect the mills with the markets. These mills cut pine in the uplands and cypress in the swamps. About 1890, George F. Mugnier, a well-known New Orleans photographer, recorded scenes of

1
2
3

4

lumbering in Louisiana. Some of his photographs show cypress-logging in a swamp (1); workers attaching a conical metal cap to a log and hitching it to a wire rope (2) (the metal cap was useful for warding off obstructions); the pull boat used to snake the capped logs out of the swamp by means of a long wire rope (3); and a bayou sawmill (4), one of many where the logs were cut into rough timber so that they could be transported to market. Sometimes logs were hauled out of the woods by a team of oxen (5).

5

GULF SALT SCHOONER.

UNCOVERED SURFACE OF SALT DEPOSIT.

FOOT OF MAIN SHAFT.

BREAKING DOWN AN UNDER-CUT.

A HEADING.

1

SIDE DRIFTS

4

The Avery Island salt mine in Iberia Parish was the first salt mine discovered in the western hemisphere. Production, begun during the Civil War, was in full swing by 1883, at the time when these engravings of mining operations were made (1). Salt was transported in schooners, one of which can be seen at the upper left. One of the views of the operations, reproduced above (2), shows the miners working in low-ceilinged tunnels off a main chamber. Oil was discovered near Jennings in the southwestern part of the state in 1901. A photograph of the period shows the first oil well in operation (3). A year later, lightning struck a wooden oil tank in the Jennings field and a spectacular fire broke out (4), spreading to one of the wooden oil derricks as well. Before the fire could be put out, experts had to be brought in from outside the state, with special fire-extinguishing equipment.

3

Steamboats

1

2

3

After the Civil War, steamboating on the Mississippi enjoyed a period of lively growth. One of the most exciting episodes was the race between the *Natchez* and the *Rob't E. Lee* from New Orleans up to St. Louis (1). The trip, which the *Rob't E. Lee* made in 3 days, 18 hours, and 13 minutes, demonstrated exactly how fast the powerful steamboats could go. Usually the boats traveled only about 10 miles an hour upstream and passengers had ample time to lounge on decks (2) or loll in comfortable and ornate cabins like that of the *Grand Republic,* built in 1867 (3). Boats became bigger and more luxurious. The *John W. Cannon* (4), with its twin chimneys, was typical. Louisiana bayous were also served by steamboats. An 1881 engraving shows cotton being loaded aboard a steamer on the Teche (5).

4

5

219

The Eads Jetties

The passes (1) at the mouth of the Mississippi had always been difficult to navigate and all efforts to deepen them had failed. A ship aground on a sandbar in one of the passes could hold up dozens of others. After the Civil War, larger ships with deeper drafts were being built; since many could not negotiate the passes, they kept away from the Mississippi and New Orleans. The whole Mississippi Valley suffered from the resulting loss in trade. In 1874, James B. Eads (2), a great self-taught engineer, proposed the construction of jetties in one of the mouths of the Mississippi. He claimed that they would deepen the channel to permit the biggest ships to enter and that they would carry the sandbar away into the sea. After much opposition, Eads finally won a contract from the government on March 3, 1875. In 4 years at South Pass, with herculean labor, his men completed the project. Within a year, 840 ships had passed through the jetties and New Orleans's commerce began to revive. Details of the construction of the Eads jetties (3) show [1] the Port Eads lighthouse; [2] a bird's-eye view of the jetties; [3] a dredging steamer; [4] dredging apparatus; [5] the former channel and the new one; [6] the seaward end of the jetties; [7] making the "mattress" on which the jetties rested; [8, 9] cross-sections of jetties; [10] the channel made by the current; [11] concrete works; [12] inside the willow sand barriers; [13] a view within the jetties.

Loading Cargo

3

In their heyday Mississippi River steamers carried huge quantities of cotton and other cargo. The *America,* pictured here taking on a load of cottonseed in a turn-of-the-century photograph (1), was already laden "to the guards" with bales of cotton. Passengers waiting to board the steamer watch the loading. At the New Orleans docks, curious onlookers visited the levee to see steamers being loaded (2), and roustabouts (3) waited for boats to come in so that they could get work toting cargo. Notices of steamboat sailings appeared in the papers (4), notifying shippers about the availability of boats to carry their cargo.

Showboats

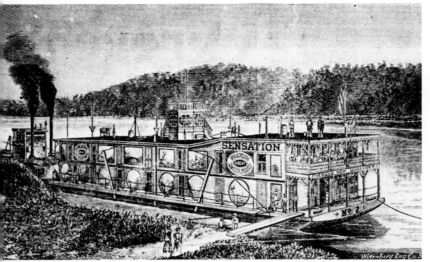

The showboat, a floating theatre built on a barge and towed from one river town to the next, provided a popular form of amusement along the rivers during the latter part of the century. Showboats brought plays and vaudeville to an isolated rural population hungry for entertainment. Many of the showboats spent the winter months down South, and Captain A. B. French, owner of a series of boats all called *French's New Sensation* (1, 2), found enthusiastic audiences waiting for his boats when they came down bayous Lafourche and Teche. Around 1908 the entire cast and orchestra of another showboat, the *Eisenbarth-Henderson Floating Theatre,* lined up for a group photograph on stage around 1908 (3). Another picture shows them on the deck of their boat (4). One of the most impressive showboats was the *New Sunny South Floating Theatre* (5). Lettering painted near the entrance promised patrons that performances would be both moral and refined.

1

2

3

4

The years just before and after the Civil War saw a great expansion in railroad construction throughout Louisiana. By the end of the nineteenth century, railroads crisscrossed the state. Photographs opposite and above show an engine of the Opelousas line (1); a ferry which transported trains across the Mississippi at New Orleans (2); and a train wreck somewhere in Louisiana (3). Directly above is the *Sabine* (4), a locomotive that served the New Orleans, Opelousas, and Great Western Railroad before the Civil War and was eventually kept on display near the railroad station in Lafayette. During World War II, when metal was in short supply, the *Sabine* was scrapped for the metal it contained. At right is an old-fashioned iron cage at a railroad switching point, built to keep unauthorized people from reaching the switch and perhaps causing a train wreck (5).

Railroad development in northern Louisiana began with the chartering of the Vicksburg, Shreveport, and Texas Railroad in 1852. This line suffered as a result of the Civil War, and it was not until 1884 that it was completed from Meridian, Mississippi, to Shreveport. The "Vicksburg route" (1), later known as the Vicksburg, Shreveport, and Pacific in Louisiana and the Alabama and Vicksburg in Mississippi, was absorbed by the Illinois Central Railroad in 1926. Railroads—small or large—played an important part in the state's economy. At left is a sawmill dummy engine (2) backing in a load of logs to be dumped into the sawmill pond for easier handling at the mill. On this page some New Orleans depots are depicted: the Illinois Central and Yazoo Mississippi Valley (3), the Southern Pacific Ferry Depot (4), and the station of the Louisville and Nashville Railroad (5).

Outside New Orleans the biggest cities were Shreveport and Baton Rouge. Along with the state capitol, Baton Rouge boasted fine churches (1); gingerbread-style wooden buildings like the ornate office of the Burton Lumber Company (2); and streetcars, pulled by mules, which transported citizens through the often muddy streets (3). Shreveport grew considerably in the years after the Civil War. An 1872 view (4) shows most of the town clustered along the riverfront. Forty years later fine new brick buildings lined Texas Street (5), one of the main business streets. Both cities were vulnerable to flooding. In 1874 floods overflowed the levees at both Shreveport (6) and Baton Rouge (7), causing much damage.

1
2
3

6

7

In the Rural Regions

Through much of the ninteenth century, back country Louisiana remained rural and undeveloped, with cypress swamps (1), where alligators swam, and woods covering hundreds of square miles. Simple dwellings were scattered through the countryside; often there was little difference between houses occupied by whites (2) and blacks (3). Simple rural churches were built at crossroads settlements (4). Those country folk who were too far from a general store to shop easily were called on by itinerant peddlers (5). When they did get to town, they could make their purchases at establishments like the ambitiously named City Store (6), in the village of Eugenia.

1

2

3

4

5

6

The Art of William Aiken Walker

1

One of the South's most active artists late in the nineteenth century was William Aiken Walker (1), who vividly recorded many scenes of Louisiana life. Walker's view of the New Orleans levee was used as the basis of a lithograph by Currier and Ives (2). Walker was particularly interested in the cotton fields and the blacks who worked in them. One of his paintings, *Negro Cotton Workers* (3), shows a woman balancing a heavy basket of cotton on her head. *The Cotton Kingdom* (4) shows on one canvas almost every aspect of life on a cotton plantation, including the owner's house, at far left, and the cabins of the field workers at far right.

3

4

OLD SPANISH COURT HOUSE

New Orleans has always been a city of special interest to the rest of the country, and it attracted many artists in the years after the Civil War; their sketches of scenes in the city were often engraved and printed in national magazines. The view of Jackson Square (1) by W. P. Snyder appeared in *Harper's Weekly* in 1885. John W. Alexander's depiction of the old French Market (2) was done for the same magazine in 1882. Charles Dudley Warner's sketch of a lounger on the levee (3) dates from 1887. The picturesque building often called the Old Spanish Courthouse (4) was sketched by A. R. Waud in 1867. Photographers also admired New Orleans's quaintness. Old Spanish houses on Dumaine Street (5) were recorded by the local photographer George F. Mugnier around 1890.

1

2

"The abode of mirth and laughter," one nineteenth-century Louisianan called the French Opera House (1); it was built in 1859 and generations of Louisianans were entertained there. The house seated 2,000 and premieres and opening nights were gala affairs, as can be seen from the photograph of a splendidly dressed crowd at the opera in 1910 (2). The Opera House reflected the characteristic Creole love of music and pageantry. Its programs (3) appeared in French. Adelina Patti (4) sang in New Orleans for a season in 1860, launching her on a career as one of the foremost singers in opera history. Less exalted entertainment was provided by popular theatres, where troupes such as McCabe and Young's operatic minstrels appeared; the program shown here (5) dates from around 1885.

The Lottery

1

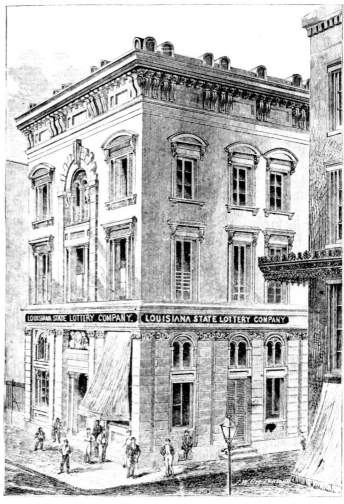

2

REMEMBER

That the presence of Generals Beauregard and Early, who are in charge of the drawings, is a guarantee of absolute fairness and integrity, that the chances are all equal, and that no one can possibly divine what number will draw a prize.

"REMEMBER, also, that the payment of Prizes is GUARANTEED BY FOUR NATIONAL BANKS OF NEW ORLEANS, and the Tickets are signed by the President of an Institution whose chartered rights are recognized in the highest courts; therefore, beware of all imitations and anonymous schemes."

3

Gambling had always been part of New Orleans life. By 1880 there were 83 large gambling houses in the city. In 1868, the Reconstruction Republican administration granted the Louisiana Lottery Company a franchise to operate a lottery for 25 years. Lottery ticket venders (1) roamed the streets of New Orleans and the lottery company occupied its own building (2). General Beauregard and General Jubal Early, both ex-Confederate heroes, were hired to supervise the drawings. One lottery advertisement reproduced here shows children counting the money that their father won in the lottery (3). At regular drawings the two generals called out the winning numbers (4). There was fierce opposition to the lottery; opponents portrayed it as an octopus (5) whose corrupting influence reached across the country. In 1890 the opponents of the lottery finally succeeded in passing a law that would force it out of existence.

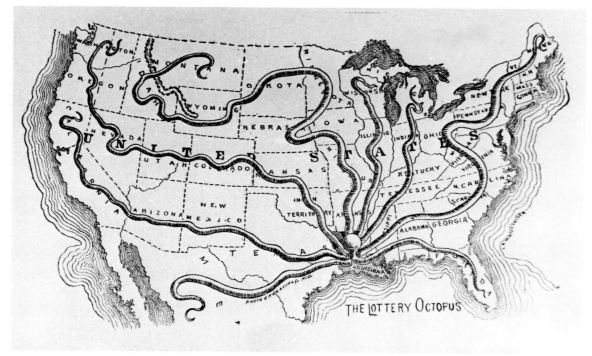

THE LOTTERY OCTOPUS

5

1

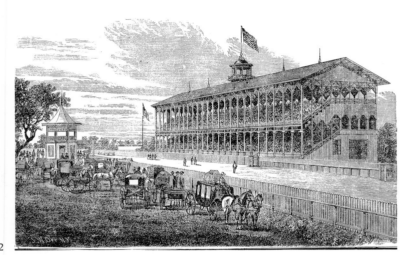

2

3

Horse racing was always a popular sport in Louisiana, and the sport reached its zenith at the fashionable Louisiana Jockey Club (1) shown along with its racecourse (2) in 1872 engravings. In 1905 the City Park Racetrack was built; its grandstand, crowded with fans, is shown in a photograph taken a year after the opening (3). There were many bookmakers in New Orleans, who took bets both on local races and on races throughout the world; one was the Crescent Turf Exchange, whose elaborately designed advertisement is seen here (4). New Orleans citizens interested in more active sports could bowl at the New Orleans Bowling Alley, shown in a 1903 advertisement (5). Or they could try their skill at gambling games or billiards at the Crescent Billiard Hall (6), which, according to its advertisement, was "acknowledged to be the largest and finest in the world." Or they could take a whirl on roller skates at the Crescent City Skating Rink which was constructed in 1869 (7).

The Sporting Life

New Orleans Bowling Alley

....FOR LADIES and GENTLEMEN....

225-227-229 BARONNE STREET,
1 Block from Tulane and Crescent Theatres.

Six Finest Alleys in the South.

5

Crescent Billiard Hall,

COR. ST. CHARLES AND CANAL STREETS, NEW ORLEANS.

ACKNOWLEDGED TO BE

THE LARGEST AND FINEST

IN THE WORLD.

20 TABLES
ON ONE FLOOR,
—WITH—
A MAGNIFICENT CLUB ROOM
FOR EXHIBITIONS.

PARLOR BAR, OYSTER and CIGAR STAND.

J. A. WALKER, - Proprietor.

6

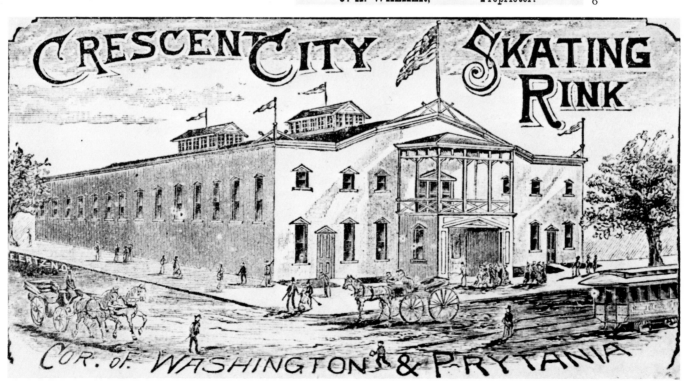

CRESCENT CITY SKATING RINK

COR. OF WASHINGTON & PRYTANIA

7

1

2

3

4

New Orleans has always been a city noted for good hotels, fine stores, excellent food and drink. In the early 1900's Madame Begue's restaurant was patronized by local and visiting gourmets, including the stylishly dressed trio shown standing before the restaurant door (2). Those more interested in drink than in fine food could patronize one of the city's many saloons. The one shown here has spittoons beneath the bar rail for the convenience of customers (1). Guests at the fashionable St. Charles Hotel could take their ease in the establishment's spacious sun parlor, furnished with wicker armchairs and potted palms (3). If they wanted to shop, they could stroll out Canal Street to visit its numerous retail establishments, such as the elegant Maison Blanche (4); or they could visit the West End Amusement Park (5) to eat and drink, listen to a band concert, ride the ferris wheel, and take in an outdoor movie.

Mardi Gras

Lavish Mardi Gras celebrations became a feature of New Orleans life in the decades that followed the Civil War, a tradition that has never lapsed. Engravings show citizens, on New Orleans's characteristic wrought-iron balconies (1), watching the Mardi Gras parade, which featured, in the year 1873, a bull, the *boeuf-gras,* adorned with a wreath (2), a grotesque crowned rhinoceros (3), and Rex, dressed in medieval fashion and preceded by pages carrying his crown and other regalia (4). A masked ball at the Varieties Theatre played a prominent part in the festivities (5). New Orleans wasn't the only place where Mardi Gras was celebrated. The small town of Washington in St. Landry Parish celebrated each year with a masquerade and a fancy dress ball. An invitation to the ball is shown here (6).

4

5

6

⊹ G R A N D ⊹

Masquerade & Fancy Dress Ball

⇥ :TO BE GIVEN BY: ⇤

THE COTTON PICKERS' CLUB,

— AT —

PERSEVERANCE PALACE, WASHINGTON, LOUISIANA,

Tuesday Evening, February 22d, 1887.

Admit _Mr. Jules Pettetui & Family_

⊹- Strictly Personal. -⊹

1

Festivals

As the century wore on, Mardi Gras celebrations became more and more elaborate. The lithographed invitation at left, for a Rex Ball, shows a jolly Rex with butterfly wings (1). It dates from 1882. New Orleans celebrated other festivals besides Mardi Gras. Illustrations from the period just before and after the Civil War show the annual May Festival celebrated by the German community of New Orleans (2); a May Day pageant put on in 1866 by young girls of the city's highest society (3); and the annual fire department parade on St. Charles Street in 1883 (4).

2

1

4

2

3

5

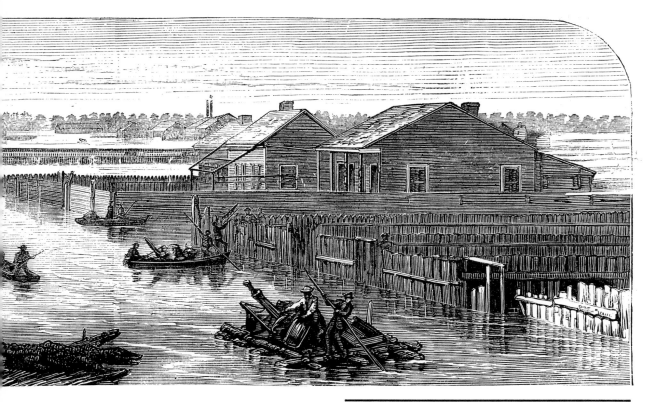

Louisiana life was not all carefree celebration. Along the riverbanks of the state, floods were frequent and devastating. New Orleans has been flooded nine times in its history and the other cities and rural areas of the state have suffered a similar fate. In New Orleans a serious flood in 1871 inundated Canal Street (1) and Custom House Street (4). A view of the interior of a flooded house on Bienville Street (2) shows the inhabitants perched on the furniture for safety, with whatever goods they could gather stored in trunks to keep them dry. Three years later another major flood struck southern Louisiana. An 1874 engraving shows flood refugees gathering in New Iberia for safety (3). In 1882 another and even more terrible flood on the Mississippi put more than 200,000 acres of Louisiana land under water. A steamboat, chartered by the *New Orleans Times-Democrat,* distributed supplies to victims stranded by the flood waters and rescued people whose houses, like the one shown here (5), were in danger of being carried away.

Since early levees were constructed by the owners of riverfront land and not made to strict standards, many of them gave way when the Mississippi rose to flood stage; a "crevasse," or break, in the levee ensued, as can be seen in the 1884 engraving above (1). Laborers piled up sandbags to repair the damage; an 1891 photograph shows them at work (2). When a crevasse occurred crops could be wiped out for miles around and sometimes the water would not go down for weeks. For this reason many plantation houses were constructed on raised pillars (3). Some levees had wooden revetments to strengthen them (4). Sometimes entire families would take refuge on the levees, the only bit of dry ground in the vicinity. An 1897 photograph shows one such group (5).

3

1

2

3
4

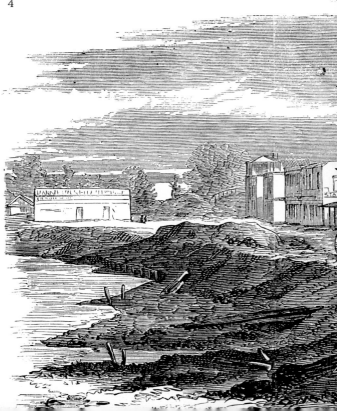

Yellow fever was a constant scourge in Louisiana until it was finally conquered in the twentieth century. In 1873 the disease broke out in Shreveport and carried off almost one-sixth of the population. Magazine illustrations of the time show Texas Street in Shreveport being fumigated with smoke from burning tar in an attempt to ward off the epidemic (1); the city's telegraph operator falling sick at his post (2); and a child, the last survivor of a family struck down by the disease, playing at building a house of cards, oblivious to the bodies of the dead (3). At right, a funeral procession winds along the levee (4). Netting, like that shown over the beds in the dormitory room depicted here (5), was used to keep out mosquitoes that carried the fever, but people were still very vulnerable to the disease. Death notices such as that of Edward Turner, who died of yellow fever, were common (6).

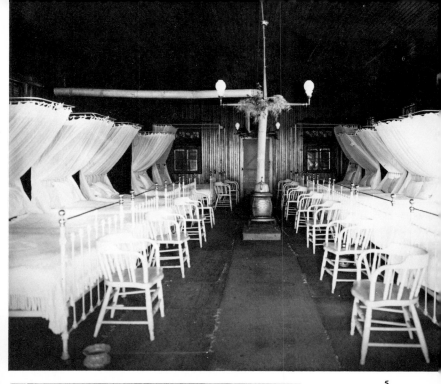

5

DIED.

November 1st, 1871, of yellow fever, in Iberville parish, La., **EDWARD TURNER,** son of LEMUEL P. and FANNIE E. CONNER, aged 11 years 7 months and 29 days.

6

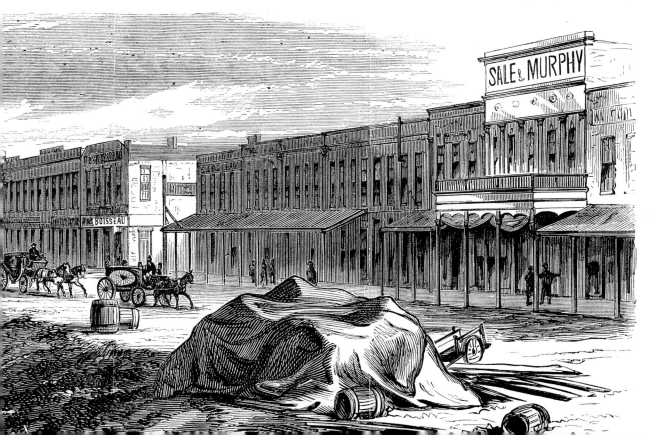

1

Throughout southern Louisiana it is the custom to decorate the graves of deceased family members on All Saints' Day, November 1. An 1885 engraving from *Harper's Weekly* magazine (1) shows New Orleans people bringing wreaths and bouquets to honor the dead in one of the old cemeteries of the city. Often the ornaments were *immortelles,* wreaths, or other adornments fashioned from wire with beads and glass to form decorations that lasted year round. They were sold in the French Market, as can be seen in an 1890 magazine illustration (2). Among the French population, deaths and funerals were announced with small black-bordered handbills (3, 4), which were displayed in public places as in France. Two examples are seen here. At Pine Grove in Vernon Parish, the dead rest under little wooden roofs, encased with picket fences to keep the graves safe from wild animals and cattle (5). The hand-wrought iron cross opposite comes from an Acadian cemetery at Grand Couteau (6).

2

Décédée,

Ce matin à 8 heures, à l'âge de 73 ans,

DAME Vᵛᵉ LABÉDOYÈRE HUCHET ᴅᴇ KERNION

Née Euphémie Aimée Lambert.

Ses amis et connaissances, ainsi que ceux de ses deux fils, Dangeville L. Kernion et A. L. H. Kernion, ainsi que ceux de ses gendres, MM. P. O. Peyroux et E. T. Bernard, sont priés d'assister à son Enterrement qui aura lieu DEMAIN, JEUDI, 5 Juillet, à 9 heures du matin.

Le corps est exposé à sa dernière demeure, No. 213, rue des Remparts, entre Dumaine et St-Philippe.

NLLE-ORLEANS, 4 Juillet 1877.

M

Vous êtes prié d'assister au convoi et à l'enterrement de feu

OCTAVE LA BÉDOYÈRE HUCHET KERNION

décédé hier après-midi à 4 heures.

à l'âge de 49 ans.

L'enterrement aura lieu **Cet Après-Midi**, JEUDI, à 5 heures précises.

Le corps est exposé sur l'Avenue St. Bernard, entre Claiborne et Prosper.

De la part de sa Famille.

Nouvelle-Orléans, le 29 Avril, 1875.

Avendre par J. Bonnot, No. 51 Rue St. Anne, entre Royale et Chartres

Funeral Rites

1

2

During a trip to southern Louisiana in 1866, the English artist A. R. Waud sketched many scenes of Acadian life, some of which were reproduced in *Harper's Weekly* magazine. Waud's scenes include a picture of Acadian women returning from church along the Bayou Lafourche wearing typical Acadian sunbonnets that protect their necks and faces from sunburn (1); two men walking on the levee hauling a sailboat alongside them (2); Cajun women washing clothes in the Bayou Lafourche, pounding dirt out of the clothes with a paddle called a *battoir* (3); and a family traveling by ferryboat, along with their horse and oxcart, across Atchafalaya Bay near Morgan City (4).

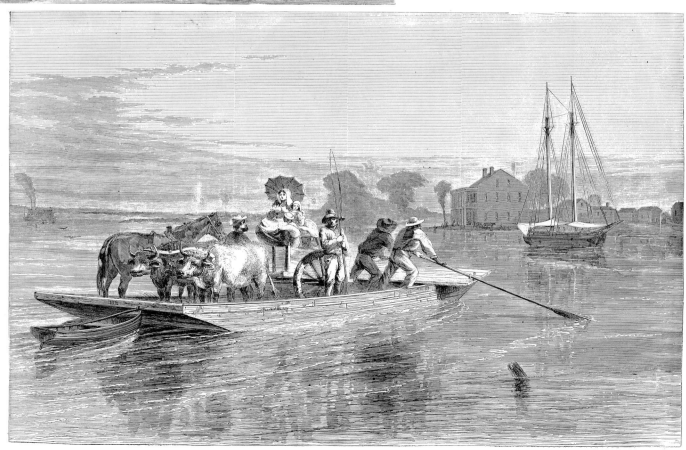

The Survival of French Culture

Both outside New Orleans and within the city, traditional French culture remained a vital force in Louisiana life. Public-school students were taught in French, by such men as the Creole schoolteacher (1) shown in an illustration by A. R. Waud. On a steamboat journey along the Bayou Teche another magazine illustrator, W. T. Smedley, sketched two Cajuns conversing with each other in French (2). French architecture survived in the countryside; the Acadian store shown here (3) is located in a building that was constructed in the typical French manner, with timber-supported brick walls covered by plaster. In this building some of the plaster has fallen away, leaving the bricks exposed. Sermons at churches, such as the beautiful and well-known St. Martinville Church (4), were delivered in French. *Comptes Rendus* (5) was founded in 1876 as a journal devoted to Louisiana French culture; it is the only French publication surviving in the state today. In New Orleans, satirical journals, such as *Le Carillon* (6), were also published in French.

La Nouvelle-Orléans, Mars 1955

COMPTES RENDUS
de
L'ATHÉNÉE LOUISIANAIS

Fondé en 1876

SOMMAIRE

Ephémérides—Saison 1953-1954

Concours de 1955

Lionel Charles Durel
Nécrologie par James F. Bezou

Hommage aux Acadiens
Dagmar Renshaw LeBreton

Les Contes Populaires de la Louisiane
Calvin Claudel

En Marge d'une Affiche de Théâtre de 1799
René J. Le Gardeur, Jr.

Le Théâtre d'Orléans en Tournée
dans les Villes du Nord 1827-1833
Sylvie Chevalley

Revue Littéraire:
A Propos de Deux Livres
Simone de la Souchère Deléry
Une Nouvelle Histoire de la Louisiane
George Raffalovich

La livraison: $1.50
Siège Social, 1925 Esplanade Avenue
New Orleans 16, Louisiana

Imprimerie E. P. Rivas, Inc., La Nouvelle-Orléans

3

Immigrants

4

5

During the late nineteenth century, Louisiana's population became even more cosmopolitan with a new influx of immigrants. Chinese laborers were imported to work in the sugar-cane fields of southern Louisiana (1), and Filipino fisherman settled in St. Malo near the coast (2). Thousands of Italians immigrated to New Orleans and southern Louisiana, where they now form a prominent segment of the community. An unfortunate occurrence in the year 1891 involving some Italian immigrants was the assassination of the New Orleans superintendent of police. In March, 1891, when a jury, perhaps as a result of intimidation or bribery, found the Italians who had been accused of the crime innocent, a mob gathered on Canal Street and set out to lynch them (3). The mob battered its way into the yard of the Parish Prison (4) and killed 11 of the Italians (5). The incident caused a serious breach in relations between Italy and the United States.

263

African Heritage

In the New World, Louisiana blacks retained many cultural inheritances from the African homeland which their ancestors had left centuries before, particularly in their music, religion, and dancing. Illustrations from an 1886 issue of *Century Magazine* show blacks in New Orleans, before a circle of singing onlookers, dancing the bamboula: a traditional dance performed to the rhythm of drums (4). Sometimes Western instruments were used, as can be seen from the fiddler shown at upper left (1). The dancing couple seen next to him are performing a traditional African courting dance (2). In the practice of voodoo there were strong survivals of African religious rites. Many unknowledgeable Americans considered these traditional rites merely superstitions, but they were directly traceable to elements of African religion that the ancestors of the slaves had followed. Often as part of the rites, ceremonial dances (3) were performed to traditional music. A voodoo priestess can be seen sitting at the right. The tomb of the voodoo priestess Marie Laveau, who died in 1881, is marked with a tablet on which believers scrawl crosses for good luck (5). The only example of traditional African architecture in Louisiana is African House, near Natchitoches, with a typical overhanging roof (6).

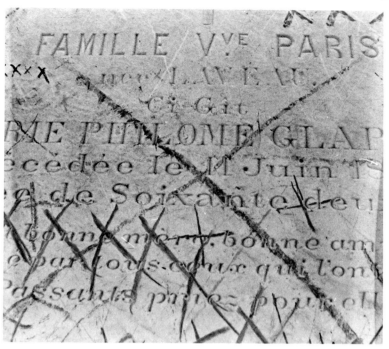

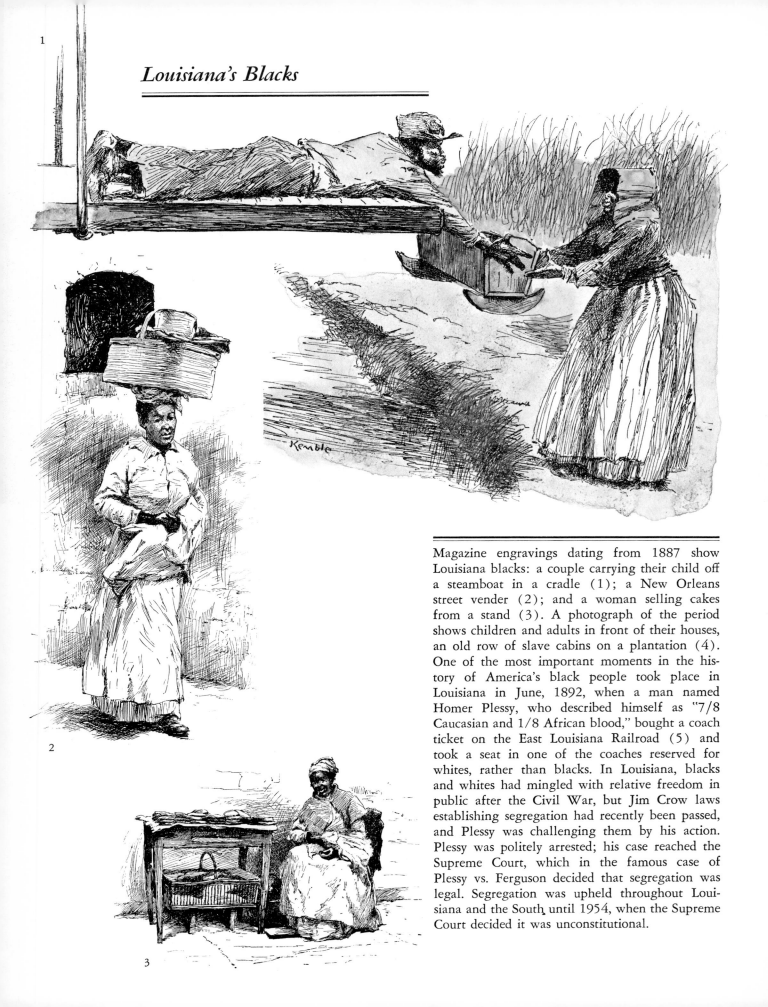

Louisiana's Blacks

Magazine engravings dating from 1887 show Louisiana blacks: a couple carrying their child off a steamboat in a cradle (1); a New Orleans street vender (2); and a woman selling cakes from a stand (3). A photograph of the period shows children and adults in front of their houses, an old row of slave cabins on a plantation (4). One of the most important moments in the history of America's black people took place in Louisiana in June, 1892, when a man named Homer Plessy, who described himself as "7/8 Caucasian and 1/8 African blood," bought a coach ticket on the East Louisiana Railroad (5) and took a seat in one of the coaches reserved for whites, rather than blacks. In Louisiana, blacks and whites had mingled with relative freedom in public after the Civil War, but Jim Crow laws establishing segregation had recently been passed, and Plessy was challenging them by his action. Plessy was politely arrested; his case reached the Supreme Court, which in the famous case of Plessy vs. Ferguson decided that segregation was legal. Segregation was upheld throughout Louisiana and the South until 1954, when the Supreme Court decided it was unconstitutional.

4

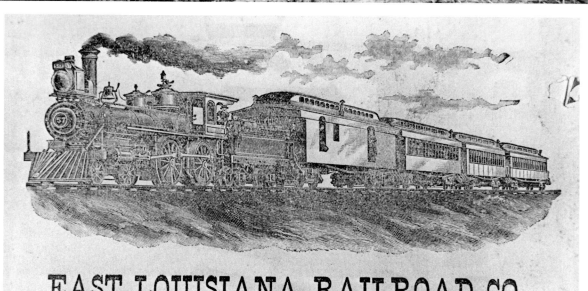

5

EAST LOUISIANA RAILROAD CO.

EXCURSIONS
$1.00.

—TO THE—
GREAT ABITA SPRINGS.

E. S. FERGUSON,
G.P.A.

Home Sweet Home

1

3

As elsewhere in America, in Louisiana the prosperous middle class lived comfortably as the nineteenth century came to a close. The New Orleans architect-photographer C. Milo Williams recorded the lives of New Orleans people in the 1890's and photographed their homes. Some of his pictures show a peaceful family musicale with a girl playing the piano and her father strumming a mandolin (1) and two family groups: one includes a drummer boy and a top-hatted dandy (2); a second shows a boy wearing a sailor suit posing with his mother and grandmother (3). Williams's photographs of house interiors show the ornate decoration that was typical of the period. A beaded hanging lamp lights the paneled and carpeted stairway in one house (4); in another, the piano, mantelpiece, marble-topped commode, and side table are all draped with decorative fabrics and adorned with chinaware and statuary; beneath a Chinese lantern is a chair made from the horns of longhorn steer (5).

Diversions

1

3

Like many other Americans, Louisianans were fond of hunting and fishing. In the Teche country, sportsmen shot at great flocks of passenger pigeons (1). Unfortunately they and other American hunters were so successful that the passenger pigeon is now extinct. A more leisurely sport was fishing: the fishermen above, who characteristically seem as interested in lolling and drinking beer as they are in fishing, were photographed around 1900 (2). A sport that could be enjoyed only in Louisiana and a few other states was alligator hunting. An 1893 engraving shows a steamboat on Bayou Tunica carrying a party of alligator hunters (4); at that time alligator-hunting was the chief sport of the region. Bicycling provided better and more peaceful exercise than hunting. The Columbia chainless bicycle (3), shown in an 1898 advertisement from a New Orleans newspaper, claimed to make hill-climbing easy. Amateur theatricals were also popular. A C. Milo Williams photograph (5) shows a group of splendidly costumed actors performing in a yard, before a backdrop made from Oriental rugs.

4

5

271

School Days

1

2

3

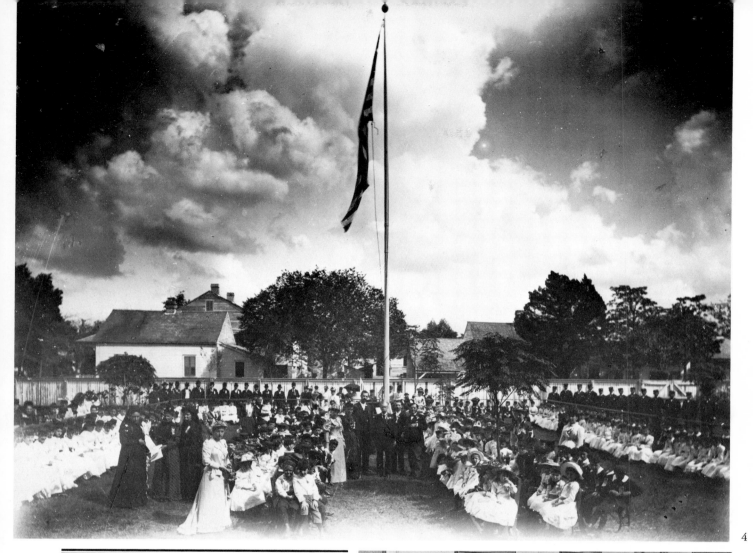

It was not until 1845 that a system of free public education was adopted in Louisiana. A prosperous New Orleans businessman, Samuel Jarvis Peters (1), was an important patron of popular education; another rich businessman, John McDonogh (2), left $750,000 in 1850 for the building of public schools in New Orleans. His money paid for 35 schools, the first of which is shown in the photograph opposite (3). Soon, with the spread of free education, most children were attending school. A C. Milo Williams photograph, dating from the 1890's, shows a ceremonial flag-raising on school grounds (4). In another school, a class of students is seen writing an essay on "The Cause of the War between the States" (5). Not all children were fortunate enough to get schooling. Around the same time as the well-dressed New Orleans children were in class writing their essay, other Louisiana children were working full time in a cannery as oyster shuckers, at a meager wage (6).

Louisiana's Colleges

SILLIMAN COLLEGIATE INSTITUTE,

For YOUNG LADIES,

CLINTON, LOUISIANA.

SESSION 1890-91.

ADVANTAGES.

LARGE ENDOWMENT.   HEALTHFUL LOCATION.
MODERATE TERMS.   FREE SCHOLARSHIPS.
EASY ACCESSIBILITY.

Centenary College,

REV. W. L. C. HUNNICUTT, D. D., PRESIDENT.

JACKSON, LA.

FACULTY.

Rev. W. L. C. HUNNICUTT, D.D. *Professor of Mental and Moral Science.*
G. H. WILEY, A. M., - *Professor of Ancient and Modern Languages.*
R. H. McGIMSEY, A. B., - *Professor of Mathematics.*
J. M. SULLIVAN, B. A. - *Professor of Chemistry and Physics.*
A. R. HOLCOMBE, M. D. - *Professor of Physiology and Hygiene.*
Rev. B. M. DRAKE, A. B. - *Professor English Law and Literature.*
Rev. ROBERT H. WYNN, B. A. - *Principal of Preparatory Department.*
Mrs. E. M. HUNNICUTT, - *Assistant in Preparatory Department.*
Mrs. R. H. McGIMSEY, - *Teacher of Vocal Music.*

CHARGES.

College Classes, 5 months,	$30 00
Preparatory Classes, 5 months,	20 00
Contingent Fee, 5 months,	2 50
Matriculation (College Class,)	5 00
Table Board, per month,	10 00
Board in Private Families, all things furnished,	$13.00 to 16 00

LOUISIANA STATE SEMINARY.

4

Before the 1880's there were few high schools in the state outside New Orleans. There were a number of small denominational colleges though, such as Silliman Collegiate Institute (1, 2), as well as preparatory departments of colleges, such as Centenary (3). In 1847, the legislature opened the school that was later to become Louisiana State University (4). In 1884, the philanthropist Paul Tulane (5) gave $500,000 worth of real estate to pay for the foundation of Tulane University. Its campus, built in the Romanesque style in the years 1894 and 1895, is shown in a contemporary photograph (6).

5

6

1

2

3

A Historic Heritage

4

6

In the decades around 1900, there was an awakening of interest in the riches of Louisiana's historical heritage. In 1911, the Louisiana State Museum (1) was established, through the efforts of the Louisiana Historical Society. Well before that time artists were recording characteristic old New Orleans buildings. The famous etcher Joseph Pennell depicted a typical two-story service annex at the rear of a large New Orleans house (2) and a small shop with an adjoining balconied house (3). Around 1881, an antiquarian sketched one of the first churches in Louisiana outside New Orleans, the Pointe Coupée Church, which had been built in 1760 near the Mississippi above Baton Rouge (5). Pictures showing scenes of Louisiana history appeared in many books; above is an engraving showing the Acadians of Nova Scotia, learning that they were about to be exiled to Louisiana (4). Writers composed vivid descriptions of Creole life. One of the most famous was Lafcadio Hearn (6), who worked for New Orleans newspapers between 1877 and 1887. One quaint Louisiana custom that has since disappeared is illustrated in a late nineteenth-century engraving (7): offering lagniappe—candy, cake, or a small souvenir—to children or servants making a purchase at a store.

Prison Life

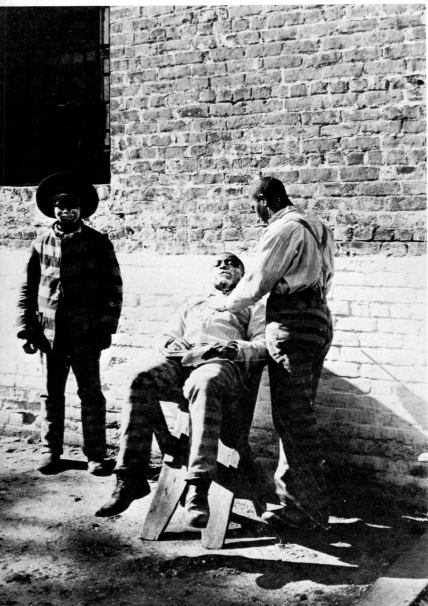

Traditionally, prison labor was used in public-works programs, particularly for tasks that were too difficult and dirty to attract hired workers. Engravings show prisoners, wearing striped convict suits that would make them easily identifiable if they should escape, building a levee under the watchful eyes of an armed guard (1) and making a cut through Chopin Hill on the Cane River near Alexandria during the building of the New Orleans Pacific Railway (2). The prisoners working on the railway were leased from the penitentiary by the railroad company. Within the state penitentiary in downtown Baton Rouge, a convict barber shaved fellow inmates in the morning sun (3). Some inmates worked in the prison shoe factory (4). The New Orleans parish prison was filled with prisoners who—as this photograph from the 1890's shows (5)—had little to do but sit around waiting for their sentence to end.

4

5

1

2

3

When the war with Spain began in 1898, thousands of Louisianans responded to President William McKinley's call for volunteers. Camp Foster (1) was opened on the Fair Grounds in New Orleans and about 2,000 men received military training there. Other Louisiana outfits received their training in the countryside (4). The hero of the war, Theodore Roosevelt (2), passed through New Orleans on his way to embark for Cuba, where most of the battles of the war were to take place. Within six months, the war was over. No Louisiana outfits actually took part, and only one Louisianan, Lieutenant Numa Augustin (3), died on the field of battle. Lack of action did not dampen the military spirit in the state, however. A photograph, dating from around 1910 (5), shows military cadets at Louisiana State firing artillery pieces in front of Garig Hall, the university assembly hall.

Industrial Expansion

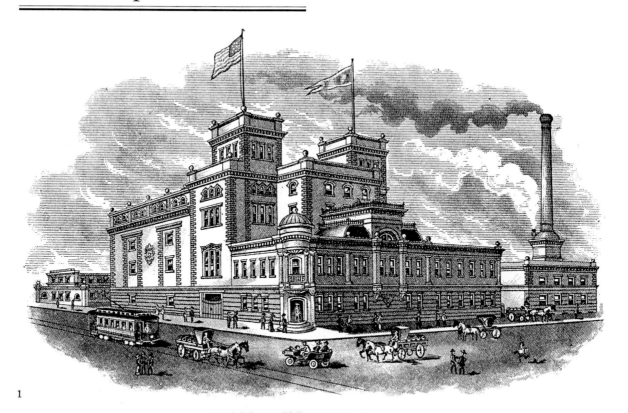

1

2

3

4

5

6

The turn of the century was an age of great industrial growth in Louisiana. Companies from banks to breweries flourished and brought new wealth to the state. Beautifully engraved stock certificates from the period, often adorned with vignettes depicting a corporation's business premises or activities, show the variety of enterprises in Louisiana. Certificates show the Consumers Brewing Company in New Orleans (1) and a cane field of the Dunbar Cane Products Corporation (2) with harvesters and a sugar mill in the background. The Columbia Cotton Oil Mill adorned its certificates with a scene of a cotton field (3). Its contemporary, the Madison Cotton Oil Company, displayed a cotton plant (4). Two banks, the Metropolitan Bank (5) and the Third District Savings of New Orleans (6), proudly showed the fine buildings in which they transacted business. The Pan American Life Insurance Company (7), more subtly, surrounded its policies with a lacy border that looked very much like the tracery on the dollar bills that the policy holders' beneficiaries would one day receive.

7

1

2

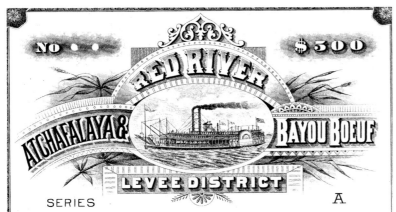

3

4

5

Canals, levees, railroads, and other public improvements were built in great numbers during the second half of the nineteenth and the early part of the twentieth centuries. Bonds were issued to pay for some of the improvements. Bonds of the Bossier Levee District showed a busy levee scene with workers loading cotton onto a steamboat (1); those of the Atchafalaya & Bayou Boeuf Levee District on the Red River showed a steamboat proceeding down the river (2). Bonds were also issued by a land-drainage organization in Plaquemines Parish (3) and by the Harvey Canal Land and Improvement Company (4). The building of canals often made Louisiana's marshy lands suitable for cultivation and construction, once water was drained away. Sometimes changes impeded development, however. Bayou Lafourche was navigable in the nineteenth century, as this picture of the steamboat *Assumption* sailing on the bayou shows (5); in 1904 the bayou was sealed off at Donaldsonville because residents along its banks feared floods when the Mississippi overflowed, and navigation ended. The New Orleans Public Belt Railroad (6) began operating in 1908 under the sponsorship of the city. It was built to enable the railroads entering the city to transfer cars from one line to another, as well as to wharves and industrial sidings.

6

1

2

3

After the turn of the century, horses were used less and less for transportation, although some could still be seen pulling buggies, as in the picture above of Canal Street, New Orleans (1). In Louisiana, as elsewhere in the country, trolleys were coming into use for urban transportation and some trolley lines even went between towns. Stock certificates from the first decade of the twentieth century show trolleys that traveled along the bank of the Bayou Teche (2) and through the streets of Alexandria (3). Automobiles were beginning to be seen on the dirt roads of the countryside. Opposite at top, a motorcade of five "touring cars" stops for a rest beneath a grove of oaks (4). At center, two cars are parked in front of a country store (5), Landeche Brothers' Good Time Store, which offered its customers a bottle of beer or a pack of cigarettes for five cents and merchandise "cheap for cash." Ferries (6), pulled across rivers and bayous by means of a cable, carried cars and horses and buggies in regions where bridges had not yet been built.

4

5

6

1

2

288

World War I

THE NEW ORLEANS ITEM **FINAL**

PRESIDENT DETAILS ARMISTICE

Washington, Nov. 11.—President Wilson issued a formal proclamation at 10 o'clock this morning announcing that the armistice with Germany had been signed. The proclamation follows:—

"My fellow countrymen:— "The armistice was signed this morning. Everything for which America fought has been accomplished. It will now be our fortunate duty to assist, by example, by sober friendly council and by material aid in the establishment of just democracy throughout the world."—WOODROW WILSON

6

Eighty thousand Louisiana men served in the armed forces during the First World War, and a great many of them went to the front lines in France. To demonstrate preparedness, citizens and soldiers paraded down the streets of New Orleans and other cities; a contemporary photograph (1) shows marchers in New Orleans parading on Canal Street on both sides of the trolley tracks, the so-called neutral ground. Camps were set up for local draftees. More than 7,000 men were trained on the Tulane campus where fourteen wooden barracks were set up to house them (2). Women volunteered to serve as Red Cross nurses and canteen workers (3), and many nurses went to the front. Civilians bought thousands of Liberty Bonds, which were issued to raise money to pay for the war; a sign on St. Charles Avenue in New Orleans urged the purchase of Liberty Bonds to keep German boots from trampling on American liberty (4). The signing of the armistice, ending the war on November 11, 1918, was greeted with great joy. The *New Orleans Item,* reporting the armistice, displayed a picture of the victorious American flag on the front page (5). A group of navy yeomen and women volunteers celebrated the armistice by riding around the city in an open truck (6).

CAPT.
gone

Jazz and New Orleans are almost synonymous, and the city has long been famous for its native music. Numerous bands played in the city and entertained the populace—both black and white. Perhaps the most famous jazz great who originated in New Orleans was Louis Armstrong, who appears in a 1931 photograph (2)—written over in ink. Armstrong is shown revisting the New Orleans Colored Waif's Home where he had spent part of his childhood and where he was taught to play the trumpet by Peter Davis, who is seen standing at his right. Louis Armstrong's Hot Five appear in a 1926 picture (1); from left to right are Johnny St. Cyr, Kid Ory, Armstrong, Johnny Dodds, and Lil Hardin Armstrong, Louis's wife. One of New Orleans's well-patronized jazz landmarks was the Gypsy Tea Room (3) where Kid Rena (who stands at far right in the photograph above) played along with his band in the 1920's and 1930's. Another well-known band that played "dreamy moon-beam blue music" was that of Johnny De Droit (4), shown in a 1917 photograph. Jazz funerals have long been a feature of the New Orleans scene; the crowded street funeral procession seen here featured the Eureka Brass Band (5). The spirit of New Orleans jazz is caught in a joyous 1937 photograph (6), which shows a pianist playing for an admiring youngster.

1

2

3

The State University

Louisiana State Seminary of Learning and Military Academy, the forerunner of Louisiana State University, was opened on January 2, 1860, near Pineville. Its first superintendent was Colonel William Tecumseh Sherman, who departed at the start of the Civil War since his sympathies were with the Union. Fire destroyed the seminary building on October 5, 1869, and the school moved to Baton Rouge. In 1870 the seminary officially became "Louisiana State University" and in 1877 the university merged with the Agricultural and Mechanical College, which was then located in New Orleans. The present campus, dedicated in 1926, saw tremendous growth in the 1930's. The 120 or so principal buildings, comprising the main part of L.S.U.'s Baton Rouge Campus (1), are grouped on a 300-acre plateau—originally part of a plantation—half a mile east of the Mississippi. L.S.U.'s most significant landmark is the Memorial Tower (2), in the heart of the campus. The architecture of the campus reflects Louisiana's varied heritage. Himes Hall (3) and David F. Boyd Hall (4) reflect Spanish architecture, as does the tile roof and arched entrance of Foster Hall (5). La Maison Française (6) is built in the style of the early French Renaissance.

1

2

3

In early spring, Chicago & Southern will inaugurate a new fleet of giant Douglas DC-3, 21 Passenger Planes.

IT PAYS TO **FLY**
EVERYWHERE
via
"The Valley Level Route"

North, south, east or west—fast, comfortable planes are waiting to carry you swiftly and safely to your destination.

Flying saves time, and time is money for business men. Successful men fly because they know the man who flies gets there first, sees more customers, signs more orders, makes more money for himself and his family. And they enjoy many real advantages over earthbound travelers because they avoid many tiresome days and nights on the road. They arrive at the end of their journey rested and refreshed, fit and eager for work or play.

next time you plan a trip
FLY
Low Air Travel Fares

New Orleans-Chicago	$44.60
New Orleans-New York	73.85
New Orleans-Memphis	19.76
New Orleans-Jackson	9.61

3 Flights—Each Way—Each Day

10% reduction on round trips
For Reservations Call
Your Travel Agent or

CHICAGO
and
SOUTHERN
Air Lines
"The Valley Level Route"

PAN-AMERICAN
AIR RACES

44

SHUSHAN AIRPORT
NEW ORLEANS

INTERNATIONAL AVIATION SPECTACLE
FEB. 9·10·11·12·13
MARDI-GRAS SEASON 1934
SPEED!   THRILLS!   ACTION!

The age of aviation reached New Orleans in 1910, when a group of stunt flyers, under the leadership of John B. Moisant (1), put on a flying circus. The circus ended tragically when Moisant lost his life trying to set a record for sustained flight time. In 1912 an attempt was made to carry airmail between New Orleans and Baton Rouge, and by 1923 the New Orleans Airlines was taking mail to the mouth of the Mississippi to be loaded on ships headed for Central America (2). Pilots are shown standing in front of one of the airline's seaplanes (3). James R. Wedell (4) of Louisiana, a great aviation ace of the 1930's, is shown standing by his plane. In 1932 Wedell flew 266.03 miles an hour over a 100-kilometer course, breaking the world record. Wedell and his brother Walter designed and built their own planes, which flew from a field at Patterson, Louisiana (5). In 1934, as this advertisement (6) shows, the Pan American Air Races, an international aviation meet, was held at New Orleans. Regular passenger service out of New Orleans began in the thirties (7).

The Long Era

Huey P. Long (2) was probably the most colorful and controversial, shrewd and ruthless political figure in the history of Louisiana. Born in obscurity in Winnfield, he rose to be virtual dictator of the state when he became governor in 1928, and he maintained control after he became a senator in Washington. A self-appointed champion of "pore folks," Huey hated corporations, Wall Street, and the rich. He ran for governor (1) with a campaign calling for free education and medical care for all, the building of good roads, providing free schoolbooks to children, and taxing the rich to pay for everything. Long got the legislature (3) to reorganize the state government; self-government was almost abolished, and Long secured command of the state militia and control of the judiciary, election officials, tax assessors, policemen, firemen, and schoolteachers. Long made many enemies both through his program and through his uncouth and dictatorial tactics. In 1929 an attempt was made to impeach him. He is shown here shaking the hand of a well-wisher during the impeachment attempt (4). A great builder, Long was responsible for bridges, roads, and a new state capitol and governor's mansion (5). Over his grave on the capitol grounds, a bronze statue of him faces the towering state capitol he built (6).

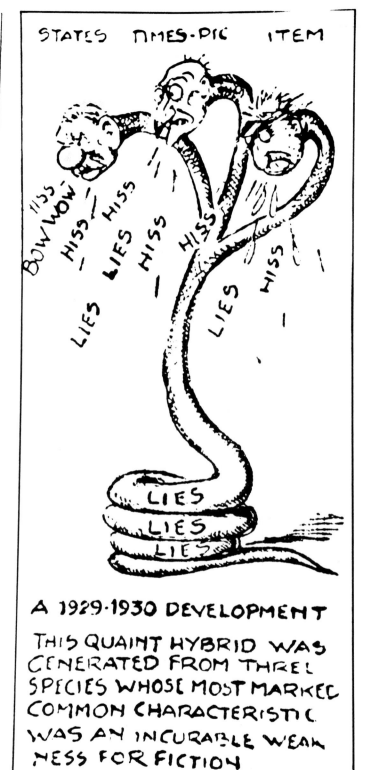

Long's relations with the press, which bitterly opposed him, inspired him to start his own newspaper: the *Louisiana Progress.* The first issue, March 26, 1930, featured a cartoon on its front page showing Governor Long distributing free schoolbooks to grateful school children, while the opposition, "The League of Notions," stands by disconsolately (1). Another pro-Long cartoon shows the governor kicking his opponents out of the way (2). Caricatures depict one of Long's opponents as an ineffective old man (3) and three Louisiana newspapers that opposed the governor as a three-headed snake, spewing out lies (4).

5

In the 1930's there was a great revival of interest in American folklore and traditional crafts, and writers and photographers recorded many aspects of Louisiana Cajun life. Photographs made during the decade show an Acadian woman, on the bank of a bayou, laundering clothes by pounding them with a *battoir* (1), as in the engraving on page 259; another woman, wearing a characteristic Acadian sunbonnet and standing beside a buggy (2); an Acadian farmer with a mule-drawn plow (3); a carpenter with typical handmade Acadian chairs (4)—their seats were of cowhide and some cowhide can be seen stretched on a board beside the carpenter. Other photographs show a woman working at a homemade loom (5); another woman at a spinning wheel (6); and a boat-maker (7) with his four sons building a dugout pirogue.

6

7

4

In the Cajun Country

1

2

3

Acadian houses were almost invariably built with a sloping roof overhanging the gallery (1). An outdoor stairway led to the spacious attic which was used as a boys' bedroom or as a storeroom. The older structures were built with a heavy timber framework, with the space between filled with a mixture of mud and moss; then the exterior was covered with clapboards. Many houses had a *tablette,* an outdoor platform on which dishes were washed (2). Houses were generally expanded by lengthening them, and many double-length houses survive in Louisiana (3). At upper left a child is seen sitting on the outdoor stairway of an old house (4). Before 1890 nearly all fences in southwestern Louisiana were built without nails. They were called *pieux* fences and consisted of cypress rails fitted into posts that had been drilled with large holes (5). Few survive now. Until around 1940 the horse and buggy was the most common mode of transportation in the prairie section of the Acadian country. A 1935 photograph (6) shows a line of horses and buggies in front of a clapboard Cajun church on a Sunday morning.

303

Acadian folk music is distinctive, with simple repetitive tunes and lyrics that deal mostly with love and marriage. Dance bands generally play with 4 instruments: the accordion, guitar, fiddle, and triangle. Acadian dances, called *Fais-do-do,* took place in dance halls such as this simple wooden building in Rayne (1) and featured bands like the Rayne-Bo Ramblers (2). A Saturday night Acadian dance is shown in a 1945 photograph (3). The first to record Acadian music were Joe and Cleoma Falcon, who are pictured at right with guitar and accordion (4). At Bayou Barataria there is an annual pirogue race (5) at which paddlers demonstrated their skill in the tricky business of handling a pirogue. Some contestants, like the man seen in the foreground, failed to maintain their balance.

In the early 1930's the effect of the worldwide depression began to be felt in Louisiana. By 1933, 11 percent of the population was on relief, and agencies such as the Works Progress Administration—the W. P. A.—were set up to aid the unemployed, who constructed sewers, water mains, bridges, public buildings, and new roads, like the men seen working here (1). Much progress was made on building up the New Orleans lakefront area (2) out of marshland. The Bonnet Carré spillway was built as a flood-control measure, to carry excess Mississippi River water into Lake Pontchartrain; a 1950 aerial photograph shows the spillway half-filled with water (3). The Huey P. Long Bridge (4) over the Mississippi near New Orleans was opened to carry both trains and automobile traffic. Money was scarce and people made do with what they had. A 1935 photograph (5) shows a Cajun man wearing a pair of homespun trousers made by his wife more than 30 years before. The family spinning wheel can be seen on the gallery behind him. Farmers were especially hard hit; cotton was selling so cheaply and so many bales were unsold that the legislature passed a bill prohibiting the planting of more cotton during the year 1932. Governor Long is seen late at night in his bedroom (6) signing the bill, which had just been passed. Because other states refused to go along with the idea, the law eventually was abandoned.

World War II

1

2

3

With war raging in Europe and threatening the United States, in September, 1941, the army brought 19 divisions—almost 400,000 men—to western Louisiana for war games that would test out the army's ability to meet and repel an enemy invasion. With mock battles (1), the army had the chance to evaluate the performance of officers, soldiers, and equipment. When war did break out, Louisiana responded swiftly by expanding its shipyards. A small New Orleans boat builder, Andrew Jackson Higgins, gathered a force of 40,000 men and women and turned out PT boats and landing craft at a lively rate; one PT boat is shown on a trial run on Lake Pontchartrain (2). Women took over the jobs of men who were in the service; one is shown here learning to handle a trolley rope for her new job as a streetcar conductor (3). Civilians, like the helmeted group shown at upper right (4), became air raid wardens preparing for enemy bombing raids which, fortunately, never came—although many ships were torpedoed by German submarines off the Louisiana coast. Patriotic symbols were displayed everywhere; an enormous 7-story-high flag hung outside Godchaux's store on Canal Street in New Orleans (5). In 1945, victory first over Germany, and later over Japan, was greeted with bonfires, parades, and impromptu celebrations (6).

1

2

4

3

Almost a third of Louisiana's land is farmland. The leading money crop is not cotton or sugar, but cattle, such as those shown here grazing in a riverside pasture (1). Cattle and dairy products bring in about 30 percent of the state's farm income. A half million Louisiana acres are devoted to cotton and production is now almost completely mechanized. Above at left is a cotton-picking machine (2). At left is a field of sugar cane—another major crop—with a sugar mill behind it (3). Louisiana rice is harvested from

Farming Today

July onward; the rice is threshed in the field and then taken to be dried (4). Some agricultural products are unique to the state, such as the dark perique tobacco, shown above being prepared in a tobacco shed (5), and Avery Island's famous tabasco sauce (6), which is fermented in barrels for at least 3 years. Although eastern Louisiana's strawberry acreage has decreased in the last few decades, Louisiana strawberries, such as those shown being picked at right (7), are still famous.

Oil

When studies indicated that the coastal-shelf region of the Gulf of Mexico contained oil, rigs were developed to drill the ocean floor. The first commercially productive oil well out of sight of land was Kerr-McGee's historic rig number 16 (1) which began operation off the Louisiana coast in 1947. To determine the best locations for offshore wells, underwater explosions were set off in the following years (2), until it was found that such explosions destroyed too much marine life. Thereafter improved methods of detection

were developed. In time gigantic deepwater-drilling rigs were constructed with living quarters for the crew and a helicopter landing pad (3). The rigs contained numerous valves, called Christmas trees, to regulate the flow of oil (4). Wellhead chambers (5) safely carry workmen far down into the ocean to assemble wellhead equipment. By the early 1970's there were almost 40,000 producing oil, natural gas, and condensate wells in the state; the field shown here is near Lees-ville (6).

1

2

3

Since World War II, Louisiana's industrial growth has been phenomenal. The Mississippi riverfront is now lined with manufacturing plants and with terminals, such as the storage facility shown under construction here (1), for handling raw materials and grain for shipment abroad. One of the world's largest aluminum reduction plants is Kaiser's Chalmette Works (2), below New Orleans; the plant covers 280 acres. Louisiana's largest employer is the Avondale Shipyards, where 10,000 people build ocean-going craft, such as the destroyer-escort *Trippe,* shown here at its launching (3). The 900-acre Michaud assembly plant has been used for fabricating booster rockets for flights to the moon (5). In the Baton Rouge area are refineries, such as the Exxon refinery (4), rubber factories, chemical plants, and both light and heavy metal works. Below, the bustling Union Carbide plant near Taft is visible behind a typical Louisiana cemetery (6).

Above and Below the Earth

Mining liquid sulphur has been an important Louisiana industry for 70 years. The Grand Ecaille sulphur mine (1) is one facility of the Freeport Sulphur Company, whose shipping and storage center (2) is at Port Sulphur below New Orleans. Grand Isle (5), an offshore sulphur mine, stands 7 miles out to sea; sulphur is obtained from great depths and pumped ashore through a heated, insulated pipeline. In the salt mines at Avery Island, salt is undercut by electrical machinery (3) and then blasted loose with dynamite. The Avery Island salt dome (4), covered by trees and ponds, can be seen in the aerial photograph at left. The cutting of lumber and the manufacture of pulpwood is another important Louisiana industry. Below, lumber is neatly stacked outside a sawmill (6).

Louisiana's commercial fishermen supply the fine seafood for which the state is famous, as well as the commercially important catch of menhaden, an inedible fish used to make fertilizer and fish oil. Oyster luggers, shown in the old photograph above (1), used to line the New Orleans waterfront, their sails furled. These sailboats have now been replaced by motor boats. The shrimp fleet, made up of trawlers such as the *North Sea* (2), has not changed in design for many years. Each year at Morgan City, priests bless the shrimp fleet (3), in a ceremony that is paralleled in other fishing ports all over the country, north and south. A 1920 photograph shows fishermen treading shrimp that had been spread out in the sun to dry, breaking the shells to extract the dried shrimp (4); more sanitary methods of obtaining the shrimp meat now prevail. The scene was photographed in the Filipino fishing village shown in the engraving on pages 262 and 263. Another 1920 photograph shows the Filipino fishermen unloading their catch (5).

319

A Growing State

Since the end of World War II, the skylines of Louisiana's cities have changed radically, with skyscrapers crowding the downtown sections. A cluster of skyscrapers marks the business district of Shreveport (1), the state's second largest city, and a superhighway, with its overpasses and cloverleaf exits, speeds traffic around the city. A row of skyscrapers overlooks the Mississippi at Baton Rouge (2); since this picture was taken in 1972 several more towering structures have been built. In Monroe a new channel was constructed to facilitate traffic on the Ouachita River (3); and the city now boasts a new city hall (4) and a modern arena (5) that seats 8,000 people. In 1961 Shreveport opened a fine new art gallery displaying, among other works, a notable collection of American paintings (6). Throughout the state, modern buildings have sprung up, including this architecturally unique, nondenominational roadside chapel (7), located outside Alexandria.

5

6

7

New Orleans (1) is now the world's third rank-ing port; dozens of ships arrive or depart from the city each week (2). The new New Orleans International Airport (3) is served by 12 airlines; both buses and trains arrive downtown at the Union Passenger Terminal (4). A magnificent new theatre has been constructed for the perform-ing arts (5), and a vast sports arena now towers over downtown New Orleans. The impressive view of New Orleans on the opposite page was taken in 1973 (6).

4

5

6

Education

3

The greatest change that has come over Louisiana education in the postwar years has been in the growing integration of the schools, despite the opposition of many whites, such as those shown picketing in front of a New Orleans public school on the day segregation ended there in 1961 (1). Many new colleges have been founded and old ones have expanded enrollment, as more and more Louisianans of both races attend college after high school. The Wyly Tower of Learning dominates the campus of Louisiana Tech in Ruston (2). The University Center at the University of New Orleans (3) is unmistakably modern, though its columns recall Louisiana's architectural past. Equally modern is Blackham Coliseum, part of the University of Southwestern Louisiana at Lafayette (4). The buildings of the campus of Centenary College reflect an older style of architecture (5). New Orleans is a noted center of medical education. The tallest building in the photograph opposite is Charity Hospital (6). Tulane Medical School is at its left, and Louisiana State University Medical School is at its right.

4

5

6

Louisiana Heritage

Louisiana folk traditions still flourish, both in the big cities and the countryside. Best known is Mardi Gras, lavishly celebrated in New Orleans; at upper left the 1971 Rex pauses during the parade to receive a toast from members of the Louisiana Club (1). A more simple but equally fervent celebration goes on in rural areas: in the region around Church Point costumed horsemen, such as the one shown above (2), tour the countryside gathering chickens for a gumbo feast. There is still lively interest in Cajun music and dancing; the band at left was photographed in 1972 at the Breaux Bridge Crawfish Festival (3). Jazz funerals still occur from time to time—the Olympia brass band is shown marching in one in 1969 (4)—and on All Saints' Night, some rural Louisianans still light candles at tombs (5). Old-time religious ceremonies, such as the riverside baptism shown opposite, can occasionally be seen (6), and numerous towns celebrate festivals built around local foods. Opposite, a man in a straw hat stirs a pot of jambalaya (7), his entry in the World Champion Jambalaya Chef Contest held annually in the town of Gonzalez, south of Baton Rouge.

6

4

5

7

The Governors of Louisiana

Here is a list of the governors of Louisiana since 1699; most of their portraits appear on the following pages. The portraits of a few of them are unavailable. In cases where a governor's portrait has already appeared on one of the preceeding pages, that page number is indicated.

The Governors of Louisiana as a French Colony

1699	Pierre le Moyne, sieur d'Iberville (founder) (see page 34)
1699–1701	Ensign Sauvolle (picture unavailable)
1701–1713	Jean Baptiste le Moyne, sieur de Bienville (see page 34)
1713–1716	Antoine de la Mothe Cadillac
1716–1717	Jean Baptiste le Moyne, sieur de Bienville (acting) (see page 34)
1717–1718	Jean Michiele, sieur de Lapinay (picture unavailable)
1718–1725	Jean Baptiste le Moyne, sieur de Bienville (see page 34)
1725–1726	Pierre Dugue, sieur de Boisbriant (acting) (picture unavailable)
1726–1733	Etienne de Périer (picture unavailable)
1733–1743	Jean Baptiste le Moyne, sieur de Bienville (see page 34)
1743–1753	Pierre Rigaud, Marquis de Vaudreuil (see page 54)
1753–1763	Louis Billouart de Kerlérec (see page 54)
1763–1765	Jean Jacques-Blaise Dabbadie (died in office) (picture unavailable)
1765–1769	Charles-Philippe Aubry (acting) (picture unavailable)

The Governors of Louisiana as a Spanish Colony

1766–1768	Antonio de Ulloa (did not assume full power) (see page 56)
1769	Alexander O'Reilly (military commander sent by Spain) (see page 56)
1769–1777	Luis de Unzaga (picture unavailable)
1777–1785	Bernardo de Galvez (see page 67)
1785–1791	Estevan Miro (see page 57)
1792–1797	Francisco Luis Hector, Baron de Carondelet (see page 57)
1797–1799	Manuel Luis Gayoso de Lemos (died in office)
1799	Francisco Bouligny (acting) (picture unavailable)
1799–1801	Sebastian de la Puesta y O'Farrill Marques de. Casa Calvo (picture unavailable)
1801–1803	Juan Manuel de Salcedo (picture unavailable)

The Governor of Louisiana before the Louisiana Purchase

1803	Pierre Clement de Laussat (November 30–December 20) (see page 68)

The Governor of Louisiana as a Territory

1803–1812	William Charles Cole Claiborne (see page 75)

The Governors of Louisiana as a State

1812–1816	William Charles Cole Claiborne (see page 75)
1816–1820	Jacques Philippe Villeré
1820–1824	Thomas Bolling Robertson (resigned)
1824	Henry Schuyler Thibodeaux (as president of the Senate succeeded Robertson)
1824–1828	Henry S. Johnson
1828–1829	Pierre Derbigny (died in office)
1829–1830	Armand Beauvais (as president of the Senate succeeded Derbigny) (picture unavailable)
1830–1831	Jacques Dupré (as president of the Senate succeeded Beauvais)
1831–1835	André Bienvenu Roman
1835–1839	Edward Douglass White
1839–1843	André Bienvenu Roman

1843–1846	Alexandre Mouton
1846–1850	Isaac Johnson
1850–1853	Joseph Marshall Walker
1853–1856	Paul Octave Hébert
1856–1860	Robert Charles Wickliffe
1860–1864	Thomas Overton Moore (see page 152)
1862–1864	George F. Shepley (military governor within Union lines) (see page 162)
1864–1865	Henry Watkins Allen (elected governor within Confederate lines)
1864–1865	Michael Hahn (elected governor within Union lines, resigned) (see page 162)
1865–1867	James Madison Wells (as lieutenant governor succeeded Hahn)
1867–1868	Benjamin F. Flanders (military governor)
1868	Joshua Baker (military governor)
1868–1872	Henry Clay Warmoth (impeached) (see page 185)
1872–1873	P. B. S. Pinchback (acting) (see page 185)
1873	John McEnery (elected, but counted out) (see page 185)
1873–1877	William Pitt Kellogg (de facto governor) (see page 185)
1877	Stephen B. Packard (de facto governor, ousted) (see page 185)
1877–1880	Francis Tillou Nicholls (see page 188)
1880–1881	Louis Alfred Wiltz (died in office)
1881–1884	Samuel Douglas McEnery (as lieutenant governer succeeded Wiltz)
1884–1888	Samuel Douglas McEnery
1888–1892	Francis Tillou Nicholls (see page 188)
1892–1900	Murphy J. Foster
1900–1904	William Wright Heard
1904–1908	Newton Crain Blanchard
1908–1912	Jared Young Sanders
1912–1916	Luther E. Hall
1916–1920	Ruffin G. Pleasant
1920–1924	John M. Parker
1925–1926	Henry L. Fuqua (died in office)
1926–1928	Oramel H. Simpson (as lieutenant governor succeeded Fuqua)
1928–1932	Huey P. Long (resigned to take seat in U. S. Senate)
1932	Alvin O. King (as president of the State Senate succeeded Long)
1932–1936	Oscar K. Allen (died in office)
1936	James A. Noe (as lieutenant governor succeeded Allen)
1936–1939	Richard Webster Leche (resigned)
1939–1940	Earl K. Long (as lieutenant governor succeeded Leche)
1940–1944	Sam Houston Jones
1944–1948	Jimmie H. Davis
1948–1952	Earl K. Long
1952–1956	Robert F. Kennon
1956–1960	Earl K. Long
1960–1964	Jimmie H. Davis
1964–1972	John J. McKeithen
1972–present	Edwin W. Edwards

Portraits appear on the following two pages

Cadillac

Gayoso

Villeré

Robertson

Thibodeaux

Johnson, H.

Derbigny

Dupré

Roman

White

Mouton

Johnson, I.

Walker

Hébert

Wickliffe

Allen, H.

Wells

Flanders

Baker

Wiltz

McEnery

Foster

Heard

Blanchard

Sanders

Hall

Pleasant

Parker

Fuqua

Simpson

Long, H.

King

Allen, O.

Noe

Leche

Long, E.

Jones

Davis

Kennon

McKeithen

Edwards

Bibliography

ADAMS, WILLIAM H. *The Whig Party of Louisiana.* Lafayette, La., 1973.

ALWES, BERCHTOLD C. "The History of the Louisiana State Lottery." *Louisiana Historical Quarterly* 27, no. 4 (October 1944).

ARNDT, KARL J. R. "The Genesis of Germantown Louisiana or the Mysterious Past of Louisiana's Mystic, Count de Leon." *Louisiana Historical Quarterly* 24, no. 2 (April 1941).

ARSENAULT, BONA. *History of the Acadians.* Translated in collaboration with Brian M. Upton and John G. McLaughlin. Quebec, Canada, 1966.

ASBURY, HERBERT. *The French Quarter: An Informal History of the New Orleans Underworld.* New York, 1936.

BALLOWE, HEWITT L. *Creole Folk Tales: Stories of the Louisiana Marsh Country.* Baton Rouge, 1948.

BAUDIER, ROGER. *The Catholic Church in Louisiana.* New Orleans, 1939.

BEDSOLE, VERGIL, and RICHARD, OSCAR. *Louisiana State University—A Pictorial Record of the First Hundred Years.* Baton Rouge, 1959.

BERGERIE, MAURINE. *They Tasted Bayou Water: A Brief History of Iberia Parish.* New Orleans, 1962.

BEZOU, MONSIGNOR HENRY C. *Metairie: A Tongue of Land to Pasture.* Gretna, La., 1973.

BIEVER, REVEREND ALBERT HUBERT, S.J. *The Jesuits in New Orleans and the Mississippi Valley.* New Orleans, 1924.

BOURGEOIS, LILLIAN. *Cabanocey, the History, Customs and Folklore of St. James Parish.* New Orleans, 1957.

BOYCE, SIR RUBERT W., M.B., F.R.S. *Yellow Fever and Its Prevention.* London, 1911.

BOYLE, JAMES E. *Cotton and the New Orleans Cotton Exchange.* Garden City, N.Y., 1934.

BRAGG, JEFFERSON DAVIS. *Louisiana in the Confederacy.* Baton Rouge, 1941.

BRIDAHAM, LESTER B., ed. *New Orleans and Bayou Country.* Photographs (1880–1910) by George François Mugnier. Barre, Mass., 1972.

BROOKS, CHARLES B. *The Siege of New Orleans.* Seattle, 1961.

BROWN, H. B. *A Brief Discussion of the History of Cotton, Its Culture, Breeding, Harvesting and Uses.* Rev. ed. by John S. Roussel. Baton Rouge, 1965.

BUTLER, BENJAMIN F. *The Autobiography and Personal Reminiscenses of Major-General Benjamin F. Butler.* Boston, 1892.

CABLE, GEORGE W. *Old Creole Days.* New York, 1897.

CAFFEY, H. R. *Rice.* 19th rev. ed. Baton Rouge, 1969.

CALDWELL, STEPHEN A. *A Banking History of Louisiana.* Baton Rouge, 1935.

CALHOUN, JAMES, ed., and CALHOUN, NANCY, asst. ed. *Louisiana Almanac 1973–74.* Gretna, La., 1973.

CAPERS, GERALD M. *Occupied City: New Orleans under the Federals 1862–1865.* Lexington, Ky., 1965.

CARRUTH, VIOLA. *Caddo: 1,000. A History of the Shreveport Area from the Time of the Caddo Indians to the 1970's.* Shreveport, La., 1970.

CARTER, CLARENCE E., ed. *The Territory of Orleans, 1803–1812.* The Territorial Papers of the United States, vol. 9. Washington, D.C., 1940.

CARTER, HODDING, and CARTER, BETTY WERLEIN. *So Great a Good—A History of the Episcopal Church in Louisiana and of Christ Church Cathedral, 1805–1955.* Sewanee, Tenn., 1955.

CARTER, HODDING, ed. *The Past as Prelude: New Orleans 1718–1968.* New Orleans, 1968.

CASE, GLADYS CALHOUN. *Après la Roulaison: The Story of Sugar.* Detroit, 1970.

CASEY, POWELL A. *Louisiana at the Battle of New Orleans.* New Orleans, 1965.

———. *Louisiana in the War of 1812.* Baton Rouge, 1963.

CASTELLANOS, HENRY C. *New Orleans as It Was.* New Orleans, 1895.

CAUGHEY, JOHN W. *Bernardo de Gálvez in Louisiana, 1776–1783.* Berkeley, Calif., 1934.

CHASE, JOHN C. *Frenchmen Desire Goodchildren and Other Streets of New Orleans.* New Orleans, 1949.

———. *Louisiana Purchase: An American Story Told in That Most American Form of Expression . . . The Comic Strip.* New Orleans, 1954.

CHASE, JOHN C.; DEUTSCH, HERMAN B.; DUFOUR, CHARLES L.; and HUBER, LEONARD V. *Citoyens, progrès et politique de la Nouvelle Orleans 1889–1964.* New Orleans, 1964.

CHRISTIAN, MARCUS. *Negro Soldiers in the Battle of New Orleans.* New Orleans, 1965.

———. *Negro Ironworkers in Louisiana 1718–1900.* Gretna, La., 1972.

CHRISTOVICH, MARY LOUISE; TOLEDANO, ROULHAC; SWANSON, BETSY; and HOLDEN, PAT. *The American Sector (Faubourg St. Mary).* New Orleans Architecture, vol. 2. Essays by Samuel Wilson, Jr., and Bernard Lemann. Gretna, La., 1972.

CLAPP, THEODORE. *Autobiographical Sketches and Recollections during a Thirty-five Years' Residence in New Orleans.* Boston, 1857.

CLEMENS, SAMUEL LANGHORNE [Mark Twain]. *Life on the Mississippi.* Boston, 1883.

CLEMENT, WILLIAM E., and LANDRY, STUART OMER. *Plantation Life on the Mississippi.* New Orleans, 1952.

COCHRAN, ESTELLE M. FORTIER. *The Fortier Family and Allied Families.* Privately printed, 1963.

Code of Honor, Its Rationale and Uses by the Tests of Common Sense and Good Morals with the Effects of Its Preventive Remedies, The. New Orleans, 1883.

COOLEY, ESTHER. *Come Aboard the Steamer America.* Baton Rouge, 1962.

CORLISS, CARLTON J. *Main Line of Mid-America: The Story of the Illinois Central.* New York, 1950.

CROUSE, NELLIS M. *Lemoyne d'Iberville: Soldier of New France.* Ithaca, N.Y., 1954.

CRUISE, BOYD. *Index of the Louisiana Historical Quarterly.* New Orleans, 1956.

CURTIS, NATHANIEL CORTLAND. *New Orleans: Its Old Houses, Shops and Public Buildings.* Philadelphia, 1933.

DABNEY, THOMAS EWING. *One Hundred Years: The Story of the Times Picayune from Its Founding to 1940.* Baton Rouge, 1944.

DAVIS, EDWIN ADAMS. *Louisiana: A Narrative History.* Baton Rouge, 1965.

———, ed. *The Rivers and Bayous of Louisiana.* Baton Rouge, 1968.

DAVIS, JEFFERSON. *The Rise and Fall of the Confederate Government.* 2 vols. New York, 1881.

DEILER, J. HANNO. *Die Deutschen Kirchengemeinden im Staate Louisiana.* New Orleans, 1894.

———. *The Settlement of the German Coast of Louisiana and the Creoles of German Descent.* Philadelphia, 1909.

DESDUNES, RODOLPHE LUCIEN. *Our People and Our History.* Translated and edited by Sister Dorothea Olga McCants, Daughter of the Cross. Baton Rouge, 1972.

Detroit Institute of Arts. *The French in America, 1520–1880.* Detroit, 1951.

DEUTSCH, HERRMANN B. *The Huey Long Murder Case.* Garden City, N.Y., 1963.

DEVOL, GEORGE H. *Forty Years a Gambler on the Mississippi.* 2nd ed. New York, 1926.

DIBBLE, ERNEST F., and NEWTON, EARL W., eds. *Spain and Her Rivals on the Gulf Coast.* Pensacola, Fla., 1971.

DICKSON, HARRIS. *The Story of King Cotton.* New York and London, 1937.

DIXON, RICHARD R. *The Battle on the West Bank.* New Orleans, 1965.

DORSEY, FLORENCE L. *Master of the Mississippi: Henry Shreve and the Conquest of the Mississippi.* Boston, 1941.

DOWLER, DR. BENNET. *Researches upon the Necropolis of New Orleans, with Brief Allusions to Its Vital Arithmetic.* New Orleans, 1850.

DUFFY, JOHN. *The Rudolph Matas History of Medicine in Louisiana.* 2 vols. Baton Rouge, 1958 and 1962.

———. *Sword of Pestilence: The New Orleans Yellow Fever Epidemic of 1853.* Baton Rouge, 1966.

DUFOUR, CHARLES L. *The Night the War Was Lost.* New York, 1960.

———. *Ten Flags in the Wind: The Story of Louisiana.* New York, 1967.

———, ed. *St. Patrick's of New Orleans 1833–1958: Commemorative Essays for the 125th Anniversary.* New Orleans, 1958.

DUFOUR, CHARLES L., and HUBER, LEONARD V. *If Ever I Cease to Love: One Hundred Years of Rex, 1872–1971.* New Orleans, 1970.

———, eds. *Battle of New Orleans Sesquicentennial Historical Booklets.* 9 booklets. New Orleans, 1965.

DU PRATZ, ANTOINE SIMON LE PAGE. *The History of Louisiana.* 3 vols. Paris, 1758.

DYER, JOHN P. *Tulane: The Biography of a University, 1834–1965.* New York, 1966.

EADS, JAMES BUCHANAN. *Mouth of the Mississippi Jetty System Explained.* St. Louis, 1874.

ELLER, ADMIRAL E. M.; MORGAN, DR. W. J.; and BASOCO, LIEUT. R. R. *Sea Power and the Battle of New Orleans.* New Orleans, 1965.

ESKEW, GARNETT LAIDLAW. *The Pageant of the Packets: A Book of American Steamboating.* New York, 1929.

FICKLEN, JOHN R. *History of Reconstruction in Louisiana (through 1868).* Baltimore, 1910.

FORTENBERRY, W. H. *The Story of Cotton.* Marketing Bulletin no. 37, United States Department of Agriculture. Washington, D.C., 1967.

FORTIER, ALCÉE. *A History of Louisiana.* 4 vols. New York, 1904.

FOSSIER, ALBERT E. *New Orleans: The Glamour Period 1800–1840.* New Orleans, 1957.

FREMAUX, LEON J. *New Orleans Characters.* New Orleans, 1876.

Friends of the Cabildo *Louisiana Indians: 12,000 Years.* Catalog of exhibition held at the Presbytere. Louisiana State Museum. New Orleans, 1966.

GAYARRÉ, CHARLES. *History of Louisiana.* 4 vols. 5th ed. New Orleans, 1965.

GIBSON, JOHN. "Historical Epitome." In *Gibson's Guide and Directory of the State of Louisiana and the Cities of New Orleans and Lafayette.* New Orleans, 1838.

GIRAUD, MARCEL. *Histoire de la Louisiane Française.* 3 vols. Paris, 1953, 1958, 1965.

GLEIG, GEORGE ROBERT. *The Campaign of the British Army at Washington and New Orleans in the Years 1814–1815.* London, 1836.

GOTTSCHALK, LOUIS MOREAU. *Notes of a Pianist.* Edited by Jeanne Behrend. New York, 1964.

GOULD, CAPTAIN E. W. *Fifty Years on the Mississippi or Gould's History of River Navigaton.* St. Louis, 1889.

GREEN, THOMAS MARSHALL. *The Spanish Conspiracy. A Review of Early Spanish Movements in the South-West.* 2nd ed. Gloucester, Mass., 1967.

HAMILTON, PETER J. *Colonial Mobile: An Historical Study.* Rev. ed. Mobile, 1962.

HERR, KINCAID A. *Louisville & Nashville Railroad, 1850–1963.* Louisville, Ky., 1964.

HIGGINBOTHAM, JAY. *Fort Maurepas: The Birth of Louisiana.* Mobile, 1968.

————, trans. and ed. *The Journal of Sauvole, Historical Journal of the Establishment of the French in Louisiana.* Mobile, 1969.

HOLMES, JACK D. L. *Gayoso: The Life of a Spanish Governor in the Mississippi Valley, 1789–1799.* Baton Rouge, 1965.

————. *A Guide to Spanish Louisiana.* New Orleans, 1970.

HUBER, LEONARD V. *Advertisements of Lower Mississippi River Steamboats, 1812–1920.* West Barrington, R.I., 1959.

————. "The Battle of the Handkerchiefs." *Civil War History* 8, no. 1 (March 1962).

————. "The Golden Age of Opera, Theatre and the Performing Arts." *New Orleans Magazine* 3, no. 12 (September 1969).

————. "Heyday of the Floating Palace." *American Heritage* 8, no. 6 (October 1957).

————. *Impressions of Girod Street Cemetery and a Plan to Rescue Some of Its Moments.* New Orleans, 1951.

————. "Mardi Gras: The Golden Age." *American Heritage* 16, no. 2 (February 1965).

————. *New Orleans as It Was in 1814–1815.* New Orleans, 1965.

————. *Notable New Orleans Landmarks.* New Orleans, 1974.

HUBER, LEONARD V., and BERNARD, GUY F. *To Glorious Immortality: The Rise and Fall of the Girod Street Cemetery.* New Orleans, 1961.

HUBER, LEONARD V., and HUBER, ALBERT R. *The New Orleans Tomb.* New Orleans, 1956.

HUBER, LEONARD V.; McDOWELL, PEGGY; and CHRISTOVICH, MARY LOUISE. *The Cemeteries.* Edited by Mary Louise Christovich. New Orleans Architecture, vol. 3. Gretna, La. 1974.

HUBER, LEONARD V., and WAGNER, CLARENCE. *The Great Mail: A Postal History of New Orleans.* State College, Pa., 1949.

HUBER, LEONARD V., and WILSON, SAMUEL, JR. *Baroness Pontalba's Buildings.* New Orleans, 1964.

HUBER, LEONARD V.; WILSON, SAMUEL, JR.; and TAYLOR, GARLAND F. *Louisiana Purchase.* New Orleans, 1953.

HUNTER, LOUIS C. *Steamboats on the Western Rivers: An Economic and Technological History.* Cambridge, 1939.

INGRAHAM, JOSEPH HOLT. *The South-West by a Yankee.* New York, 1835.

JACKSON, JOY J. *New Orleans in the Gilded Age: Politics and Urban Progress, 1880–1896.* Baton Rouge, 1969.

JACOBS, JAMES RIPLEY. *Tarnished Warrior: Major-General James Wilkinson.* New York, 1938.

JEWELL, EDWIN L., ed. *Jewell's Crescent City Illustrated: The Commercial, Social, Political and General History of New Orleans, Including Biographical Sketches of Its Distinguished Citizens.* New Orleans, 1874.

KANE, HARNETT T. *Louisiana Hayride: The American Rehearsal for Dictatorship, 1928–1940.* New York, 1941.

KENDALL, JOHN SMITH. *Golden Age of the New Orleans Theatre.* Baton Rouge, 1952.

————. *History of New Orleans.* 3 vols. Chicago, 1922.

KEYES, FRANCES PARKINSON. *All This Is Louisiana.* New York, 1950.

KING, GRACE. *New Orleans: The Place and the People.* New York, 1904.

KMEN, HENRY A. *Music in New Orleans: The Formative Years, 1791–1841.* Baton Rouge, 1966.

KORN, BERTRAM WALLACE. *Benjamin Levy: New Orleans Printer and Publisher.* Portland, Me., 1961.

————. *The Early Jews of New Orleans.* Waltham, Mass., 1969.

KROUSE, RITA MOORE. *Fragments of a Dream.* Ruston, La., 1962.

LaCOUR, ARTHUR BURTON, and LANDRY, STUART OMER. *New Orleans Masquerade.* New Orleans, 1952.

LANDRY, STUART O. *The Battle of Liberty Place: The Overthrow of Carpet-Bag Rule in New Orleans—September 14, 1874.* New Orleans, 1955.

LATOUR, A. LaCARRIERE. *Historical Memoir of the War in West Florida and Louisiana in 1814–1815.* Philadelphia, 1816, and Gainesville, Fla., 1964.

LATROBE, J. H. B. *The First Steamboat Voyage on the Western Waters.* Baltimore, 1871.

LAUGHLIN, CLARENCE, and COHN, DAVID L. *New Orleans and Its Living Past.* Boston, 1941.

LAUSSAT, PIERRE-CLÉMENT DE. *Mémoires sur ma vie à mon fils pendant les années 1803 et suivantes. . . .* Pau, France, 1831.

LeBLANC, DUDLEY J. *The Acadian Miracle.* Lafayette, La., 1966.

LE CONTE, RENÉ. "The Germans in Louisiana in the Eighteenth Century." Translated and edited by Glenn R. Conrad. *Louisiana History* 8, no. 1 (Winter 1967).

LE GARDEUR, RENÉ J., JR. *The First New Orleans Theatre: 1792–1803.* New Orleans, 1963.

LEVASSEUR, A. *Lafayette in America in 1824 and 1825 or Journal of Travels in the United States.* New York, 1829.

LIEBLING, A. J. *The Earl of Louisiana.* Baton Rouge, 1970.

LLOYD, JAMES T. *Lloyd's Steamboat Directory and Disasters on the Western Waters.* Cincinnati, 1856.

LONG, E. B., and LONG, BARBARA. *The Civil War Day by Day: An Almanac.* New York, 1971.

LONG, EDITH ELLIOT. *Madame Olivier's Mansion: 828 Toulouse.* New Orleans, 1965.

LONG, HUEY P. *Every Man a King—The Autobiography of Huey.* New Orleans, 1933.

LONGINO, LUTHER, M. D. *Thoughts, Visions and Sketches of North Louisiana.* N.p. [1930].

LONN, ELLA. *Reconstruction in Louisiana after 1868.* 2nd ed. Gloucester, Mass., 1967.

LYON, E. WILSON. *The Man Who Sold Louisiana.* Norman, Okla., 1942.

MARTIN, FRANÇOIS-XAVIER. *The History of Louisiana.* New Orleans, 1827–1829.

MAYO, H. M. *Mme. Bégué and Her Recipes.* Chicago, 1900.

MCCAUGHAN, RICHARD B. *Socks on a Rooster, Louisiana's Earl K. Long.* Baton Rouge, 1967.

MCDERMOTT, JOHN FRANCIS, ed. *The French in the Mississippi Valley.* Urbana, Ill., 1965.

————, ed. *Frenchmen and French Ways in the Mississippi Valley.* Urbana, Ill., 1969.

MCLAUGHLIN, JAMES J. *The Jack Lafaience Book.* New Orleans, 1922.

MCMURTRIE, DOUGLAS C. *Early Printing in New Orleans 1764–1810 with a Bibliography of the Issues of the Press.* New Orleans, 1929.

MCWILLIAMS, RICHEBOURG GAILLARD. *Fleur de Lys and Calumet.* Baton Rouge, 1953.

MEADE, GEORGE P. "A Negro Scientist of Slavery Days." *Scientific Monthly* (April 1946).

————. *Sugar: Its Importance in Food Processing History.* Privately printed, Savannah, Ga., 1959.

MORRISON, JOHN H. *History of American Steam Navigation.* New York, 1903.

NAU, JOHN F. *The German People of New Orleans, 1850–1900.* Leiden, 1958.

New Orleans City Guide. Federal Writers' Project of the Works Progress Administration for the City of New Orleans. Boston, 1938.

NIEHAUS, EARL F. *The Irish in New Orleans, 1800–1860.* Baton Rouge, 1965.

NOLTE, VINCENT. *Fifty Years in Both Hemispheres.* New York, 1854.

NORMAN, N. PHILIP. "The Red River of the South." *Louisiana Historical Quarterly* 25, no. 2. (April 1942).

OUDARD, GEORGE. *Four Cents an Acre.* Translated by Margery Bianco. New York, 1931.

OWEN, WILLIAM MILLER. *In Camp and Battle with the Washington Artillery of New Orleans.* Boston, 1885.

PARKMAN, FRANCIS. *La Salle and the Discovery of the Great West.* Edited by John A. Hawgood. New York, 1962.

PARTON, JAMES. *General Butler in New Orleans.* New York, 1864.

PHARES, ROSS. *Cavalier in the Wilderness.* Baton Rouge, 1952.

Picayune's Guide to New Orleans. 6th ed. New Orleans, 1904.

PIPES, FORT. *The Year Book of the Louisiana Sugar Cane Industry, 1939.* New Orleans, 1940.

PITOT, HENRY CLEMENT. *James Pitot (1761–1831): A Documentary Study.* New Orleans, 1968.

POESCH, JESSIE J. *Early Furniture of Louisiana, 1750–1830.* New Orleans, 1972.

POST, DR. LAUREN C. *Cajun Sketches from the Prairies of Southwest Louisiana.* Baton Rouge, 1962.

QUAGLIA. *Le Père Lachaise ou recueil de dessins aux traits et dans leurs justes proportions des principaux monuments de ce cimetière. . . .* Paris, 1828.

QUICK, HERBERT, and QUICK, EDWARD. *Mississippi Steamboatin': A History of Steamboating on the Mississippi and Its Tributaries. . . .* New York, 1926.

RAMSEY, CAROLYN. *Cajuns on the Bayous.* New York, 1957.

READ, WILLIAM A. *Louisiana–French.* Rev. ed. Baton Rouge, 1963.

————. *Louisiana Place-Names of Indian Origin.* University Bulletin, Louisiana State University and Agricultural and Mechanical College, vol. 19 n.s., no. 2 (February 1927). Baton Rouge.

REED, MERL E. *New Orleans and the Railroads: The Struggle for Commercial Empire 1830–1860.* Baton Rouge, 1966.

REEVES, MIRIAM G. *The Governors of Louisiana.* New Orleans, 1962.

————. *The Governors of Louisiana.* Gretna, La., 1972.

REINDERS, ROBERT C. *End of an Era: New Orleans, 1850–1860.* New Orleans, 1964.

RIPLEY, ELIZA. *Social Life in Old New Orleans, Being Recollections of My Girlhood.* New York, 1912.

ROBIN, CLAUDE C. *Voyage to the Interior of Louisiana, 1802–1806.* Translated by Stuart O. Landry, Jr. New Orleans, 1966.

ROBINSON, WILLIAM L. *Diary of a Samaritan.* New York, 1860.

ROUSSEVE, CHARLES B. *The Negro in New Orleans.* New Orleans, 1969.

RUSSELL, RICHARD JOEL, and HOWE, HENRY V. *Lower Mississippi River Delta.* Reports on the geology of Plaquemines and St. Bernard Parishes.

336

Louisiana Department of Conservation. New Orleans, 1936.

SALA, GEORGE AUGUSTUS. *America Revisited.* London, 1886.

SAMUEL, RAY. *The Great Days of the Garden District and the Old City of Lafayette.* New Orleans, 1961.

———. *. . . . to a Point called Chef Menteur.* New Orleans, 1959.

SAMUEL, RAY; HUBER, LEONARD V.; and OGDEN, WARREN C. *Tales of the Mississippi.* New York, 1955.

SAMUEL, RAY, and SAMUEL, MARTHA ANN. *The Uptown River Corner: The Story of Royal and Bienville.* New Orleans, 1964.

SAXON, LYLE. *Fabulous New Orleans.* New York, 1928.

———. *Old Louisiana.* New York, 1929.

SAXON, LYLE; DREYER, EDWARD; and TALLANT, ROBERT. *Gumbo YaYa.* Boston, 1945.

SCOTT, VAL MCNAIR [Lady Pakenham]. *Major-General Sir Edward Pakenham.* New Orleans, 1965.

SCULLY, ARTHUR, JR. *James Dakin, Architect: His Career in New York and the South.* Baton Rouge, La., 1973.

SHORES, J. B. *From Ox-teams to Eagles, a History of the Texas and Pacific Railway.* N.p., n.d.

SINCLAIR, HAROLD. *The Port of New Orleans.* Garden City, N.Y., 1942.

SOMDAL, DEWEY A. "A Century of Steamboating on Red River to Shreveport and the Coming of the Railroads." *Louisiana Historical Quarterly* 18, no. 4 (October 1935).

SOMERS, DALE A. *The Rise of Sports in New Orleans 1850–1900.* Baton Rouge, 1972.

STODDARD, T. LOTHROP. *The French Revolution in San Domingo.* Boston and New York, 1914.

TALLANT, ROBERT. *Voodoo in New Orleans.* New York, 1946.

TEXADA, DAVID KER. *Alexandre O'Reilly and the New Orleans Rebels.* Lafayette, La., 1970.

THOMAS, MAURICE. *The Story of Louisiana.* Boston, 1888.

TINKER. EDWARD LAROCQUE. *Creole City: Its Past and Its People.* New York, 1953.

———. *Lafcadio Hearn's American Days.* New York, 1924.

———. *Louisiana's Earliest Poet.* New York, 1933.

TROLLOPE, FRANCES. *Domestic Manners of the Americans: With a History of Mrs. Trollope's Adventures in America.* Edited by Donald Smalley. New York, 1949.

TROVAIOLI, AUGUST P., and TOLEDANO, ROULHAC B. *William Aiken Walker, Southern Genre Painter.* Baton Rouge, 1972.

VILLIERS DU TERRAGE, BARON MARC DE. *Les Dernières Années de la Louisiane.* Paris, 1904.

VOORHIES, FELIX. *Acadian Reminiscences with the True Story of Evangeline.* Opelousas, La., 1907.

VOSS, REVEREND LOUIS. *Presbyterianism in New Orleans and Adjacent Points.* New Orleans, 1931.

WALDO, J. CURTIS. *History of the Carnival in New Orleans from 1857 to 1882.* New Orleans, 1882.

WARMOTH, HENRY CLAY. *War, Politics and Reconstruction: Stormy Days in Louisiana.* New York, 1930.

WEBB, CLARENCE H. *The Story of Poverty Point.* N.p., n.d.

WHITAKER, ARTHUR PRESTON. *The Mississippi Question, 1795–1803: A Study in Trade, Politics and Diplomacy.* New York, 1934.

———. *The Spanish-American Frontier: 1783–1795: The Westward Movement and the Spanish Retreat in the Mississippi Valley.* 2nd ed. Gloucester, Mass., 1962.

WIESENDANGER, MARTIN, and, WIESENDANGER, MARGARET. *19th Century Louisiana Painters and Painting.* New Orleans, 1971.

WILLIAMS, T. HARRY. *P. G. T. Beauregard: Napoleon in Gray.* Baton Rouge, 1954.

———. *Huey Long.* New York, 1969.

WILSON, NEILL C., and TAYLOR, FRANK J. *Southern Pacific: The Roaring Story of a Fighting Railroad.* New York, 1952.

WILSON, SAMUEL, JR. "Almonester, Philanthropist and Builder in New Orleans." In *The Spanish in the Mississippi Valley 1762–1804.* Edited by John Francis McDermott. Urbana, Ill., 1974.

———. "An Architectural History of the Royal Hospital and the Ursuline Convent of New Orleans." *The Louisiana Historical Quarterly* 29, no. 3 (July 1948).

———. *The Capuchin School in New Orleans, 1725.* New Orleans, 1961.

———. "Colonial Fortifications and Military Architecture in the Mississippi Valley." In *The French in the Mississippi Valley.* Edited by John Francis McDermott. Urbana, Ill., 1965.

———. *A Guide to Architecture of New Orleans, 1699–1959.* New York, 1959.

———. "Gulf Coast Architecture." In *Spain and Her Rivals on the Gulf Coast.* Edited by Ernest F. Dibble and Earle W. Newton. Pensacola, Fla., 1971.

———. "Ignace François Broutin." In *Frenchmen and French Ways in the Mississippi Valley.* Edited by John Francis McDermott. Chicago, 1969.

———. "Louisiana Drawings of Alexander DeBatz." *Journal of the Society of Architectural Historians* 22, no. 2 (May 1963).

———. *Old New Orleans Houses.* 30 monographs in *The New Orleans States* (February 7 to November 14, 1953).

———. *Plantation Houses on the Battlefield of New Orleans.* New Orleans, 1965.

———. *The Vieux Carré New Orleans: Its Plan, Its Growth, Its Architecture.* Washington, D.C., 1968.

WILSON, SAMUEL, JR., ed. *Impressions Respecting New Orleans by Benjamin Henry Boneval Latrobe, Diary & Sketches 1818–20.* New York, 1951.

———. *Religious Architecture in French Colonial*

Louisiana. From Winterthur Portfolio 8. Charlottesville, Va., 1973.

WILSON, SAMUEL, JR., and HUBER, LEONARD V. *The Basilica on Jackson Square and Its Predecessors 1727–1965.* New Orleans, 1965.

WILSON, SAMUEL JR.; HUBER, LEONARD V.; and GORIN, ABBEY A. *The St. Louis Cemeteries of New Orleans.* New Orleans, 1963.

WILSON, SAMUEL, JR., and LEMANN, BERNARD. *The Lower Garden District.* Compiled and edited by Mary Louise Christovich, Roulhac Toledano, and Betsy Swanson. New Orleans Architecture, vol. 1. Gretna, La., 1971.

————. *The Cabildo on Jackson Square.* New Orleans, 1970.

WINTERS, JOHN D. *The Civil War in Louisiana.* Baton Rouge, 1963.

Writers' Program. *Louisiana, A Guide to the State.* New York, 1945.

YOUNG, PERRY. *The Mistick Krewe: Chronicles of Comus and His Kin.* New Orleans, 1931.

New Orleans Newspapers

L'Abeille
The Bulletin
Clarion Herald
The Courier
The Daily Democrat
The Daily Item
The Daily Picayune
The Daily States
The Daily Times
The Delta
Le Carillon
The Louisiana Gazette
Le Louisianais, St. James, Louisiana
The Mascot
L'Omnibus
The Orleanian

The States-Item
Sunday Sun
The Times-Democrat
The Times-Picayune
The True American
The True Delta

Periodicals

Ballou's Pictorial Drawing Room Companion
The Century Magazine
The Daily Graphic (New York)
Emerson's Magazine and Putnam's Monthly
Every Saturday (Boston)
Frank Leslie's Illustrated Newspaper
Gleason's Pictorial Drawing Room Companion
Harper's Weekly
Illustrated London News
Le Monde Illustré (Paris)
New Orleans City Directories, 1823–1969
New York Illustrated News
Scientific American
Scribner's Magazine
Waterways Journal

Miscellaneous Sources

Archives Nationales, Paris
Archivo General de Indias, Seville
Spanish Judicial Records in the Louisiana State Museum
Museo National de Historia, Mexico City
Miscellaneous Documents, Manuscripts Division, Library of Congress, Washington, D.C.
Records of the Deliberations of the Cabildo (1769–1803)
Mayor's Messages to Municipality No. 1 (1804–1853)
New Orleans City Council Minutes and Resolutions

Picture Credits

Here is a list of abbreviations used in the picture credits:

BN: Bibliothèque Nationale, Paris
CSS: Charles Scribner's Sons art files
HTML: Special Collections Division, Howard-Tilton Memorial Library, Tulane University, New Orleans
LC: Library of Congress
LSU: Louisiana State University, Baton Rouge
NOPL: Louisiana Division, New Orleans Public Library
NYPL: New York Public Library

26–27 1–4. Photograph by Don Nugent. School of Geoscience, LSU. 5. School of Geoscience, LSU. 6. Photograph by Don Nugent. School of Geoscience, LSU. 28–29 1. *Relations de la Louisiane et du Fleuve Mississippi* chez Jean Frederick Bernard, Amsterdam, 1720. HTML. 2. *History of Louisiana* by Le Page Du Pratz, 1758. 3. Sketch by James E. Taylor. Probably from *Harper's Weekly,* ca. 1866. 4. *History of Louisiana* by Le Page Du Pratz, 1758. 5. United States Department of Agriculture. 6. *Moeurs des Sauvages Amériquains comparées des premiers Temps* by Joseph François Lafitau, 1724. 30–31 1. *Relations de la Louisiane et du Fleuve Mississippi* chez Jean Frederick Bernard, Amsterdam, 1720. HTML. 2,3. Smithsonian Institution Press, *Drawings by A. DeBatz in Louisiana, 1732–1735* by David I. Bushnell, Jr., Smithsonian Miscellaneous Collection, Vol. 80, No. 5, 1928. 4. HTML. 5. *Relations de la Louisiane et du Fleuve Mississippi* chez Jean Frederick Bernard, Amsterdam, 1720. HTML. 6. Copper engraving from *Northern America,* 18th century. Collection of the author. 32–33 1. From a painting by W. H. Powell. Lithograph by A. Lemoine, 1850. Collection of the author. 2. Artist unknown. Bibliothèque Municipale de Rouen. 3. Attributed to Nicholas Maes, ca. 1674–1678. Museum of the City of Mobile, Ala. 4. Painting by Robert Nanteuil. Musée Condé, Chantilly, France. 5. Artist unknown. HTML. 6. *Extrait de la Carte des Voyages de M. de la Salle par Franquelin, 1684,* in *De la Salle et ses Relations Inédites de la Découverte du Mississippi (Extrait de la Géologie Pratique de la Louisiane),* Paris, 1859. LC. 34–35 1,2. Collection of the Compte Le Moyne de Martigny, Paris. 3. Museum of the City of Mobile, Ala. 4. Collection of the Compte Le Moyne de Martigny, Paris. 5. *Histoire de L'Amérique Septentrional* by B. de la Potherie, N. D., 18th century. 6. BN. Photograph courtesy of Henry Pitot. 36–37 1. Courtesy of Gallier Hall, New Orleans. 2,3. BN. 4. Courtesy of the Louisiana State Museum. 5. Archives Nationales, Section Outre-Mer, Paris. 6. BN. 7. Map by H. Moll, 1714. Collection of Henry Pitot. 38–39 1.

Engraving by Leon Schenck, Paris, 1720. Collection of the author. 2. *Lettres Patentes en Forme d'Edit, Portant Establissement d'une Compagnie de Commerce, sous le nom Compagnie d'Occident* (1717). Historic New Orleans Collection. 3. Detail from a map of Louisiana on the Mississippi River, 1719. LC. 4. Artist unknown. Collection of Henry Pitot. 5. Museum of the City of Mobile, Ala. 6. Engraving by Bernard Picart, 1720. *Hetgroote Tafereel Der Dwaasheid vertoonende de opkomst, voortgang en ondergang or actil, bubbel en windnegotie, in Vrankryk, Engeland en de Nederlanden gepleegt in den jare MDCCXX* (Amsterdam), 1720. HTML. 40–41 1. Historic New Orleans Collection. 2. *The Settlement of the German Coast of Louisiana and the Creoles of German Descent* by J. Friedrich Gleditschen's seel. Sohn, 1720, Leipsic. Manuscripts and Rare Books Department, Howard-Tilton Memorial Library, Tulane University, New Orleans. 3. Engraving by Jean Baptiste Le Buteux, 1920. E. E. Ayer Collection, The Newberry Library, Chicago. 4. Historic New Orleans Collection. 42–43 1. Cartouche sketch from map "Nouvelle de la Partie de Ouest de la Province de la Louisiane, sur les Observations et decouvertes du Sieur Bernard de la Harpe" by de Beuvilliers, 1720. HTML. 2. Detail of watercolor by Jean Pierre Lassus. Archives Nationales, Section Outre-Mer, Paris. 3. Archives Nationales, Section Outre-Mer, Paris. 4. BN. 5. Archives Nationales, Section Outre-Mer, Paris. 44–45 1–3. Archives Nationales, Section Outre-Mer, Paris. 4,5. Dépôt des Fortifications des Colonies—*Atlas Moreau de Saint Méry,* Archives Nationales, Paris. 6. Photograph by Richard Relf. Collection of the author. 46–47 1. Plan by Ignace Francois Broutin, November 10, 1745. Archives Nationales, Section Outre-Mer, Paris. 2. LC. 3,4. Ursuline Academy, New Orleans. 5. Plans by Adrien de Pauger, May 29, 1724. Archives Nationales, Section Outre-Mer, Paris. 6,7. Ursuline Academy, New Orleans. 8. Church of St. Martin, St. Martinville, La. Courtesy of the Louisiana State Museum. 48–49 1. United States Department of Agriculture, Agricultural Stabilization and Conservation Service. 2. Courtesy of Louisiana State Parks and Recreation Commission and Koch and Wilson, Architects. 3. BN. 4. NOPL. 5. Collection of Ruth Robertson Fontenot, Opelousas, La. 6. Photograph by Ruth Robertson Fontenot. 7. *Les Dernières Années de la Louisiane Française* by Baron Marc de Villiers du Terrage, Paris, 1903. 8. Plan by Adrien de Pauger, May 29, 1724. Archives Nationales, Section Outre-Mer, Paris. 9. Archives Nationales, Section Outre-Mer, Paris. 50–51 1,2. Photograph by Betsy Swanson. Hermitage Louisiana Collection. 3. Photograph by Betsy Swanson. Collection of Mr. Thomas Edward Smith, Hammond, La. 4. Photograph by Betsy Swanson. Hermitage Louisiana Collection. 5,6. Photograph by Betsy Swanson. Collection of Dr. Ambrose Howell Storck, New Orleans. 7. Photograph by Betsy Swanson. Collection of Mr. Hugh Allison Smith, Hammond, La. 52–53 1. Smithsonian Institution Press, *Drawings by A. DeBatz in Louisiana, 1732–1735* by David I. Bushnell, Jr., Smithsonian Miscellaneous Collection, Vol. 80, No. 5, 1928. 2. Lithograph by Oursel. *Cabinet des Estampes,* BN. Photograph courtesy of Henry Pitot. 3. HTML. 4. Artist unknown, ca. 1797. Courtesy of the Louisiana State Museum. 54–55 1. Painting by Louis Michel Van Loo. Reproduced by permission of the Trustees of the Wallace Collection. 2–5. *Les Dernières Années de la Louisiane Française* by Baron Marc de Villiers du Terrage, Paris, 1903. 6. LC. 7. Source unknown. Photograph courtesy of Henry Pitot. 8. Courtesy of the Louisiana State Museum. 56–57 1. Museo Naval, Madrid. 2. *Early Printing in New Orleans 1764–1810* by Douglas C. McMurtrie, New Orleans, 1929. 3. Courtesy of the Louisiana State Museum. 4. *Les Dernières Années de la Louisiane Française* by Baron Marc de Villiers du Terrage, Paris, 1903. 5. *The History of Louisiana* by Alcee Fortier, 1904. 6. Courtesy of Comtesse Paul de Leusse. 7. Historic New Orleans Collection. 8. *Early Printing in New Orleans 1764–1810* by Douglas C. McMurtrie, New Orleans, 1929. 58–59 1. Photograph by Jack Beech. Collection of the author. 2. Plan by Juan M. Perchet. Photograph courtesy of James C. Massey. Archivo General de Simancas, Simancas, Valladolid, Spain. 3. HTML. 4. Plan by Barthelemy Lafou, 1795. Courtesy of the Louisiana State Museum. 5. Artist unknown. Archdiocese of New Orleans. 6. Painted and engraved by Edmund Brewster. Courtesy of Monsignor Henry C. Bezou. 7. Facsimile reproduction of a copy since destroyed; illustrated in the *Publications of the Louisiana Historical Society,* Vol. 1, Part IV, 1896. 60–61 1. Historic New Orleans Collection. 2. Artist unknown, ca. 1798. Courtesy of the Louisiana State Museum. 3. Artist unknown, ca. 1795. Courtesy of the Louisiana State Museum. 4. Portrait by José de Salazar. Archdiocese of New Orleans. 5. Portrait in Colomb family collection. Courtesy of Sidney L. Villeré. 6. Artist unknown, ca. 1790. Courtesy of the author. 62–63 1,2. Photograph by Howard Coleman. Thelma Hecht Coleman Collection. 3. HTML. 4. Photographer unknown. Collection of the author. 64–65 Collection of Mrs. Warren M. Faris. 66–67 1. *Gentlemen's Magazine,* London, 1772. 2. LC. 3. Courtesy of Antonio Perez Elias, Chief of the Department of Disclosure and Cultural Promotion of the National Institute of Anthropology and History, Mexico City. 68–69 1. Portrait by Jean-François-Gille Colson (1786). HTML. 2. Courtesy of the Louisiana State Museum. 3. *Les Dernières Années de la Louisiane Française* by Baron Marc de Villiers du Terrage, Paris, 1903. 4. BN. 5. Muséum du Havre, France. 70–71 1. Portrait by Rembrandt Peale, 1800. White House Collection. 2. Portrait by Gilbert Stuart, 1817. The Metropolitan Museum of Art, Bequest of Seth Low, 1929. 3. Engraving by E. McKenzie from painting by J. Vanderlyn. Collection of the author. 4. Engraving by W. H. Mote. Picture collection, NYPL. 5. Lithograph by Delpech. Collection of the author. 6. Treaty Series 86, General Records of the United States Government (Record Group 11), National Archives. 7. Sculpture by Chauvet. Courtesy of the Louisiana State Museum. 72–73 Historic New Orleans

Collection. 74–75 1. Plan by J. L. Bouqueto de Woieseri (1803). Courtesy of the Louisiana State Museum. 2. Plan by J. Pilié, ca. 1820. Courtesy of the Louisiana State Museum. 3. Engraving by Charles B. J. Fevret de Saint-Memin, 1798. LC. 4. Louisiana Room, LSU Library. 5. Engraved by Wellmore from drawing by J. B. Longacre. Photograph in the collection of the author. 76–77 1. From a watercolor drawing by Charles Turner Warren. The Mariners Museum, Newport News, Va. 2. *Lloyd's Steamboat Directory and Disasters on the Western Waters* by James T. Lloyd (Cincinnati, 1856). 3. Maps, Manuscripts and Archives Division, NYPL, Astor, Lenox and Tilden Foundations. 4. Drawing by United States Engineers Department, Topographical Bureau, 1817. National Archives. 5. Maps, Manuscripts and Archives Division, NYPL, Astor, Lenox and Tilden Foundations. 6. Portrait by Ralph E. W. Earle. Brooks Memorial Art Gallery, Memphis, Tenn. 7. Engraving after a portrait by Thomas Heaphy, 1816. Source unknown. Photograph in the collection of the author. 78–79 1. Courtesy of the New York Historical Society. 2. CSS. 3. Lithograph by Case & Green, Hartford, Conn., from painting by Hyacinthe Laclotte, 1815. Collection of the author. 4. Photograph by W. Woodbridge Williams. Printed by permission of United States Department of the Interior, National Parks Service. 5. Photograph by George A. Grant. Printed by permission of United States Department of the Interior, National Parks Service. 6. Engraving by W. Ridgeway from painting by F. O. C. Darley. Collection of the author. 7. I. N. Phelps Stokes Collection. Prints Division, NYPL, Astor, Lenox and Tilden Foundations. 80–81 1. Map by Jacques Tanesse (1817). I. N. Phelps Stokes Collection, Prints Division, NYPL, Astor, Lenox and Tilden Foundations. 2. Painting by Ambroise Louis Garneray, ca. 1820. Historic New Orleans Collection. 3. City of New Orleans. 4. Painting by John Wesley Jarvis. Courtesy of the Louisiana State Museum. 82–83 1. I. N. Phelps Stokes Collection, Prints Division, NYPL, Astor, Lenox and Tilden Foundations. 2. Courtesy of the Architect of the Capitol. LC. 3. I. N. Phelps Stokes Collection, Prints Division, NYPL, Astor, Lenox and Tilden Foundations. 4. Photograph by Rudolph Hertzberg. HTML. 5,6. Historic New Orleans Collection. 84–85 1. *Hall's Forty Etchings in Camera Lucida in North America,* 1827–1828. Courtesy of the New York Historical Society. 2. Collection of the author. 3. Print by B. F. Read (Cincinnati, 1873). LC. 4. Engraving, ca. 1822. I. N. Phelps Stokes Collection, Prints Division (cat. no. P1822 F-34), NYPL, Astor, Lenox and Tilden Foundations. 5. Collection of the author. 6. Photograph in the collection of the author. 86–87 1. Lithograph by Thomas Williams, 1845. Courtesy of the Louisiana State Museum. 2. Lithograph by Félix-Achille Beaupoil de Saint-Aulaire. Courtesy of the Louisiana State Museum. 3. Lithograph by Pierre Vigneron. Courtesy of the Louisiana State Museum. 4,5. Courtesy of the Louisiana State Museum. 6. Engraving by Bonneville. Collection of the author. 88–89 Painting by Alfred Boisseau (1847). New Orleans Museum of Art. Gift of William E. Groves. 90–91 1. Engraving from a painting by Chappell. Collection of the author. 2–7. Courtesy of the Louisiana State Museum. 92–93 1. Sketch by Fleury Generelly. HTML. 2–4. Courtesy of The Henry Francis Du Pont Winterthur Museum. 5. *Harper's New Monthly Magazine,* 1853. 6. Mrs. Robert H. Bolton. 94–95 1. Photograph by David M. Kleck. Collection of the author. 2. Collection of the author. Gift of Dr. Tom Gandy, Natchez, Miss. 3,4. Photograph by Howard Coleman. Thelma Hecht Coleman Collection. **96–97** 1. Photograph by Charles L. Franck. Collection of the author. 2. Pencil and watercolor by Pietro Gualdi. Anglo-American Art Museum, LSU. 3. Photographer unknown. Collection of the author. **98–99** 1. Mr. & Mrs. I. J. Persac, Baton Rouge. 2. Original painting believed to be destroyed. Photograph by C. Bennette Moore. Collection of the author. 3. Courtesy of the Louisiana State Museum. **100–101** 1–4. Rural Life Museum, LSU. 5. *Harper's Monthly,* March, 1858. **102–103** 1. *Das Illustrirte Missisippithal* by Henry Lewis, Dusseldorf, 1857. 2,3. *Harper's Monthly,* March, 1854. 4. *Ballou's Pictorial Drawing Room Companion,* April 12, 1856. 5. Source unknown. Photograph in the collection of the author. 6. *New Orleans City Directory,* 1842. **104–105** 1–4. *Harper's Monthly Magazine,* November, 1853. 5. Photograph by Guy F. Bernard. *New Orleans City Directory,* 1838. **106–107** 1. *Slave States of America* by J. S. Buckingham, Vol. I, London, 1842. 2. *Illustrated London News,* April 6, 1861. 3. *New Orleans Bee,* April 2, 1851. 4. *New Orleans Bee,* April 2, 1836. 5. Photograph by Elemore M. Morgan. By permission of The Keyes Foundation, Inc. 6. Watercolor sketch by Franz Holzlhuber. Glenbow-Alberta Institute, Calgary, Alberta. **108–109** Painting by John Antrobus (1850's). Historic New Orleans Collection. **110–111** 1. I. N. Phelps Stokes Collection, Prints Division, NYPL, Astor, Lenox and Tilden Foundations. 2. Collection of Samuel Wilson, Jr. 3. Louisiana Tourist Development Commission, Baton Rouge. 4. Photograph by Gerald E. Arnold, 1970. 5. *Thoughts, Visions and Sketches of Northern Louisiana* by Dr. Luther Longino, 1930. **112–113** 1. NOPL. 2–4. *New Orleans City Directory,* 1857. 5. HTML. 6. NOPL. **114–115** 1. *A History of Yellow Fever in New Orleans during the Summer of 1853,* HTML. 2. *Ballou's Pictorial Drawing Room Companion,* ca. 1858. 3. *Harper's Weekly,* September 3, 1859. 4. *New Orleans City Directory,* 1853. 5. Photographer unknown. Collection of the author. **116–117** 1. NOPL. 2. Photograph by Richard Koch. Courtesy of Koch and Wilson, Architects. 3. Photograph by Gerald E. Arnold, 1970. 4. Original portrait destroyed. Photograph in the collection of Mrs. Louis Früchter. 5. Photograph by Mrs. Louis Früchter. 6. Photograph by the author. 7. Collection of the author. **118–119** 1. Engraving by Ch. Colin from drawing by K. Fichot. Collection of the author. 2. Attributed to José de Salazar, 1796. Courtesy of the Louisiana State Museum. 3. Plan by J. N. de Pouilly, July 28, 1847. Courtesy of the Louisiana State Museum. 4. Lithograph by Louis Schwartz, New Orleans, 1862. Collection of the author. 5. *Scribner's Monthly,* November, 1873. 6. Confederate Museum, Louisiana Historical Association, New Orleans. **120–121** 1. *Norman's New Orleans and Environs* by B. M. Norman, 1845. 2. *New Orleans City Directory,* 1938. 3,4. *Norman's New Orleans and Environs* by B. M. Norman, 1845. 5. Drawing by James Gallier, April 21, 1846. Historic New Orleans Collection. 6. Prints Division, NYPL, Astor, Lenox and Tilden Foundations. 7. *Jewell's Crescent City Illustrated* by Edwin L. Jewell, New Orleans, 1873. Collection of the author. **122–123** 1. Drawing by H. Reinagle, 1830. Historic New Orleans Collection. 2. I. N. Phelps Stokes Collection, NYPL, Astor, Lenox and Tilden Foundations. 3. Lithograph by G. Tolti, printed by D. Theuret, 1850. HTML. 4. Reproduced from the program of the revival of the play by the New Orleans Little Theatre, N. D., ca. 1935. 5. HTML. 6,7. Probably from *Gleason's Pictorial Drawing Room Companion,* 1853. Col-

lection of the author. 8. Source unknown. Collection of the author. **124–125** 1. Courtesy of the Louisiana State Museum. 2. Photograph by H. J. Patterson. Times-Picayune Publishing Corporation. 3. Photograph by Rudolf Hertzberg. HTML. 4. *Jewell's Crescent City Illustrated* by Edwin L. Jewell, New Orleans, 1873. **126–127** 1. Photograph by Rudolf Hertzberg. HTML. 2. Photographer unknown. Collection of the author. 3. Photograph by Rudolf Hertzberg. HTML. 4–7. Photograph by Guy F. Bernard. **128–129** 1. Courtesy of the Louisiana State Museum. 2. Poydras Home for Elderly Ladies, New Orleans. 3. Courtesy of the Louisiana State Museum. 4. Historic New Orleans Collection. 5. Courtesy of the Louisiana State Museum. 6. Historic New Orleans Collection. **130–131** 1–6. Courtesy of the Louisiana State Museum. **132–133** 1. Courtesy of Baton Rouge Chamber of Commerce. 2. Drawing by J. A. Maurel. Lithograph by X. Magny. HTML. 3. Photograph by Elemore M. Morgan. By permission of The Keyes Foundation, Inc. 4. NOPL. **134–135** 1. Illinois Central Gulf Railroad. 2. Courtesy of the Louisiana State Museum. 3. Notarial Archives for the Parish of Orleans. 4. HTML. 5. Confederate Museum, Louisiana Historical Association, New Orleans. **136–137** Painting by Hyppolite Sebron. HTML. **138–139** Artist unknown. Corcoran Gallery of Art. Gift: the Estate of Emily Crane Chadbourne. **140–141** 1. Lithograph by J. Lion. Collection of the author. 2. Lithograph by Félix-Achille Beaupoil de Saint-Aulaire, ca. 1821. BN. 3. Notarial Archives for the Parish of Orleans. 4. *Paxton's New Orleans City Directory,* 1823. 5,6. Muséum du Havre, France. **142–143** 1,2. *Ballou's Pictorial Drawing Room Companion,* 1858. 3. Courtesy of the Louisiana State Museum. 4. Photograph in the collection of the author. **144–145** 1. Engraving by J. E. Boehler, published by Louis Grunewald. Collection of the author. 2. Engraving by B. W. Thayer & Co., Boston, 1842. Courtesy of the Louisiana State Museum. 3. *Almanach de la Louisiane,* New Orleans, 1867. HTML. 4. Photograph by Dan S. Leyrer. 5. Relief by Robert A. Launitz. Photograph by Gerald E. Arnold. **146–147** 1. Engraving from sketch by J. Wells Champney. *Scribner's Monthly,* December, 1873. 2. Source unknown. Photograph in the collection of the author. 3. Photographer unknown. Collection of the author. 4. Wharton Diary, 1855, p. 48. Manuscripts and Archives Division, NYPL, Astor, Lenox and Tilden Foundations 5. Prints Division, NYPL, Astor, Lenox and Tilden Foundations. **148–149** 1. I. N. Phelps Stokes Collection, Prints Division, NYPL, Astor, Lenox and Tilden Foundations. 2. Source unknown. 3. *New Orleans Weekly Delta,* December 13, 1847. 4. Courtesy of the Louisiana State Museum. **150–151** 1. Aquatint by W. J. Bennett from sketch by A. Mondelli, ca. 1841. HTML. 2. Sketch by J. Dallas. *Emerson's Magazine and Putnam's Monthly,* Vol. V, No. 4, October, 1857. 3. Collection of the author. 4. Probably from *Gleason's Pictorial Drawing Room Companion,* 1850's. 5. *Illustrated News,* March 19, 1853. **152–153** 1. *Jewell's Crescent City Illustrated* by Edwin L. Jewell, New Orleans, 1873. 2. Department of Archives and Manuscripts, LSU Library. 3. *A History of Louisiana* by Alcee Fortier, Vol. IV, New York, 1904. 4. Artist unknown. Confederate Museum, Louisiana Historical Association, New Orleans. 5. *A History of Louisiana* by Alcee Fortier, New York, 1904. 6. Painting by Pierre Cordelli, 1840. Courtesy of the Louisiana State Museum. 7. Source unknown. Collection of the author. 8. Courtesy of the Louisiana State Museum. 9–13. Collection of the author. **154–155** 1. *Harper's Weekly,* April 27,

1861. 2. Lithograph by Adrien Persac. Photograph in the collection of the author. 3. Cline Room, Centenary College, Shreveport. 156–157 1. *A History of Louisiana* by Alcee Fortier, 1903. 2. Engraving by George E. Perine after an original drawing. CSS. 3. *Le Monde Illustre*, Paris, 1862. 4. *Frank Leslie's Illustrated Newspaper*, May 24, 1862. 158–159 1. *Harper's New Monthly Magazine*, August, 1866. 2. *Frank Leslie's Illustrated Newspaper*, May 24, 1862. 3. Engraving by Samuel Sartain after a drawing by F. B. Schell. Collection of the author. 160–161 1. Photograph by A. D. Lytle, Baton Rouge. Department of Archives and Manuscripts, LSU Library. 2. *Harper's Weekly*, 1862. 3. Contemporary woodcut, source unknown. Collection of the author. 162–163 1. Engraving by H. B. Hall from sketch by Thomas Nast, 1863. Source unknown. Photograph in the collection of the author. 2,3. *Harper's Weekly*, 1864. 4. *Harper's Weekly*, January 24, 1863. 5. Confederate Museum, Louisiana Historical Association, New Orleans. 6. *Frank Leslie's Illustrated Newspaper*, May 9, 1863. 164–165 1. *Frank Leslie's Illustrated Newspaper*, January 31, 1863. 2. *Frank Leslie's Illustrated Newspaper*, June 25, 1864. 3. Sketch by Adalbert Johann Volck, ca. 1862. Source unknown. Collection of the author. 4. Collection of the author. 5. *Harper's Weekly*, July 12, 1862. 6. *Frank Leslie's Illustrated Newspaper*, April 25, 1863. 166–167 *Harper's Weekly*, May 7, 1864. 168–169 1. Sketch by Francis H. Schell. Anglo-American Art Museum, LSU. 2. Painting by E. Arnold, 1864. Anglo-American Art Museum, LSU. 3. Sketch by J. R. Hamilton. *Harper's Weekly*, April 18, 1863. 4. Photographer unknown. Collection of the author. 170–171 1. Sketch by J. R. Hamilton. *Harper's Weekly*, June 27, 1863. 2. Sketch by J. R. Hamilton. *Harper's Weekly*, August 8, 1863. 3. *Harper's Weekly*, July 18, 1863. 4. Sketch by Fred B. Schell. *Frank Leslie's Illustrated Newspaper*, August 15, 1863. 172–173 1. Sketch by Henri Louie. *Frank Leslie's Illustrated Newspaper*, April 11, 1863. 2. Sketch by J. R. Hamilton. *Harper's Weekly*, June 20, 1863. 3. Sketch by J. R. Hamilton. *Harper's Weekly*, June 13, 1863. 4. *Harper's Weekly*, February 14, 1863. 5. Sketch by William M. Hall. *Harper's Weekly*, May 16, 1863. 174–175 1. Collection of Kenneth Trist Urquhart. 2. *Frank Leslie's Illustrated Newspaper*, November 14, 1864. 3. Sketch by C. E. H. Bonwill. *Frank Leslie's Illustrated Newspaper*, May 21, 1864. 4. *Harper's Weekly*, May 7, 1864. 176–177 1. *Harper's Weekly*, May 14, 1864. 2. Source unknown. Photograph in the collection of the author. 3. Sketch by C. E. H. Bonwill. *Frank Leslie's Illustrated Newspaper*, June 18, 1864. 4. *Frank Leslie's Illustrated Newspaper*, June 18, 1864. 5. Sketch by C. E. H. Bonwill. *Frank Leslie's Illustrated Newspaper*, April 30, 1864. 178–179 1. Sketch by Theodore R. Davis. *Harper's Weekly*, August 16, 1862. 2. *Frank Leslie's Illustrated Newspaper*, May 7, 1864. 180–181 1. Sketch by William L. Challoner. Courtesy of the Louisiana State Museum. 2. Sketch by Theodore R. Davis. *Harper's Weekly*, August 25, 1866. 3,4. Sketch by Theodore R. Davis. *Harper's Weekly*, September 1, 1866. 182–183 1. Sketch by F. H. Schell. *Frank Leslie's Illustrated Newspaper*, May 21, 1864. 2. Sketch by Lilienthal. *Harper's Weekly*, April 21, 1866. 3. *Harper's Weekly*, January 30, 1864. 4. Sketch by W. L. Sheppard. Probably *Harper's Weekly*, ca. 1868. 5. Sketch by S. W. Bennett, *Frank Leslie's Illustrated Newspaper*, December 2, 1876. 6. *Harper's Weekly*, May 10, 1873. 184–185 1. From a lithograph in the Cabildo. Courtesy of the Louisiana State Museum. 2. *America Revisited* by George Augustus Sola, London,

1886. 3. *A History of Louisiana* by Alcee Fortier, Vol. IV, New York, 1904. 4. *Jewell's Crescent City Illustrated* by Edwin L. Jewell, New Orleans, 1873. 5. *Harper's Weekly*, October 10, 1874. 6,7. *The Daily Graphic*, September 25, 1874. 186–187 1. *Frank Leslie's Illustrated Newspaper*, October 3, 1874. 2. Sketch by Nathan W. Mills. *Frank Leslie's Illustrated Newspaper*, January 23, 1875. 3. *Harper's Weekly*, October 3, 1874. 4. Photograph in the collection of the author. 188–189 1. *A History of Louisiana* by Alcee Fortier, 1904. 2. Painting by Paul Poincy. *A History of Louisiana* by Alcee Fortier, 1904. 3,4. *Frank Leslie's Illustrated Newspaper*, January 27, 1877. 5. *Frank Leslie's Illustrated Newspaper*, May 19, 1877. 6. *Frank Leslie's Popular Monthly*, February 3, 1877. 190–191 1. *Frank Leslie's Illustrated Newspaper*, August 22, 1868. 2–8. *Jewell's Crescent City Illustrated* by Edwin L. Jewell, New Orleans, 1873. 192–193 1. *Every Saturday*, July 1, 1871. 2,3. *New Orleans Characters* by Leon J. Frémaux, 1876. 4,5. "The Great South: Louisiana Old and New" by Edward King, *Scribner's Monthly*, Vol. VII, No. 1, November, 1873. 194–195 1–3. *Harper's Weekly*, April 14, 1876. 4,5. *Every Saturday*, July 29, 1871. 6. *Every Saturday*, September 23, 1871. 7. Sketch by A. R. Waud. *Picturesque America*, William Cullen Bryant, ed., New York, 1874. 196–197 1. New Orleans Museum of Art, Gift of Mr. Bernard Bruen. 2. Courtesy of the Louisiana State Museum. 3. New Orleans Museum of Art, Gift of William E. Groves. 4. New Orleans Museum of Art, Gift of Sam Freidberg. 5. New Orleans Museum of Art. 198–199 1. HTML. 2. *Frank Leslie's Illustrated Newspaper*, January, 1881. 3. *Jewell's Crescent City Illustrated* by Edwin L. Jewell, New Orleans, 1873. 4,5. Collection of the author. 200–201 1. *Harper's Weekly*, June 23, 1883. 2. *Harper's Weekly*, July 7, 1883. 202–203 1. Musée des Beaux-Arts, Pau, France. 2. *New Orleans Characters* by Leon J. Frémaux, New Orleans, 1876. 204–205 1. Collection of the author. 2. *The Daily Graphic*, May 22, 1882. 3. *Frank Leslie's Illustrated Newspaper*, April 30, 1881. 4. *Jewell's Crescent City Illustrated* by Edwin L. Jewell, New Orleans, 1873. 5. *The Daily Picayune, Momus Edition*, February 17, 1887. 206–207 1. Collection of the author. 2. *Harper's Weekly*, January 31, 1885. 3. *Harper's Weekly*, January 3, 1885. 4. *Frank Leslie's Illustrated Newspaper*, May 30, 1885. 5. Photograph by Elemore M. Morgan. By permission of The Keyes Foundation, Inc. 208–209 Sketch by C. Upham. *Frank Leslie's Illustrated Newspaper*, January 24, 1885. 210–211 1,2. Photograph by C. Milo Williams. Louisiana Landmarks Society Collection, HTML. 3–5. *Century Magazine*, February or April, 1886. 6,7. Photograph by George F. Mugnier. Courtesy of the Louisiana State Museum. 212–213 1. *Every Saturday*, July 29, 1871. 2. *Jewell's Crescent City Illustrated* by Edwin L. Jewell, New Orleans, 1873. 3. *New Orleans Characters* by Leon J. Frémaux, New Orleans, 1876. 4. Photographer unknown, ca. 1885. Collection of the author. 5. From a painting by W. A. Rogers. *Harper's Weekly*, (date unknown). Collection of the author. 214–215 1–4. Photograph by George F. Mugnier. Courtesy of the Louisiana State Museum. 5. HTML. 216–217 1,2. Drawing by Charles Graham from sketches by J. O. Davidson. *Harper's Weekly*, April 28, 1883. 3,4. Jennings Chamber of Commerce. 218–219 1. Currier & Ives, 1870. 2. Sketch by A. R. Waud. *Every Saturday*, September 2, 1876. 3. Collection of Captain Frederick Way, Jr. 4. Photograph by D. B. Fischer. Collection of the author. 5. *Frank Leslie's Popular Monthly*, November, 1881. 220–221 1. Drawing by J. O. Davidson.

Harper's Weekly, 1884. 2. *A History of the Jetties at the Mouth of the Mississippi River* by E. L. Corthell, C.E., New York, 1880. 3. Drawing by J. O. Davidson. *Harper's Weekly*, December 8, 1883. 222–223 1,2. Photographer unknown. Collection of the author. 3. Photograph by Stoughton Cooley, ca. 1892. Courtesy of Miss Esther Cooley. 4. Collection of the author. 224–225 1–5. Collection of the author. 226–227 1,2. Courtesy of the Southern Pacific Transportation Company. 3. Photograph by C. Milo Williams. Louisiana Landmarks Society Collection, HTML. 4. Courtesy of the Southern Pacific Transportation Company. 5. Photograph by C. Milo Williams. Louisiana Landmarks Society Collection, HTML. 228–229 1–5. Collection of the author. 230–231 1. Photograph by A. D. Lytle, Baton Rouge. Department of Archives and Manuscripts, LSU. 2. Photograph by A. D. Lytle, Baton Rouge. The Louisiana Room, LSU Library. 3. Photograph by A. D. Lytle, Baton Rouge. Department of Archives and Manuscripts, LSU. 4. Louisiana State Land Office. 5. HTML. 6. Engraved from a photograph by Christian Olsen. *Frank Leslie's Illustrated Newspaper*, May 16, 1874. 7. Engraved from a photograph by A. D. Lytle. *Frank Leslie's Illustrated Newspaper*, May 16, 1874. 232–233 1. From sketch by A. R. Waud. *Harper's Weekly*, December 8, 1866. 2. Photograph by C. Milo Williams. Louisiana Landmarks Society Collection, HTML. 3. Photographer unknown. Collection of the author. 4. Rural Life Museum, LSU. 5. From sketch by E. W. Kemble. *Harper's Weekly*, November 3, 1888. 6. Photograph by C. Milo Williams. Louisiana Landmarks Society Collection, HTML. 234–235 1. Collection of Mrs. W. H. Cogswell, Charleston, S. C. Photograph courtesy of Mrs. Ben C. Toledano, New Orleans. 2. Property of Mrs. Ben C. Toledano. 3. Collection of Herman A. Schindler. Photograph courtesy of Mrs. Ben C. Toledano, New Orleans. 4. Collection of Herman A. Schindler. Photograph courtesy of Mrs. Ben C. Toledano, New Orleans. 236–237 1. *Harper's Weekly*, January 24, 1885. 2. *Harper's Weekly*, January 21, 1882. 3. *Harper's New Monthly Magazine*, January, 1887. 4. Sketch by A. R. Waud, ca. 1867. 5. Photograph by George F. Mugnier. Courtesy of the Louisiana State Museum. 238–239 1. Photographer unknown, ca. 1900. 2. HTML. 3. Albert L. Voss Collection. 4. Source unknown. Collection of the author. 5. John Minor Wisdom Collection, Howard-Tilton Memorial Library. 240–241 1. Sketch by W. T. Smedley. Probably *Harper's Monthly*, ca. 1890. 2. *Jewell's Crescent City Illustrated* by Edwin L. Jewell, New Orleans, 1873. 3. Collection of the author. 4. Sketch by Hal Hurst. *The Illustrated American*, September 20, 1890. 5. *The Louisiana State Lottery Company Examined and Exposed* by Reverend Beverly Caradine, D.D., 1890. 242–243 1,2. *Jewell's Crescent City Illustrated* by Edwin L. Jewell, New Orleans, 1873. 3. NOPL. 4. *New Orleans Police Department Souvenir Book*, 1900. 5. *Rex Carnival Paper*, February 24, 1903. 6. *Soard's New Orleans City Directory*, New Orleans, 1883. 7. *Rex Carnival Paper*, 1885. 244–245 1. Photograph by George F. Mugnier. Courtesy of the Louisiana State Museum. 2–4. Photographer unknown. Collection of the author. 5. Detroit Photographic Co. LC. 246–247 1–5. *Scribner's Monthly*, November, 1873. 6. Collection of the author. 248–249 1. Collection of the author. 2. *Frank Leslie's Illustrated Newspaper*, May 28, 1859. 3. *Harper's Weekly*, June 23, 1866. 4. *Frank Leslie's Illustrated Newspaper*, March 17, 1883. 250–251 1. *Frank Leslie's Illustrated Newspaper*, July 1, 1871. 2. *Every Saturday*, July 8, 1871. 3. *Frank Leslie's Illustrated Newspaper*, May 16,

1874. 4. *Frank Leslie's Illustrated Newspaper*, July 1, 1871. 5. *Harper's Weekly*, March 4, 1882. Collection of the author. 252–253 1. *Harper's Weekly*, March 15, 1884. 2,3. Collection of the author. 4. NOPL. 5. Photograph in the collection of the author. 254–255 1–4. *Frank Leslie's Illustrated Newspaper*, October 4, 1873. 5. NOPL. 6. Collection of the author. 256–257 1. *Harper's Weekly*, November 7, 1885. 2. *Frank Leslie's Illustrated Newspaper*, April 19, 1890. 3,4. Collection of the author. 5. Photograph by Gerald E. Arnold. Times-Picayune Publishing Corporation. 6. Photograph by the author. 258–259 1. *Harper's Weekly*, January 19, 1867. 2. *Harper's Weekly*, October 13, 1866. 3,4. *Harper's Weekly*, October 20, 1866. 260–261 1. *Every Saturday*, June 10, 1891. 2. *Harper's New Monthly Magazine*, November, 1893. 3. *Harper's Weekly*, March 27, 1884. 4. Photograph by Howard Coleman. Thelma Hecht Coleman Collection. 5. Courtesy of *Comptes Rendus de L'Athénée Louisianais*, New Orleans. 6. HTML. 262–263 1. Sketch by A. R. Waud. *Every Saturday*, July 29, 1871. 2. Drawn by Charles Graham from sketch by J. O. Davidson. *Harper's Weekly*, March 3, 1883. 3. Drawn after instantaneous photographs by T. De Thulstrup. *Harper's Weekly*, March 28, 1891. 4. *Scribner's Monthly*, February, 1896. 5. Sketch by Charles Graham. *Harper's Weekly*, March 28, 1891. 264–265 1–4. Sketch by Edward W. Kemble. *Century Magazine*, April, 1886. 5. Photograph by Adolph J. Claverie. Collection of the author. 6. Photograph by Elemore M. Morgan, 1945. By permission of The Keyes Foundation, Inc. 266–267 1. Sketch by Edward W. Kemble. *Century Magazine*, April, 1886. 2,3. *Harper's New Monthly Magazine*, January, 1887. 4. Photograph by George F. Mugnier, ca. 1890. Courtesy of the Louisiana State Museum. 5. *New Orleans Police Department Souvenir Book*, 1900. 268–269 1–5. Photograph by C. Milo Williams. Louisiana Landmarks Society Collection, HTML. 270–271 1. *Frank Leslie's Illustrated Newspaper*, November, 1881. 2. Photographer unknown. Collection of the author. 3. *Daily Picayune*, February 22, 1898. 4. *Down the Great River* by Captain Willard Glazier, 1893. 5. Photograph by C. Milo Williams. Louisiana Landmarks Society Collection, HTML. 272–273 1. Artist unknown. Portrait in S. J. Peters High School, New Orleans. 2. Portrait by Helen Maas, 1890. Collection of the author. 3. *New Orleans Times-Democrat*, 1910. Photograph in the collection of the author. 4. Photograph by C. Milo Williams. Louisiana Landmarks Society Collection, HTML. 5. Source unknown. Collection of the author. 6. International Museum of Photography at George Eastman House (Lewis Hine Collection). 274–275 1. HTML. 2. Photograph by A. D. Lytle. Department of Archives and Manuscripts, LSU. 3. Courtesy of Centenary College. 4. Lithograph by Colonel S. H. Lockett. Collection of Mrs. C. Lafayette Brown. 5. *A History of Louisiana* by Alcee Fortier, Vol. IV, 1904. 6. Photographer unknown. Collection of the author. 276–277 1. Photographer unknown. Collection of the author. 2,3. *Century Magazine*, 1883. 4. Sketch by Felix O. C. Darby. *Our Country* by Benson J. Lossing, New York, 1895. 5. Collection of Samuel Wilson, Jr. 6. Source unknown. Collection of the author. 7. Source unknown. Photograph in the collection of the author. 278–279 1. *Harper's Weekly*, March 15, 1884. 2. *Frank Leslie's Illustrated Newspaper*, December 22, 1877. 3,4. Photograph by A. D. Lytle. Department of Archives and Manuscripts, LSU. 5. Collection of the author. 280–281 1. Photograph by George F. Mugnier. Courtesy of the Louisiana State Museum. 2,3. HTML. 4. Photographer unknown. Collection of the author. 5. HTML. 282–283 1–7. Collection of the author. **284–285** 1–4. Collection of the author. 5. Photograph by D. B. Fischer, ca. 1890. Collection of the author. 6. Collection of Edwin Gebhardt. **286–287** 1. Photograph by C. Milo Williams. Louisiana Landmarks Society Collection, HTML. 2,3. Collection of the author. 4,5. Photographer unknown. Collection of the author. 6. Photograph by Dr. Lauren C. Post. Courtesy of Dr. Fred B. Kniffen, LSU. **288–289** 1. Photograph by Charles L. Franck. Collection of the author. 2. HTML. 3. Photographer unknown. Collection of the author. 4. HTML. 5. Times-Picayune Publishing Corporation. 6. Photograph by Gasquet. Collection of Miss Lillian Roan. **290–291** 1. Okeh Records Publicity Photograph. Collection of the author. 2. Peter Davis Collection, New Orleans Jazz Museum. 3. Photograph by Charles Genella, ca. 1937. 4. Courtesy of John DeDroit. 5. Photographer unknown. Collection of the author. 6. Photograph by Charles Genella, ca. 1937. **292–293** 1–6. Information Services, LSU. **294–295** 1. *New Orleans Times-Democrat,* 1910. NOPL. 2,3. Photographer unknown. Collection of the author. 4,5. Photograph by Hermann B. Deutsch. Collection of the author. 6. Collection of Arthur L. P. Scully, Jr. 7. *Roosevelt Review,* 1938. **296–297** 1,2. Photograph courtesy of Hermann B. Deutsch. Collection of the author. 3. Times-Picayune Publishing Corporation. 4. Photograph courtesy of Hermann B. Deutsch. Collection of the author. 5. HTML. 6. Photograph by Grady Smart. Louisiana Tourist Development Commission, Baton Rouge. **298–299** 1. Cartoon by Trist Wood. *The Louisiana Progress,* March 26, 1930. 2. Cartoon by Trist Wood. *The Louisiana Progress,* June 12, 1930. 3. Cartoon by Trist Wood. *The Louisiana Progress,* July 24, 1930. 4. Cartoon by Trist Wood. *The Louisiana Progress,* June 19, 1930. **300–301** 1,2. Photograph by Dr. Lauren C. Post. Courtesy of Dr. Fred B. Kniffen, LSU. 3. Photograph by Dr. Lauren C. Post, 1935. *Cajun Sketches* by Dr. Lauren C. Post, LSU Press, Baton Rouge, 1962. 4–6. Photograph by Dr. Lauren C. Post. Courtesy of Dr. Fred B. Kniffen, LSU. 7. Photograph by Louis T. Fritch, ca. 1920. Collection of the author. **302–303** 1. Photograph by Dr. Lauren C. Post. *Cajun Sketches* by Dr. Lauren C. Post, LSU Press, Baton Rouge, 1962. 2. Photograph by Elemore M. Morgan. By permission of The Keyes Foundation, Inc. 3,4. Photograph by Dr. Lauren C. Post, 1935. Courtesy of Dr. Fred B. Kniffen, LSU. 5. Photograph by Dr. Lauren C. Post. *Cajun Sketches* by Dr. Lauren C. Post, LSU Press, Baton Rouge, 1962. 6. Photograph by Dr. Lauren C. Post, ca. 1935. Courtesy of Dr. Fred B. Kniffen, LSU. **304–305** 1. Photograph by Dr. Lauren C. Post, ca. 1935. *Cajun Sketches* by Dr. Lauren C. Post, LSU Press, Baton Rouge, 1962. 2. Photograph by Dr. Lauren C. Post. Courtesy of Dr. Fred B. Kniffen, LSU. 3. Photograph by Elemore M. Morgan. By permission of The Keyes Foundation, Inc. 4. Photograph by Dr. Lauren C. Post. Courtesy of Dr. Fred B. Kniffen, LSU. 5. Photograph by Charles Genella, 1937. Louisiana Tourist Development Commission, Baton Rouge. **306–307** 1. NOPL. 2. Courtesy of Orleans Parish Levee Board. 3. United States Army Engineer District, Corps of Engineers, New Orleans. 4. Photograph by Leon Trice. NOPL. 5. Photograph by Dr. Lauren C. Post. Courtesy of Dr. Fred B. Kniffen, LSU. 6. NOPL. **308–309** 1. U. S. Signal Corps Photograph in the National Archives. 2. Navy Department Photograph in the National Archives. 3. Times-Picayune Publishing Corporation. 4. Collection of the author. 5. Times-Picayune Publishing Corporation. 6. Photograph

by Oscar J. Valeton. Times-Picayune Publishing Corporation. **310–311** 1. Photograph by Elemore M. Morgan. By permission of The Keyes Foundation, Inc. 2. Louisiana Tourist Development Commission, Baton Rouge. 3. Photograph by Gerald E. Arnold, 1972. 4,5. Photograph by Elemore M. Morgan. By permission of The Keyes Foundation, Inc. 6. Photograph from Mr. and Mrs. Beauregard L. Bassich. 7. Photograph by Elemore M. Morgan, 1945. By permission of The Keyes Foundation, Inc. **312–313** 1. Kerr-McGee Corporation. 2–4. Photograph by Manuel C. DeLerno. 5. Photograph from Shell Development Company. 6. Photograph by Elemore M. Morgan. By permission of The Keyes Foundation, Inc. **314–315** 1. Photograph by Gerald E. Arnold, 1972. 2. Kaiser Aluminum and Chemical Corporation. 3. Avondale Shipyards, Inc. 4. Courtesy of Baton Rouge Area Chamber of Commerce. 5. New Orleans Chamber of Commerce. 6. Photograph by David M. Kleck. **316–317** 1. Fairchild Aerial Surveys, Inc. 2. Courtesy of Freeport Sulphur Company. 3. International Salt Company. 4. Photograph from Mr. and Mrs. Beauregard Bassich. 5. Courtesy of Freeport Sulphur Company. 6. Photograph by Elemore M. Morgan. By permission of The Keyes Foundation, Inc. **318–319** 1. LC. 2,3. Louisiana Tourist Development Comission, Baton Rouge. 4,5. Photographer unknown. Collection of the author. **320–321** 1. Photograph by Ben Kinel. Courtesy of Shreveport-Bossier Convention-Tourist Bureau. 2. Photograph by Fred C. Frey, Jr. Courtesy of Baton Rouge Chamber of Commerce. 3. Photograph by Jon Mask. Courtesy of City of Monroe. 4,5. Photograph by Roger Kelley. Courtesy of Monroe Chamber of Commerce. 6. Photograph by Ben Kinel. Courtesy of Shreveport-Bossier Convention-Tourist Bureau. 7. Alexandria Conventions Commission. **322–323** 1,2. Photograph by Sam R. Sutton. Courtesy of Board of Commissioners, Port of New Orleans. 3. Photograph by Gerald E. Arnold. 4. Courtesy of City of New Orleans. 5. Photograph by C. F. Weber Photography, Inc. The New Orleans Philharmonic Symphony Society. 6. Photograph by Gerald E. Arnold. **324–325** 1. Photograph from Major Henry M. Morris, Chief of Detectives, New Orleans Police Department. 2. Courtesy of News Bureau, Louisiana Tech University, Ruston. 3. Information Services, The University of New Orleans. 4. Courtesy of Greater Lafayette Chamber of Commerce. 5. Courtesy of Centenary College. 6. Tulane University Medical School. **326–327** 1. Photograph by Beauregard Bassich. 2,3. Louisiana Tourist Development Commission, Baton Rouge. 4,5. Photograph by the author. 6. Photograph by Elemore M. Morgan, 1946. By permission of The Keyes Foundation, Inc. 7. Louisiana Tourist Development Commission, Baton Rouge. **330–331** General Motors: Cadillac. Courtesy of the Louisiana State Museum: Baker; Flanders; Gayoso de Lemos; Thibodeaux; Wells. NOPL: Blanchard; Edwards; Fuqua; Heard; Kennon; McEnery; McKeithen; Noe; Sanders. HTML: Pleasant; Simpson. *A History of Louisiana* by Alcee Fortier, New York, 1904: Allen, H.; Derbigny; Hébert; Johnson, H.; Johnson, I.; Mouton; Robertson; Roman; Villeré; Walker; White; Wickliffe; Wiltz. *Citoyens, Progrés et Politique de la Nouvelle Orléans* by Chase, Deutsch, Dufour, and Huber. E. S. Upton Publishing Company, Publishers, New Orleans, 1964: Allen, O.; Foster; Hall; Long, E.; Parker. *Louisiana Today,* 1939: Jones; King; Leche. By permission of The Keyes Foundation: Davis. By permission of Russell B. Long: Long, H. Source unknown. Photograph in the collection of the author: Dupré.

Index

Illustrations are designated by bold face